T0151951

Greatest Hits

twelve years of compost magazine

EDITED BY
Kevin Gallagher and Margaret Bezucha

PREFACE BY
Rosanna Warren

ZEPHYR PRESS
BROOKLINE, MA

Book design by *typeslowly*

Published in part thanks to a generous grant
from the Massachusetts Cultural Council

massculturalcouncil.org

98765432 FIRST PRINTING IN 2006

ZEPHYRPRESS
50 Kenwood Street / Brookline, MA 02446
www.zephyrpress.org

TABLE OF CONTENTS

Hear America Singing: A Gallery of the U.S.

.

I remember my first conversation, years ago, with Kevin Gallagher and Meg Bezucha, in a dim coffee shop in the early days of compost. These young people startled me with the intensity of their purpose. They had read the anthology I had edited on literary translation, and they wanted to pursue questions about the relations of literature to national and international politics, and of literature in the United States to literatures abroad. They wanted the names of good foreign writers. They wanted, too, to see how poetry could act alongside drawing, printmaking, painting, photography. They were writers and painters themselves, and though their journal was called compost, they also might have called it "frontier" or "boundaries," so earnest were they in exploring the edges where art takes us.

Twelve years of compost have yielded a remarkable compendium. For one thing, the collection is useful. If you want to learn about strong recent poetry in Vietnam, Haiti, China, Ireland, Zimbabwe, or Calcutta, turn to those sections in the compost anthology; and from Diana Der-Hovanessian you will receive a historical survey of Armenian poetry from its origins. The compost editors found masterful guides to those poetic cultures. Kevin Bowen of the Joiner Center for the Study of War and Its Social Consequences at the University of Massachusetts, Boston, brings us into the workshop, so to speak, where American and Vietnamese poets collaborate in the translation of Vietnamese poems and carry out the integrative work of the imagination on the very site of past violence. Sue Standing lays out the topography of current Zimbabwean poetry with admirable lucidity, providing not just the names of authors, titles of books, and examples of work, but the names and addresses of the crucial publishing houses. Each foreign section is similarly generous. What stands out about them is not only the clarity of each overview, but the excellence of so many of the representative poems. Many kinds of excellence, and, for the American reader, surprising and renewing excellences, a powerful antidote to the parochialism to which this self-absorbed, self-congratulatory continent so easily tends. Let one poem stand as an emblem of these many virtues. The Irish poet Medbh McGuckian's "Mating with the Well," a crabbed variation on the sonnet, crams strategic force and plenitude into its narrow boundaries: "I am Ireland-blind and stone-lined/ and open to the purity of death…" Her verbal energy—which can seem ferocious—is the opposite of the violence which is the poem's subject: "But the rhythm of war, like a corrupt star…"

In its lyrical reach to the political, as well as in its formal sophistication, this poem represents the ambitions of compost.

The section called "The Hub of the Universe" celebrates poetry in Boston with verve and a charming insouciance, stringing together a wild variety of poems by younger and older poets. The effect is, as Louis MacNeice wrote in a different context, in his poem "Snow," "incorrigibly plural," and makes us feel with delight "the drunkenness of things being various." Each of these offerings has its own life pulse. A particular vitality emanates from Martha Collins' witty pair, "Goods" and "Ills" ("Death/ is being ill all over. Ill all over and done"). Jennifer Rose brings her characteristic intelligence to bear on a dandelion, "Brittle reliquary! Dimmed nimbus!// Its tonsured head/ now bows like mine, bent to appraise/ the mysteries of faith…" William Corbett contributes high spirits and tender goofiness in his letter poem, "To Marni," an artfully artless performance. Fred Marchant extends the earlier meditation on Vietnam with his own delicate tribute, "Red River Crossing." And to keep things unstuffy, CHS presents, in "For the Blake Babies," a genially obscene paean to Allen Ginsberg.

The anthology opens out from Boston to "A Gallery of the U.S." Not the least of the pleasures of this volume is the staggered testimony offered in a series of interviews: Robert Pinsky, the playwright Ed Bullins, the philosopher Martha Nussbaum, Victor Hernandez Cruz, Alan Dugan, among others, enlarge the scope of the creative work in the journal by meditating, from different angles, on the place of art in the larger political cultures of the United States and the world. Pinsky's account of American optimism, adaptability, and immigrant resourcefulness complements Nussbaum's rich weave of intellectual autobiography and propositions about the usefulness of fiction to thinking about political and economic justice. In her panoptical survey of these themes, Nussbaum goes a long way toward defining the goals of compost and one source of its rare vitality. Those goals may be further identified, aesthetically, with the figures of James Laughlin and Kenneth Rexroth, whose spirits preside over this volume as they presided over the journal as a whole. Dedication to freshness in form and thought, openness to the foreign, belief in art as a form of knowledge—these principles, lived out in perpetual youthfulness by the elders Laughlin and Rexroth, animate compost, this venture of the young, and they join the generations in an adventure that seems likely to endure but never to grow old.

Rosanna Warren

compost mortem

Twelve years ago, a guy named Bush was president, the country was in the midst of turmoil in the Middle East, and, although the president enjoyed unprecedented support, the seeds of opposition were beginning to spread— especially overseas. Some things never change, but others do and did.

Those of us who came to found compost, a handful of young poets and artists then living in Jamaica Plain (one of Boston's southern neighborhoods), saw ourselves as part of that seemingly growing cast of those seeking a different world. How could the Berlin Wall have just fallen, Mandela have just become victorious in South Africa, Pinochet have left office, and Europe have just united into a common market, all peacefully, while the United States pursued war overseas, and seemed blissful at home?

We saw the world of poetry in the United States as no more than a mirror of this paradox. When you would have thought that poetry was about to rise in an attempt to explain the changing world, the most famous discussion of poetry was an essay turned book called *Can Poetry Matter?*— documenting how the U.S. poetry readership was at an all time low and was bordering on the irrelevant.

Meanwhile, Boston was experiencing a harsh recession and Jamaica Plain (JP) became the low rent mecca for many aspiring artists, musicians, and writers. Many of these folks ended (or started!) their days at Brendan Behan Pub, which, in hindsight had much more in common with its namesake than its name alone. This group of emerging artists saw the Boston (and national) area poetry scene as at a lull. To us, the long standing clan of university-based magazines seemed to have an iron curtain that blocked out innovation and all of our submissions.

Eventually, a blend of inspiration, naivety, technology, desperation, and indeed some vision led a small group of us to found compost magazine. Our stated mission was to help facilitate a better understanding of the world's people through art and literature.

Thanks to the recognition and efforts of Zephyr Press, this post mortem that compiles our greatest hits is a testimony of our case. Although we did not articulate it as such in the beginning, looking back, our editorial position had four planks:

- Re-place poetry in its proper artistic context: alongside visual art, theater, and discussions of society at large;
- Attempt to re-internationalize poetry in the United States;

- Showcase Boston area artists alongside emerging and established artists across the U.S. and the globe;
- Expand the traditional audience for poetry to include the community of the artists themselves and the general public.

In a modest way, for twelve years our mission was fulfilled. Our group was less than inspired by the small digest-sized journals that machine gunned more than three hundred poems at their readers without a breather. There is a long history of alternatives to that genre, and in a way we were "tweeners" among them. We came after the "zine" movement which Xeroxed and stapled poetry magazines by the thousands (in the late 1980s there were an estimated 2000 "zines" in Boston alone). However, we came before the world wide web-based literary magazine that has swept the electronic universe. As the first generation of college students fully versed in computers and desktop publishing, we could leapfrog the printing press and produce a handsome magazine in our own living room!

With our Macintosh in hand, we set out to open up the concept of poetry by printing it on a large and wide open page, by juxtaposing it with artwork, and by publishing it alongside essays, interviews, and plays. Indeed, our first three issues were printed on 11 x 17 inch brown kraft paper. Moreover, we sewed each binding with the sewing machine plugged into the same socket as the Macintosh. Our first three issues were samizdat editions that we printed ourselves. In those early issues we featured translations from the Russian, Bengali, and Bulgarian; sketches and artwork by international and Boston area artists; and poetry and interviews with established artists such as Robert Pinsky, KRS-ONE, and Rosanna Warren. We also presented this work in a performance setting at bars or parties in JP tenements that featured readings, live music, and fellow editor Margie Nicoll painting collages. After those successful early issues, it was suggested that we distribute the magazine on a larger scale. Distributors were intrigued by our energy and before we knew it you could buy a copy of our magazine in San Francisco, Ontario, and Texas. The problem was, given our size we'd be put on the rack with Rolling Stone and the other large-sized magazines. Since that wasn't who we were, beginning with our fourth issue we chopped ourselves down to (our permanent) size: 9 x 12 inches.

In addition to our physical size, beginning with our fourth issue we solidified our editorial format. Issues four through twelve were loosely divided into three sections. Each issue had a feature section on the poetry of a culture other than mass culture USA, a section called "Hear America Singing" which featured established and emerging writers from the U.S., and a section that presented Boston-area artists and writers.

It was our view that poetry in the U.S. had become extremely provincial, and we set out to help expose readers of poetry to the exciting poetries outside the U.S. We met Kevin Bowen, poet and director of the William Joiner Center for the Study of War and its Social Consequences at the University of Massachusetts, Boston. We had heard that Kevin was bringing a few poets from Vietnam to Boston to give readings, workshops, and most importantly, to review recently released documents that were captured by the U.S. forces in Vietnam in the 1970s. When we asked Kevin if we could meet one or two of the poets and ask them for a poem or two, Kevin replied by setting up countless meetings with all the poets and by handing us literally hundreds of pages of unpublished material. "Use what you like," Kevin said. Well, for a group of artists a generation removed from the Vietnam conflict, this was a moving experience. Kevin's gift sparked months of research and understanding on our part with regards to the U.S. war, the country of Vietnam, its language, and its poetry. Since we had so much material, we decided to publish a large section. Little did we know that we were the first venue in the U.S. to publish the poetry of North Vietnam. This was in 1994, more than twenty years after the conflict had ended!

We had learned so much from that experience, and received such great feedback from our peers and counterparts, that we decided to do such a feature in every issue. We went on to feature the poetry of contemporary Haiti, China, Zimbabwe, Armenia, Ireland, and women poets from Calcutta, India. In addition, we did a section on Latino poetry in the U.S. In each case, we did not pretend to be experts on the country or culture we were featuring, and worked with guest editors who were experts in each area. In addition to Kevin Bowen, we are indebted to Bei Ling, Danielle Legros Georges and Patrick Sylvain, Sue Standing, Diana Der-Hovanessian, Carolyne Wright, and Cindy Schuster for playing the role of guest editor in many issues. Selections from each of these editions are included in this volume.

Much of the inspiration for our international slant on poetry came from James Laughlin and Kenneth Rexroth. Laughlin because his New Directions introduced generations of readers in the U.S. to world literatures, and Rexroth because he did the actual translation of many of those literatures. Over the years, we have paid homage to each of these extraordinary individuals.

James Laughlin was one of the earliest enthusiasts of compost and our most frequent contributor. We wrote Laughlin early on to tell him of our effort and to ask for his endorsement. He loved our format and our blend of established and emerging artists and poets. He ended up submitting numerous poems (most of which we published), giving us contact information for other writers, and giving suggestions about publishing and who we should be reading through countless letters.

To honor Rexroth we established the Kenneth Rexroth Memorial Translation Prize—a contest rewarding the best translation submitted to us. Rexroth introduced the English reading public to a great many literatures from around the globe. His effort was among the best because his translations were also great poems in English as well. In this volume, the Chinese translations by Stroeb Taylor is a sample of our past prize winners.

Laughlin, a great friend of Rexroth, was a great supporter of this prize. Indeed, he often supplied us with photographs of Rexroth from Laughlin's personal collection for us to publish alongside the award-winning poems. He would end letters with photos by making us promise to send them back. On a winter day in 1997 I had just dropped a letter to him that included a photo of Rexroth, purchased a Boston Globe, then got on the subway. Midway on my journey I read that Laughlin had just passed away. We felt his loss deeply and decided to pay homage to Laughlin in a formal way.

compost was slated for a reading for the New Poetry Club (NEPC) at Harvard University just a few weeks later. We called noted poet Diana Der-Hovanessian (who guest edited compost's issue featuring Armenian poetry), then President of NEPC and asked if we could turn the reading into a James Laughlin tribute. She thought it was a great idea. With Bill Corbett's help we put together a gala reading that featured many of Laughlin's friends, those he published, and his admirers. In addition to Corbett and members of compost, the group included poets Forrest Gander and Rosmarie Waldrop; Tree Swenson who designed many of the covers of Laughlin's Copper Canyon Press books; his publishers Roland Pease and Elizabeth Lund, and others. We later collected these poems and essays in the tenth issue of our magazine. We will always be indebted to James Laughlin. We dedicated this volume to his memory.

Alongside the international poetry that we have featured, we always published emerging and established poets, writers, and thinkers from the U.S. In this volume you can read our interviews with the dazzling philosopher Martha Nussbaum, award winning playwright Ed Bullins, and poets Alan Dugan, Robert Pinsky, Rosanna Warren, and Eavan Boland. We always juxtaposed features of such greats with emerging poets and writers. Some of these have gone on to publish notable works. Among those included in this volume are Kevin Bowen, Denise Duhamel, Connie Deanovich, Sam McGavern, Danielle Legros Georges, and Wayne Sullins.

To us, our final modest contribution was to expand the traditional audience for poetry to include visual artists and the general public—at least in our small community. In the 1990s Jamaica Plain was analogous to an under-35 art colony, thriving with poets, writers, visual artists, and musicians. In addition to publishing our magazine, a major event for us each year was participation in the Jamaica Plain Open Studios (JPOS). During a weekend in late September each year, over 150 artists open their workspaces to the public—an event that attracts thousands to Jamaica Plain each year. As part of JPOS we would do two things. First, we would curate a show that exhibited the visual artists that we were featuring in current and past issues of compost. Some artists, like Pablo Gonzalez, were a mainstay on our walls. Second, we would hold a gala reading that would showcase our newest issue of compost. These readings would attract hundreds, and not your typical poetry reading attendees. Perhaps it was the keg beer, the rock musicians, and the fact that so many artists were in town that weekend anyway. Nevertheless, it made for a vibrant context for poetry. It was very gratifying to learn that many had never been to a poetry reading before, and that they actually enjoyed themselves at ours!

In many ways compost has fallen victim to its success. compost was always considered a "hobby" or an outlet that would not interfere with our own art and professions. We put out an issue per year alongside a JPOS blow-out, that's it. Initially, this was manageable through Monday night meetings at an apartment to go over submissions and the magazine layout. Soon things changed. The magazine gained national recognition and distribution, reaching every Barnes and Noble and Borders in the country. With this came reams of submissions, and the pressure to grow. In fact, we were almost denied a grant on grounds that we weren't willing to "take it to the next level." The next level was to hire outreach consultants, put out six issues per year, raise funds for full-time staff members, and put together a working board of directors. We always wanted the magazine to be home grown, so we resisted such pressure. In the end, the magazine became too much, as we wanted to give attention to our individual art (that we had been neglecting), to our families, and to our professions.

We hesitate to make a list thanking the many people who helped and inspired us in all these efforts because we know we would leave important people out. But, we must try. Financially compost would be nothing without the generous support of the Massachusetts Cultural Council (MCC). We bow down to Charles Coe and Penny Pimentel for their enthusiastic support over the years. Also here in Boston, Jack Powers, Bill Corbett, and Louisa

Solano have all supported us by welcoming us into longstanding traditions in Boston with open arms. Kevin Bowen, as mentioned earlier, has been a major inspiration and supporter. Jen Jackowitz has been a key design element to our effort. Jonathan Hummel was the "sound" of our public appearances. Northeastern University's Center for the Arts took us in as artists in residence for a number of years. Of course we mentioned the Brendan Behan Pub. Although Meg and Kevin served as the editors of this anthology, compost had a variety of editors: Margie Nicoll, Anastasios Kozaitis, Louis Pingatore, Christopher Hazard Seifert, and Patrick McAllister. There are so many others. We thank and love you all.

Finally, we thank Cris Mattison at Zephyr Press for recognizing the small but significant contribution that compost has made to poetry in Boston and in the U.S. as a whole. We hope this volume will reach people that we were not able to reach the first time around, and serve as a testament to our mission. Most of all we hope you enjoy it as twelve years of literature in our great language.

Kevin Gallagher, Margaret Bezucha

The House of the World

~

Vietnam

The Sky in a Bomb Crater
Lam Thi My Da
translated by Kevin Bowen and Ngo Vinh Hai

Your comrades said that you, a female roadbuilder
with fervent love for our country,
saved the Trail and the convoy that night
by lighting a torch to divert the bombs on yourself.

An army unit on the Trail passed by the bomb crater
and talked of the young girl you used to be
and pitched some stones on your barren grave,
adding love to the rising rock pile.

I gazed into the bomb crater where you died
and saw the sky in the rain water.
Our country is so benign
as sky water always washes away painful wounds.

You lay deep in the ground
as quietly as the sky in the crater
and nightly your soul shone
brightly like twinkling stars.

Could it be that your soft and fair skin
have turned into columns of white clouds?
Could it be that when one passed by this place
it was not the sun that shone through but it was your heart?

Your name is now the name of this section of the Trail
and the sky reflects your early death and your meaningful life.
Though I and my friends did not know what you looked like;
I knew that there was a trace of you on each of our faces.

Truong Son East, Truong Son West
Pham Tien Duat
translated by Nguyen Khac Vien

you and I, let us hang our hammocks in the same mountain jungle
we two—at the two ends of the long chain
the road to the front is so beautiful in this season
the Eastern Chain longs so for the Western
one single mountain, two colours of clouds
there sun, here rain, the sky too is different
that's how it is with you and me and South and North
that's how it is with two slopes of one long single forest
Western Chain—I leave, my heart tight, oh my beloved
on the other slope under ceaseless rain, the shoulder of the trail
                            beneath baskets of rice
mosquitoes by thousands in the ancient jungle—pull down your sleeves
the vegetable season over, where will you search for shoots of bamboo?

your heart knotted, my beloved, and I am on the wintry slope
streams dry, butterflies among the rocks
you know, my head is high with unknown lands
but you think of bombs that cut my path

I climb into the truck and all the sky's rain pours down
the windscreen wiper brushes my nostalgia away
and you walk down the mountain and the sun sets in splendour
branches of trees keep our sorrows apart
the trail that joins East to West carries no letters
it carries bullets and rice
on the Eastern Chain, a young girl in a green jacket, hard at work
on the Western Chain, a soldier in a green jacket...

from your side to mine
wave after wave, troops march to the front
like love that joins words without end
the East meets with the West.

The Black Ants
Nguyen Quang Thieu   [3 poems]
translated by Martha Collins

Sleepy car wheels carried away
The laughter, cries, and death of alcohol.
They carried away men's fingers
Crawling up women's legs.

Now nothing is left on the banquet table
But bowls, plates, cups, and empty bottles,
And the whirlwind of the ceiling fan
Singing about the sadness of things.

Black ants cross the banquet table
As if it were a battlefield
Filled with bits of meat
And dead bodies of basil.
The ants embrace red pepper
As if it were a tattered flag;
It makes their eyes water.
They creep over bones
They creep over skin
Under the wail of the fan.

The false sun of a 1000-watt bulb
Sets at the flick of a black switch.
The whirlwind fan turns more and more slowly,
Until it dies, spreading three black wings.

All that's left are the black ants
With watering eyes, helping each other back
Toward their burrows, dark and deep.

Motion

Like an ancient town buried underground for thousands of years that is just now waking up, the snails creep across the garden under moonlight as dazzling as sunlight in summer. The tops of their shells flash like the diamond beads of a queen's crown on a festival evening. Their soft wet bodies glide, trembling with tenderness. Their antennas rise toward the sky to catch the waves of strange sounds. What secret language, happy or sad, is calling the snails?

The moonlight is quiet, the trees are quiet. The snails creep over sleeping grass and fallen leaves. Their bodies glide over sharp-cold bits of broken glass. I can't tell whether they cry or curse. What I hear is the sound of water, rising to flood the moonlit night.

The snails were hidden in thorn-bushes, in holes in the wall. Awake now, they silently slip away. Is my garden their native land, or the next garden, or still another garden? Are they running away from their native land, or finding their native land? It doesn't matter: I sing a song tonight because their departure is as marvelous as a sudden burst of dream, or a festival evening.

The last snail creeps over the old wall surrounding my garden. As the top of its shell disappears, the last diamond light of the queen's crowns fades away. The snails leave glittering streams of light in their paths, and the streaming stars change position in the sky.

Behind the window of my house tonight, I whisper Goodbye to the snails.

Moonlight and a Doorstep
translated by Martha Collins and the author

Moonlight spills onto the doorstep.
Young leaves are silver spoons, scooping it up.
Shadows of drunken trees fall into each other.

Riding the waves of moonlight
Are romantic crickets, thirsty cockroaches,
Love coming together and parting,
The hair-knots of widows breaking into laughter,
Rippings, mendings, scatterings, dryness,

And you, who arrived before the moon,
Who breathe best in the mist of space and time.

*

I can't find any companions tonight.
As I creep across my doorstep,
A cockroach spreads her wings to fly,
Traveling with her eggs behind her,
Little streaks of quivering light.
The farther she flies, the stronger, the more transfixed—

Under the earth, tree-roots are making love.
Love is fertile, love is fallen leaves.
We reveal ourselves in dull sleep:
The more we dream, the more our footsteps falter.
There's no doorstep for me to creep across.

*

Insects, tiny streaks of light,
Run from the base of the tree to the branches,
Obediently licking moonlight from silver leaves,
While our children curl up in sleep,
Betrayed by rows of math-book numbers.
In their dreams, do they lick moonlight from the leaves?
The creation of a moon, an insect, a person—

Which is more bloody, more dark?
Crime carries goodness, fast asleep, to the other bedroom.
Dream, with bleeding feet, walks on fragments of gold bells
That vibrate on the sharp tongue of moonlight
As it slides into nothingness, making the sap flow.

*

I cannot find you, my woman, tonight.
Houses, holes of earth with straw roofs soaked in moonlight,
Are anxious and close their doors.
A river goby gets pregnant and faints;
Only the sound of sacred water echoes in the distance.
Exhaustion is our last comfort.
My two arms, my two torn fins,
Carry my fear of getting you pregnant
And seek a sad hole made of earth for us.

*

Moonlight saturates happiness, sadness.
It saturates our hesitations like batter
That thickens and brings steam to the hungry ground.
The dogs look up and howl at the moon for no reason:
They're not rabid, they're guarding nothing, they're not—

The jungle cries; souls of trees rise from rotting leaves
And open a festival night of dancing fleas.
My native village is sad, with broken wings,
My native village, bewitched, has lost its way.
In a jungle full of devils,
I can't find any companions tonight.

*

Moonlight has flowed to the other side.
Breasts are young, breath burns hot again.
On a moldy wall, ants follow their own
Rambling perceptions, as if in a fever—
Tiny ants, with immense heads.

8

Where do the right things go?
Where do the wrong things go?
And oh, the roaming crickets!
Think of your own species tonight
And don't just stroke your beard!
A guitar shaped like grass
Fills a path with its blue song.

*

I can't find any companions tonight.
I've lost half of myself
And given birth to another half.
Which half has blood, which has water?
My hands are tarnished spoons scooping moonlight.
I cry, hungry and thirsty as never before.
When tree roots seize me and crush me to water,
I rush through the trunk and rise to the highest branches.

*

I cannot find you, my woman, tonight.
I fall, the last squash-flower of summer.
An old toad, sly and indifferent, with cold hands,
Holds moonlight up to my face and looks at me.
Beginnings resemble that gesture.

*

The clouds are drifting, soft and wet.
The handkerchief of the saddest, loveliest woman in the world
Is sleeping in a desert of moonlight tonight.

There's something like a doorstep for me to cross over,
There, where moonlight is throwing itself on the ground.

9

Question and Answer
Huu Thinh
translated by Ngo Vinh Hai

I have encountered feet
that say rivers are long and thorns are sharp
Then I have talked with yellowing grass by road sides
that sobs for having been trampled on.

And I have heard from dying embers
of the deep murmur from the blue sky.

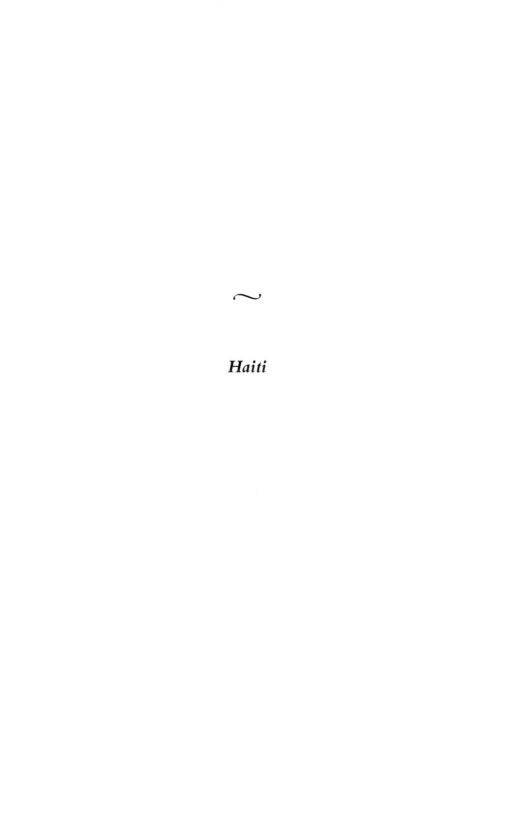

Haiti

The Valleys' Signposts—Haitian Art and Literature
Guest edited by Danielle Legros Georges and Patrick Sylvain

The themes of justice, pride, progress, liberation and solidarity manifest themselves in the Haitian arts, especially in our rich literary tradition (which began, some say, before Haiti's birth in 1804, with the poet-queen Anacaona, the Amerindian woman who sought to unite the island's southern kingdoms during the Taino and Carib struggle to overthrow Spanish colonizers in the 16th century). Haitian writers have been prolific, publishing more books per capita since the beginning of the 19th century than writers of any other country in the Americas, with the exception of the United States. Yet, ironically, for millions of Haitians, words on the printed page are hard, if not impossible to decode, a reflection of an 80 percent illiteracy rate in Haiti.

The pressing issue of literacy, the problem of audience, and to whom and for whom Haitian writers produce their work, is touched upon on the one hand by poet and activist Jean-Claude Martineau in an interview published in the following pages, and on the other hand by musicologist Gerdès Fleurant in his essay entitled "The Song of Freedom: Vodun, Conscientization and Popular Culture in Haiti." Both writers address the problematics of audience, the meaning of writing in exile, and some of the many contexts in which we produce our work. Between these two pieces fall the poetry and fiction of Haitian writers. Some of us, such as Félix Morisseau-Leroy, choose to write almost exclusively in Creole. Others, Edwidge Danticat, for example—whose novel *Breath, Eyes, Memory*, is excerpted in these pages, are writing in English. Yet others, like Marilene Phipps navigate two languages at once. Each writer brings to the table his/her experience, contributing to the Haitian canon, the literary legacy Haitians will leave for each other and for readers interested in the complex and rich culture that is Haitian culture. We are grateful to the visual artists and writers who have contributed to this issue of compost, and are pleased to have had the opportunity to travel through and present a Haitian landscape of images and words. It is our hope that these pages contribute to an ongoing dialogue.

The Long Walk Home
An interview with Jean-Claude Martineau   [1994]

c: In your opinion, what are the goals for Haiti in this new phase of its history, and what might be some constraints on these goals?

JCM: As far as I'm concerned, what I've been fighting for a number of years is to make Haiti a modern republic—a modern republic with laws for economic and social progress. The goal we've had in our dreams is still the same. The constraint that we have now is that the whole world is watching. When I say the whole world, I mean right now a world with one dominant tendency. There are a lot of ideas that people had just a few years ago that have become very unpopular. Let's say, if Haiti wanted to implement some kind of a socialist type of government, I think that the whole world would fall on us and bring us back to what we have been for a number of years—a country without a state, a country without law. Although we have beautiful laws written in the books, nobody cares about them. We have to pursue our dreams, while taking into consideration that dreams of this sort are no longer popular. They are dormant, and right now the balance of forces in the world is completely different.

We have succeeded, politically, in doing something unique. The intervention of the American forces in Haiti is not what it was in 1915. It's a very different thing today. In 1915, those who had money and power welcomed the intervention, right now they are against it. In 1915, those who had nothing fought against the intervention, now they are welcoming it. So, you see, it is a very different situation, very different. How we are going to navigate between these constraints to pursue our dream is exactly like the river, like the flood we will present. We will go down the mountain. We will avoid obstacles that are too much. We will overrun small obstacles. We will turn around mountains, but we will reach the sea which is the important thing. And, the sea, in this case, is a modern republic with social justice for all.

c: Can you expand on what your dream of a modern republic with social justice will be. Is there a model? Will Haiti have its own model, or will it be manifest in Haiti more than anywhere else?

JCM: We have to create it ourselves. There are quite a few things we've witnessed in the world that didn't work the way that they were promised to work. If we take Haiti and El Salvador, as examples, we can say the Salvadorian people took up arms and fought for a number of years. Although

13

we cannot say that they have lost; they have not won, either. They are still in negotiations, and they don't have state power. They have lost a large number of people. We have followed a different path—we didn't lose that many people, although our losses were substantial. We didn't ravage the country, and we have a president in the National Palace. So this, it seems to me, is a new path, and there are valuable lessons to be learned from this new path. It seems that in many countries in the Caribbean and South America, even in the Philippines, people are talking of the Haitian way—the Lavalas way.

Now, what is a modern republic? We are talking about bringing down the 85 percent illiteracy rate existing in the country. We must revive our agriculture to become self-sufficient in foodstuffs again. We must reduce our imports, and in Haiti almost all manufactured goods are imported: a cup, a glass, a bottle, a sheet of paper, shoes, material, everything. In Haiti, if you pull out one dollar to buy something, 75 percent of that dollar goes straight back abroad. In this case, accumulation of capital—if we should call it this, money to be invested in the country—is not accomplished. We cannot accumulate anything. Some people have said that when money comes into black communities in the U.S. it turns around only once and goes out—it doesn't stay to build. It doesn't stay to insure health, production, or good jobs. Haiti is even worse than this scenario, because when money comes into Haiti sometimes it doesn't even turn around once. The country seems to reflect money like a mirror reflects the sun—the money flies away. It has become a habit. It has become a system—there are capitalist and socialist systems. We have another system, the system of corruption. It permeates the whole society. A modern republic is a country that will control this. I don't say that corruption will be completely kicked out of the country, it is everywhere, but the level of corruption in Haiti is at 100 percent. It cannot continue this way.

So a modern republic will be all of these: education, health, work, and, more than anything else, the right to determine our life with dignity. We are not talking about a modern republic in which the country will be rich. We don't need that. It seems to me, the world has gone the wrong way by thinking that personal fortune is the solution. Personal fortune is going to be only for the minority, no matter how rich the country is. What we want to do in Haiti, what I would like to see, is a country in which everybody would have the necessities of life. We don't need a swimming pool and two cars in every house; we have the Caribbean Sea, and we will use that. We have a small island, and we can walk around the small island. But, we would have an adequate transportation system. In Haiti, we have so many cars because of the imported dream that we have. Port-au-Prince has traffic jams that you wouldn't see in major U.S. cities. We would like a modern republic admitting that we are a poor country. Our dreams will have to fit our budget, our resources. As far as resources are concerned, many people think only natural resources are important. We may not have a lot, but we don't know yet. The underground resources have not even been explored yet, but we do have human resources. We have plenty of this. Our human resources will be the cornerstone of our development.

c: You mention the corruption in the country, how do you develop democratically with this corruption? In addition, with a Structural Adjustment Plan, how do you plan to reduce imports? How can you counter such a binding plan? And, President Aristide is only in office until February 1996, do you think anyone can follow in his footsteps?

JCM: This is really unbelievable. I have made all the effort I could not to talk about Mr. Aristide. I'm talking about the dreams of my country—the way that I interpret them. The Haitian people have modeled and fashioned somebody named Jean-Bertrand Aristide. The Haitian people can do the same for others. People always see Jean-Bertrand Aristide as somebody who came from I don't know where to impose his view or to convey his dreams to the Haitian people. That's not the way it happened at all.

The Haitian people, in the search for their own future, in searching for a way to come out of this situation, have created many leaders, locally and nationally. Aristide is the product of this struggle and this search. The dream of the Haitian people, the work that we have in front of us cannot be in any way limited by somebody's term in office in any way, shape or form. It was important to bring President Aristide back to reaffirm the Haitian people's right to choose their own leader. We were not going to accept that a group of military men or a group of rich people decided that they would stage coup after coup until the person they wanted was in the National Palace, and what the Haitian people wanted would not be permissible. The struggle was to tell the elites that we, the people, are the only ones to put somebody in the National Palace, and this right that we have conquered will be maintained forever.

If you want to be president, you will have to come in front of us, and you will have to tell us what your program is; what you think about agriculture, about industry, about foreign policy for a small black nation existing in the shadow of the U.S. Then we will say, OK we agree, or no we don't. So this is not a question of Aristide, this is a question of the Haitian people who have for this time chosen Aristide to be their leader.

According to a lot of people, Aristide has become a puppet of the American government, and that he is going to implement economic programs that are going to satisfy, not the Haitian people, but the rich people that he fought and also the American interest. If we continue with the same idea of who creates leaders, everything that Mr. Aristide has agreed to do will have to be again supported by the people, and if it is not, these plans will fall. Everything will have to be understood in detail by the Haitian people. The struggle continues. I would also like to tell you that to my knowledge—I have been President Aristide's spokesperson for the past 10 months he's been in the U.S.—I am not aware of anything that he has signed. I am not aware of any compromise that he put his signature on in order to go back to Haiti. I don't think that he's going to be forced against his will to adopt measures that he, in his heart, knows are against the interest of the Haitian people. This is my strong belief.

c: You also say that one of the tenets of a modern republic, especially in Haiti, is a mass literacy project. What might the principle tenets of such a mass literacy project be, and what role will poets, playwrights, and the artistic community in Haiti play in such a project?

JCM: You see in Haiti, we probably have more artists per capita than any other country. I definitely believe that the role is going to be a very important role. A literacy campaign is not to teach people some symbols saying this is A and this is B, and if you put them together they produce this sound or that sound. It is to open the door of knowledge to people to be able to individually enrich their lives by reading. Also, they have to have, during the first period after literacy, something to read that is talking about them, to them. You cannot educate, cannot interest a peasant from the Artibonite Valley in reading while his main interest is the growing of rice. His life has to be in these books that he is reading, his interests. So, I definitely believe that the work, not only the words of poets, will be very important.

Also, there are in Haiti things that poets who have been living in Port-au-Prince or abroad don't have a clue about. It will be for these people newly arriving to writing and reading to start teaching us about what Haiti is in reality. This is a very important thing.

We are going to find a lot of difficulties too. I have noticed that right now almost all over the world, Haiti included, poets have a tendency of thinking that they are better poets when nobody understands what they are talking about. You read, and you read, and you read, and you cannot figure out, in many languages, what they are talking about. This may be good for people who are sitting in a salon and trying to impress beautiful women. But, it is not going to be good for a Haitian peasant who wants to understand every single word of what he or she is reading. I don't know exactly what is happening in the world, and what is happening in poetry, there was a time—if we are talking about literatures that I know, French literature for instance—that the greatest poets could be understood word by word. You read Lamartine or Victor Hugo or Baudelaire, everyone of them, and you will understand everything that they say. They took well-known flowers and made unique bouquets. Now the tendency is to put artificial flowers in the bouquet. They last longer than natural flowers, but not in poetry. Here, the artificial ones last the space of morning, and the natural flowers are the ones that last for centuries.

In Haiti, we do have poets writing the same way in Creole. Nobody understands what they are talking about, and although I don't have the power to decide, I hope their work will not be included in our literacy campaign. After 400 years of French forced upon the Haitian people, they who fought to make Creole a national language, will they now come to look at Creole and not understand what is being said? Suppose they say, we are stupid, we couldn't understand French and now we also can't understand our own language. The kind of poetry that does this, I personally, would advise keeping in the salons where beautiful people will be impressed by it. As far as something that is working in creating the mind that will implement this modern republic, I don't think there is a place for that kind of poetry.

c: You started writing poems in French, and what made you change to writing in Creole?

JCM: I haven't changed. I still write in French. I have just changed my ratio. I have changed what to say in French and what to say in Creole. I also write in English. I have something to say, and I don't have any intention of hiding it. I have no intention of making people think for three days and three nights in a row to find out why I put this word here and this word there. I don't think this is what poetry is about, at least not what I want to do.

I started writing in French because when I was growing up I was told that Creole was not a language, it is a dialect, it is a patois, it is this, it is that. Creole was a language that you spoke during recess at school. It was a language that you spoke everyday, except when you had something serious or cultural to do. If you were courting a girl, you had to put your Sunday language in your mouth in order to do that. I started writing in French, but later realized that the people who don't know French are the people who should know what I'm writing about. So the best way to reach them was to use their language, that was mine. I still want French people to know what is going on in Haiti, and what is going on in our mind. I would like Americans or British people to know what is going on in our mind. But, if I have to speak to my people, or if I have the chance to speak on their behalf I think I have to write in Creole. But I still write in French and English.

c: An interesting point you made is that most of the modern world has equated personal fortune with satisfaction—an end in itself. You say that that definitely has not been the case in Haiti, and it shouldn't be for its future. There is a different idea and a different dream of welfare in Haiti. Given that Haiti has a high illiteracy rate, with not everyone having access to television and mass communication—which are the elements which in part mend the fabric in industrialized countries—do you think you can help Americans and people in industrialized countries understand what the fabric of the Haitian culture is? How are the fabrics different in our two countries?

JCM: I am a story teller. I am going to tell you a few little anecdotes, and you will see the difference. I had to lecture at a university in Connecticut. There was a photographer who had an exposition in the room in which I was to lecture. There were photos of poverty, open sewers, and naked people washing their clothes in gutters, etc. This is something that is quite sensational. People have a tendency of believing that Haiti is poor, period. This is not true. There would not be a struggle in Haiti if there were no difference between the haves and the have nots. So, I walked into the room after looking at all the pictures and started my lecture by saying that I had a beautiful childhood in Haiti. There was a woman in the room who couldn't stop herself. She said, In Haiti? I said, Yes, I had a beautiful childhood. I did not have money, but it was not that important..

First, I come from a village in Haiti. We call it a town, but you see, with less than 2,000 people you don't qualify in the world as a town. So, I say a village—1,800 to 2,000 people. My mother was born there. Everybody knew not only me and my mother but the whole family tree, and they kept repeating it to me. Oh, you are Jean-Claude, the son of Christian, who was the son of Ferdinand, and Ferdinand's father was Antenor and on and on. I was bored stiff. When I came back for vacation to my village, my biggest problem was that I had to spend one hour walking from the main street to my house. I could throw a rock from main street to the top of my house, but it took me one hour to walk there. I had to go from one porch to another kissing everybody, and I didn't have to know everybody closely. And, they would all ask me the same questions: How was the year in Port-au-Prince? Fine. Did you work well? Yes. Now you may have a girlfriend now?… No… Oh come on now, tell us the truth, do you have a girlfriend now? You have to be careful with the women of Port-au-Prince. I was between 14 and 18, and I would go from this porch to the other across the very narrow street, everyone would listen to my conversation of a few minutes earlier, in detail, but they would go around and ask the same questions again until I got home. So you see, this was enough to start my vacation on the wrong foot. In that village everybody knew who I was. My biggest sin was to spend the vacation without sitting down for dinner at this table or that table. Nothing could happen to me. I belonged there. We had no money. When I pulled a cigarette, the next guy would say, OK leave me half of it. And it was the way we lived, and between the waterfall, the sun, walking and hunting birds there was nothing I needed more after 9 months of work in Port-au-Prince than to go to Plaisance and be among the people of Plaisance. As a matter of fact, I am looking for a place where I can build myself a little house and go back there and never come out again. I have seen the Eiffel Tower. I have seen the Seine. I have seen the St. Lawrence River and the Washington Monument, and my dream is to go back to Plaisance and never come out again.

This is what is different. If you don't have friendship, you need money to try to buy it or to buy the artificial friendship of a psychiatrist. If you have friends you don't need it. Have you noticed that right now the American press never writes Haiti without saying the poorest country in the western hemisphere. People may suffer from hunger but the visible effect of famine is nowhere to be found. This is because people have learned to share. It is part of our being. I was in demonstrations here in Boston when the coup occurred, and people came with food and hot beverages, because it was late September. I don't know who they were and never met them again. This is something that even 30 years of dictatorship has never been able to kill. This is what makes us who we are. This is what makes us a nation, in spite of pressures for 200 years. Our culture is a culture of sharing. We have had dictatorship, and we have had people going against that. But, whenever we have somebody like Aristide coming up, you see these instincts coming out of the woodwork. I am convinced that it cannot be killed. I used to have a group of friends in Port-au-Prince, and we would go to the sea to swim. Sometimes we had no money for public transportation, and the money we did have we had to buy cigarettes and coconuts with. So we would call a tap-tap—a little truck with a canopy on back for transportation, and there were five of us. We would tell the driver, two dead people. This would mean that three of us would pay and two wouldn't have to pay—they were dead. The driver would say come on, don't do this to me. But then the driver would agree. We would then spend the whole day enjoying the coconut water, eating an ear of grilled corn. We would spend the whole day enjoying life. So you see, there are countries where money is less important. Not everything is for sale. This is what, in my opinion, has gone wrong.

Industrialized people have come to a conclusion that everything can be bought. When they go to countries like Haiti, they try to buy things. They have succeeded in buying people, buying conscience, in buying many things, but the whole country is not for sale. All the consciences are not for sale. And that's exactly why we have existed. If we can build a country with these kinds of ideas—that happiness is not something that necessarily comes with money. If we can use our culture to democratically stop some ideas from coming in and becoming popular in the country, and if we can support our artists, our way of seeing life—and I think it can be done—I don't think the danger is whether or not they'll squash us or if we'll spread. I think that Lavalas is not necessarily a Haitian phenomenon.

c: What do you mean by that?

JCM: I think that in every country, there is a possibility for masses of people to stand up and say to their governments, you've been lying to us all this time! When the people realize that their leaders may very well be their worst enemies and when they realize that their leaders are not living their lives, because they're all millionaires, this will be the time. They will realize that most of the career politicians are using politics just for themselves and their own personal fortunes; they don't give a damn about so many people having nothing.

It has always been a puzzlement for me to go to Washington D.C. and see so many homeless people. I cannot understand it. In Haiti, yes. Here? In Haiti, we don't even have enough money to electrify the whole country. Do you know how much money is burned for electricity every second in the U.S.? Look at downtown Boston, I've been here for 32 years, most of the buildings were not there when I arrived here, and I've seen them go up like mushrooms. It takes a lot of money to do that. You mean to tell me that none of this money could be diverted to give shelter to Boston's homeless? I don't believe it. You can show me all the laws and economical laws showing how it's not possible, but humanly it is possible. If the heart and not the head were making the decisions, it would have been done already.

And that's why I think that one day, even here, people may ask, What are you doing with our country? Is it yours alone, or are we part of it? Are we co-owners of this country? What rights do we have? There are a lot of rights that are written in the books. In the U.S. you have the right to go anywhere you want, providing you have the money for the plane. And that's where your right is limited. I think that what I said I will say again, Lavalas is not a Haitian phenomenon.

c: People refer to the Haitian exile community as the 10th Department. How many people in the 10th Department will go back to Haiti, and what role should they play or could they play? In lieu of the conversation we had before about commodification and money as fortune, has the 10th Department maintained the temperament that exists in Haiti or will they bring the Western equation of welfare=money=happiness?

JCM: I think this is a struggle we will have to wage. But let's look at the tendencies. Haitians living outside of Haiti do not have anything directly connecting them with Haiti. When I say directly what I mean is even if Haiti collapses in the ocean, they will be safe, they will have a job. They will have refrigerators and everything. Why is it then that when Aristide declared his candidacy the Boston Haitian community sent close to $90,000 for his campaign? In communities like New York and Miami it was well over $1 million. When the coup occurred, demonstrations were organized in Miami, Montreal, Boston, New York, Chicago, Philadelphia, Washington with thousands and thousands of Haitians. I think the largest one gathered over 100,000 Haitians. It's hard to believe that any American politician can do that here in the U.S. with Americans.

What is the interest? I have been here for 32 years. I have worked here. I got married here, divorced here. I have a son who has never known Haiti. I could easily say my life is here. I have taught in universities. I have worked in warehouses, when I first arrived. I know my way around, and, in spite of my accent I still can speak English. Why am I so involved in what is going on in Haiti that I accepted to be the spokesperson for a president that I had never met before? He was not a personal friend. As a matter of fact, he returned to Haiti, and I didn't go. After 32 years, you cannot just pack up and go. So, I do believe that what we call the 10th Department has a lot to do with our future and our economic development.

The people living abroad are the ones responsible for there not being a famine in Haiti. They send close to $150 to $250 million per year to friends and family. That's very important. We wouldn't like to see them go back to Haiti in droves. That would cause a disaster, but we would like to attract quite a few of them—those who could create employment, create jobs. In the last few months outside Haiti, President Aristide met with Haitian doctors, nurses, engineers, teachers to interest them directly or indirectly in the plight of Haiti. One simple example: Haiti has 1.2 doctors for 10,000 inhabitants, but we still have 2,500 Haitian doctors in the U.S. We don't expect them all to go back to Haiti, but if we can attract 200–300; if we can create a structure by which they go to Haiti, spend their vacation, and do something like work in a clinic or give a lecture in the University; if we can create that revolving door of Haitian professionals living abroad to coming to Haiti; and, if we are very successful we may not even need foreign technicians.

Right now the goodwill toward Haiti is very high. For instance, Fitchburg University is ready to give scholarships to young Haitians, and participate in an exchange of students and faculty. There are quite a number of universities here in the U.S. that can do this. The 10th Department is going to be very important in our future development—not only economically—but on many other ways. They have been living in countries that have, at least, the tradition of democracy. The tradition of having the right to say what you want without being killed. They will come with that—with a new attitude of I have a right to express myself. They will come with the attitude which says, you have to be elected to be a member of the Parliament. You see, these people are going to put more distance between the Haitian people and the tradition of dictatorship by coming with new ideas. Some will come from the U.S., some will come from Canada, some from Europe, and this is the contribution that they will make.

If I invite an American to go to Haiti right now I may be embarrassed. The country doesn't look good, although physically the country's beautiful. My description of Haiti right now is a clean people forced to live in a dirty country. But, Haitians will go there. Our first tourists will have to be Haitians, and we do have enough. If we can attract annually, millions of dollars from Haitians living abroad who would visit Haiti, this would allow the country to change little by little. And, when the country is ready, we will then make tourism what it used to be, the country's second biggest source of income after coffee. This is something that has to be done. It has to be started by those who will go to Haiti without thinking it's too dirty.

There are also about 7 to 8 million Americans who can also be part of this. Those who helped us in the demonstrations. Those who helped us with everything that we have been doing in order to bring democracy back to Haiti; grassroots organizations, religious organizations all over this country. This is what the 10th Department can do: maintain the friendship with those who've helped us, and visit the country. When these people visit the country, it is completely different than when the traditional tourist visits the country. The traditional tourist is going to use only our beautiful climate. They are going to stay in Club Med, for instance, demand a continental breakfast, and after two or three days take the boat or the plane back. They'll learn nothing about Haiti. But, when these people I was talking about go, they try to figure out how to say coffee in Creole; what Haitians eat everyday; what Haitian music is; how Haitians dance. These are the friends that we want. A lot of Americans have told me that Haiti is like crazy glue. You touch it, and you're caught. Ask the American soldiers who are there now—last I heard there are two American soldiers who are going to get married in Haiti to Haitians. They probably won't come back up.

c: One of the attractions of the culture which fascinates me is something we don't experience here in the U.S. The sharing you spoke of comes into play, but on a metaphysical level. Catholicism and the Vodou religions are major pillars of the Haitian temperament. In our culture, one is either a believer in one faith or another. But, in Haiti one can be a strong believer of Catholicism while at the same time being a believer of Vodou and the lwa—the gods of Vodou. How do these two play and survive off each other?

JCM: Let me try to explain that to you. It comes from the history of these two religions. The Africans came with their beliefs. They were very different from one another, because they came from different tribes. You had Mandingos, Ibos, the Congos, the Aradas, the Kaplau, the Fon, and many other tribes. All of them had their own belief systems and their own deities. When they came to Haiti, try to imagine the kind of soup this created, but on top of this there was Catholicism being practiced by the French. Since the French were very adamant about their religion being the only right one—their god being the only true one, they had to impose their beliefs on everybody. The main difference between Vodou and the other religions is that the other religions tell you my god is your god, whether or not you know it. He created you so you owe allegiance to him. You have to kneel and praise him everyday, and if you don't he will punish you. And if you're not careful, I'll punish you in his name.

Because of this multiplicity of tribes and religious beliefs, the Africans were tolerant among themselves. No one told the other my god should be yours. Instead, they would say, Oh, this is your god? Mine is this one. That's all. Vodou is not a religion that imposes itself on others.

Now what happened in Haiti? After 300 years of slavery, and after realizing that the god of the white man was clearly against them, the Haitian Vodou formed itself. The result: gods that never knew each other in Africa met, shook hands, and learned to live together in Haiti. We have so many gods that some people say that there are more gods than Haitians. In order to form one religion out of all these beliefs, the religion had to be extremely tolerant. The way the French Catholics started dealing with Vodou—since Catholicism did not want to be included, because it believed itself superior—was that they started oppressing Vodou. Slavery was the oppressing economic and social system; the French started oppressing the Africans' religious beliefs too.

First, ten days after the slaves' arrival to the colony, they had to be baptized. Just like instant coffee. Put coffee in the cup, add water, and BOOM, coffee. They made instant Catholics—just like that. The slaves didn't understand the dogmas; they didn't understand the language; they didn't understand the concept. They didn't understand anything, but they had to be baptized. They were normally forced to go to mass. There again was a problem, for the masters were not going to accept them inside the church, so they had to stand around the church and receive mass listening to it through opened windows. They couldn't go inside. This made it very clear that not only was this religion not for them, but it was not going to mix with them.

Now with the repression coming down on them, what did they have to do? They had to take all the symbols of Catholicism and change them. This meant that all the icons and the images of the virgin which they would put in their huts allowed their masters to think they were good Catholics. But, for them the icons stood for Ezili, the Vodou Goddess of Love. Little by little, thanks to Vodou, this coexistence came into play, and some people started to believe in both. The two didn't seem to be talking about the same thing at all—so why not? One can eat bread and bananas, so why not? These people are sincere in both. The problem is that even today, Catholics don't accept Vodou and have made Vodou the darkest side of their own religion. They try to tell the people that if you believe in Ogoun or Ezili, you believe in the devil. They made Vodou the dark side of Christianity. But these guys, the Ogoun, Danmbala, and the Agwe, they have nothing to do with Catholicism. They are not the dark side of Catholicism—it's another belief system completely. Vodou has nothing to do with fallen angels. This is what Catholicism has done. From time to time they would violently repress Vodou; the army would go with priests walking in front and praying and chanting. They would go and destroy the temples, arrest the Vodou priest, and all these types of things. It is an ideology, an idea, a belief system; thus, if you come at it and try to destroy it with bullets and violence the only thing it has to do is go underground. And, like any seed that goes underground, it grows stronger. So this is what is happening with Vodou and Catholicism. The slaves started being Catholic, because it was safer for them to be. But, some started to accept Catholicism. Toussaint L'Ouverture, for example, was a Christian. Although Dessalines became a god of Vodou, there is no historical proof that Dessalines was a Vodounist. Dessalines said in his constitution that every single religion was free. That was very advanced for the time, in 1805. This is the strange mixture of these two religions, one oppressing the other.

But something is happening right now. A priest is president, and he is the first one to say that he is the president of everyone: Catholics, Protestants, Vodounists. He uses some Vodou terms in his speaking in such a way that some people say that he is a closet Vodounist. This is not true. It's the same thing as in French literature when writers used Greek or Roman mythological symbols. It's not that the writers believed in them, but they worked very well as far as symbolism was concerned. This is what President Aristide does sometimes. He is not a Vodounist. He strongly believes in religious tolerance, and that it cannot remain within the Christian denominations. It has to go everywhere. As long as somebody has a belief and this belief doesn't bother others, one must respect the belief. One has a right to practice one's belief.

c: Is that a tenet of liberation theology?

JCM: Yes, definitely.

c: Writer Joël Des Rossiers said that the young generation of artists in Haiti and abroad has begun to speak more from their interior and their personal lives. He claimed this to be the young generation's modernity. That they are presenting the "I" in their work. But, there is another trend, writers like Jacques Roumain and René Depestre's whose writing embody the concept of "WE." Writer Yanick Lahens wrote an essay that said that the challenge of art and literature and the country itself is how to mesh the "I" and the "WE." Would you comment on that?

JCM: In countries like the U.S., France, U.K., art is something that is more or less part of leisure. In countries like Haiti, it's one way to express something, to reach out for other people. This is not because we choose to, but this is what has attracted people to write. It is because of what they have seen: injustices, death, and abuse. If you look at what is going on in Western civilization, in general, I would definitely say that Western writers have nothing else to say. If you listen to the radio after a few hours, only one or two songs would not have said, Be mine tonight, Dream come true, or I'll be there. These sentences seem to appear in every song. If you were to take all these phrases, write them down on little pieces of paper, and put them in a hat, somebody could compose a song just by grabbing a bunch of these papers and putting them together. The song is made. If you look at TV and movies, I would say that the genre right now is guns, sex, and fast cars. That's what it is.

Thus for us in the third world, the industrial world doesn't have anything to tell us anymore. The Victor Hugos, the Shakespeares, the Frosts, the Longfellows, the Lamartines are gone, and what Europe is telling us (and when I say Europe, I mean European culture, in general) is just corruption. They seem to tell us the world is doomed. Take whatever you can, as fast as you can. Enjoy it, and after that to hell with the rest. Even with your family that will follow you. What they seem to be telling us is that we only have two days to live. In Haiti, we say that only for Carnivale. I don't think that I can pass the opportunity of making you realize that lately more and more writers from the third world have been getting the Nobel Prize. In our area of the world, man is living an experience. We are the ones who will be able to tell people what is going on. The so-called civilized world has run out of ideas.

I have been to poetry readings where the poet has been published left and right. The first thing I notice is that there are only 15 people attending to hear him or her, and the second thing is that I don't understand what the poet is talking about. This is the poetry of the "I." They are trying to tell you things that are going on inside their soul that are so obscure that they are not understandable. You're wondering if he or she is a human being, like you are, or another type superior to your type. I don't know. I don't understand. The form has overcome the meaning, and it has become fashionable for them to say something that nobody else can understand. This is, in my opinion, the last refuge of the "I." I believe that we are living in societies. We may not have chosen this, but that's where we are. Whatever we are doing, we are part of the society. The suffering of others must be of concern. We have, when we speak, to be part of that society. I cannot understand why 98 percent of every song is talking about problems between one man and one woman. What about poverty? What about friendship? What about love between children and their parents? What about love of nature? What about injustice and abuse? Each one of these ideas could generate millions of songs, but for some reason the songs that we listen to every day talk about

Be mine tonight, I'll be there, and/or You love me. I love you. We're happy, I love you. You don't love me; I'm unhappy. This makes it seem as if this is the only problem in the world.

My opinion is that all these things are happening in a society, and this society is going to influence and determine why this woman loves you or not. Suppose you are black and the woman is white, and all the parents are against it. See, there are backgrounds. There are frames in which the painting has to sit. I think that's where the "WE" comes from. If there are young Haitians who are coming back to the "I," I am very sorry to tell them that they will attract a group of people in Haiti that think like Europeans. Thinking they have only two or three days to live so let's get the best of it. For the large masses of Haiti, they are not going to go anywhere. They may not even be recorded in our literature, as people of any kind of significance. Haiti is living an era of the "WE," whether or not we want to write about what we want, what we feel. Haiti is now living a "WE" period. It will be very interesting to notice how many young people will try to go against the grain, and what they will harvest from that.

c: Does this "WE" have a vision. You say that no one is saying anything in the first world. Is there a commonality the third world shares in its literatures, is there a vision?

JCM: On the one hand, it's selfishness. Everything is done to become a celebrity. On the other hand, we have people who are coming together to make life better. To make tomorrow better. People who are still concerned about their sons, grandsons, granddaughters, these are the two opposing tendencies that we have. They are not new.

They have always been like that, but it so happens during the time of Shakespeare, Corneille, and Racine—all the educated people who could be writers were on one side. You can see that the majority of work they did focused on what was going on in the court or around the king. Now, we have more people from the other side who can also write. The first thing they did, as far as the forms are concerned, was break them down. They said, it doesn't have to be this way. It doesn't have to rhyme. That's the first thing they started to do. The other side was saying, you are going about it in this way because you cannot rhyme. But, they had things to say, and they didn't think it was that important for the things that they had to say to be tied up in rules and regulations. It had to come out fast—even though the form may not have been very good in the beginning. Yet, little by little the form came. The meanings were awakening. That's exactly why you can see all

27

these changes that generations after generations create in literature—those who never wrote started to write and started to talk about things that are completely different.

Today in the third world we still have slavery. I'm not talking about slavery in a very poetic manner, slavery in the way that it used to exist. There are parts of India, parts of Africa, parts of the Arabic Gulf where slavery is as pure as it used to be, and you have people starting to denounce these things. People must realize that in the time of Shakespeare there was slavery, but he never mentioned it. Corneille and Racine were living in the time of slavery—they never mentioned it. We had to wait until the 18th century with Diderot to start understanding that a little concern started to appear in Europe about the issue.

What is happening now is that sons and daughters of slaves are starting to talk. They want to talk, and they're starting to master writing in such a way that they have to be recognized. That's why I mention the Nobel Prize, although for me it is not of great importance. But, it has to be noticed. This is what is going on. You will understand, also, that the "I" and the "WE," although not allying themselves straight on this border, are also part of what's going on. In Haiti right now, you cannot tell me that I'm going to write about "I" and my personal feelings when I go around and see what happened in the last hurricane, for example. People were forced to live on dry beds of ravines, and some were taken away by the torrents and are now dead. How can I look at that and not feel part of that, isn't part of that my responsibility? I carry a bit of the guilt for it occurring, and I carry a little bit of the hope that some of the problems can be solved. I am not the type of person who would write about being caught in a house during the hurricane with a beautiful woman and how beautiful the experience was, even if it had occurred. Why not try to include the voices of those who didn't speak, those who cannot speak, and how they felt about it? It is not a question of me standing on the wall of the ravine and crying over the people who died. I try and see how I would have felt if the water were coming after me. That's exactly what makes the difference. That's what I'm talking about between the "I" and the "WE" generation. In Haiti, until a lot of things are resolved we are going to live in the era of the "WE." For me, my choice is made. I think I will spend the rest of my life trying to be the voice of those who don't speak or for whom writing is an impossibility.

c: How do you perceive your two roles as a political player and a poet? Do they contradict themselves at all? Are they one and the same?

JCM: There is no contradiction whatsoever. Because of my age and because of the amount I have still to write, I have chosen to write instead of being an active political person. But, I have to tell you, it's because I think I would be more useful in this role. However, if somebody convinced me that the best way I could help my people would be to stop writing and get involved in politics and get elected as a senator, I would. If someone could convince me of that, I would make it a priority. I am a Haitian revolutionary that has chosen writing as a weapon. I couldn't have chosen anything else. So, there is no contradiction for me at all.

c: How effective is a weapon like writing in a country with such a low literacy rate? How important is the oral tradition in Haiti?

JCM: The oral tradition is everything for the moment. I'm going to give you one example. I would say 20 or 30 years ago, when a Haitian had to write to another Haitian, they would call somebody that we call a savé—meaning somebody who knows. Then he would dictate to the guy in Creole what the savé would write down in French. The letter would be sent. Another guy would be called, and he would take the letter in French and orally translate it into Creole to the recipient of the letter. Do you know between the first dictation and the last hearing how much distortion was presented? Now, the Haitian people are still, for the majority, illiterate, but they have solved the problem. They take a cassette, they record themselves, and mail the cassette. It goes directly to the recipient. They have eliminated the two middlemen.

I put my poetry on records and everybody listens. One month before the coup, I went to a peasant gathering where they were talking about their organization, but there was a cultural part of it. A young girl of about 16 or 17 stood up and recited by heart, without hesitation, one of the longest narrative poems I've written. I was sitting there. She didn't know I wrote it. She didn't know who I was. But she knew it by heart. I don't think she read it anywhere. She listened to the record, memorized it, and recited it.

c: A friend of ours was in Haiti at a rally upon the return of Aristide and they sang your poem, "Tomorrow's Haiti."

JCM: Yes. They've made it their weapon. Technology can be used by anybody. This is what they have done. This is why, too, I put my work on cassette and records so they can listen to them. They play them on the radio, so they are more available to everybody. The oral tradition in Haiti is very important in Haiti. Not only in Haiti, but all over Africa, as well. It is a very important tool.

My Broad Back
Paul Laraque

Any way you shuffle the cards
I'm an ass with four aces

the coffee's me
the new banana's me
the sisal's me
the cotton's me
the sugar's still me
but you play with a stacked deck

one day I'll stand up
I'll say no
I'll stand up downtown
I'll stand up in the village
in the field
on the hill

that day we'll know that this time is gone
and another is going to begin

The Bull at Nan Souvenance
Marilene Phipps

I
He was brought in yesterday
as an offering
for today's Easter Sunday rites,
pulled by a rope
to these ancient and sacred grounds of Souvenance,
then tied by the Acacia tree, all day, unfed.

Now, noontime, he lies and waits,
his root-like legs make dust enclaves
next to his sweat-furrowed flank.
He no longer shows annoyance
towards the scrawny chick hopping
around and pecking at his flesh.
"PA MANYIN'L
SE LANMO WAP GADE!"—
"Don't touch him!"—
a voice threatens us—
"It is Death you're seeing!"

The bull stands up.
His nostrils reach, breathe in
towards the growing crowd.
Hands with a purpose, now untie him,
take him to another tree. He goes,
as if for his familiar fields.
"DON'T TOUCH HIM!
DON'T YOU KNOW!?"

II
Now
the bull is resisting!
all legs stiffened,
he won't get close to
this tree! Swiftly,
ropes are wound at the base of

each of his horns,

        crossed

on his forehead,

        and yanked

on either side.

                They force

the
flat part of his broad face

               against the tree

trunk.

               Men dragging

at his tail keep him

               aligned. He

can't move.

               He can't see

beyond the tree bark,

               the roots or his

hoofs.

               Midday sun

stings him.

A man straddles him, he can't move.

               He hears all
               where he can

no longer look.
The bull trembles.
The ropes are tugged tighter
and fastened behind the tree.
A shiver vibrates down his spine,
his entrails deliver their moist soil—
he defecates. Someone in the crowd, laughs.

        "METE GASON SOU NOU!"
        "We must be virile!" René
        Master of Ceremony—calls out,
        flourishing his machete
        to the Hounsis, handmaidens of Gods,
        gathered around him in white dresses.

They respond and wave their machetes,
symbolic wooden ones. Now René
shakes hands with the executioner
over the stilled body of the bull.
"LET US BE MEN!"

III

The dagger and the screams
start in the same instant.
Deep, long, helpless bellows;
thick, grey tongue extended,
recurved, stiff and drooling.

The knife misses its aim
    for the spine, at the base of the neck,
        pulls out and stabs again.
Again, twists, pulls out and stabs again.

Blood gurgles, gushes out,
    drawing a red web on the bull's back
        like lava's hands about to blanket
the city in silence.

The legs falter,
    then regroup.
        The dagger thumps down again.
Again, the legs falter and fold.

Like a great ship sinking,
    the rear lowers first—his head
        being stuck at the tree.
But he stands up again!

"TO THE THROAT!" René shouts.
    The executioner abandons
        the spot above, to start
cutting, with a small knife,

into the thick of the throat

underneath, inching the blade
    through the feeling flesh, alive.
The wind and the bellows

wrestle into the leaves
   above us. More warm dung drops
      to the ground. The vocal cords
get cut. A last gurgling hiss…

He can no longer voice what he feels.
Shut in. Further removed.
Hung by the horns, the great
black body slumps and kneels
to the live tree. The last
that the bull sees is not
this immaterial blue,
a tropical Easter Sunday sky,
but his own red blood's swamps.

The crowd cheers.

If the Pope Knew
Félix Morisseau–Leroy
translated by Patrick Sylvain

If the archbishop knew
how Haitians
love
bread
he would make hosts as big as bread
wine
people would partake in communions
during each Sunday mass
if the pope knew
how Haitians
love
rum
he would ask God to turn stale water into
rum
paradise would be filled
with saints

To and From
Danielle Legros Georges

for my mother
November, 1993

She laughs as she tells of their escape from the rural region
where they'd grown their farm of chickens and goats,
rice fields, some beans.

Despite not being a market woman she'd been shrewd,
forced to be, in a country ruled by anticipation

of food shortages,
of shortages of gasoline,
            of shortages
            of electricity,
            shortages of power;
            of power shifts.

        Her husband in his impeccable restraint recounts
        their consideration of the hen house as refuge,
        behind the barbed wire or in the plantain fields
        where humans and trees are often confused at night,

        While the gunmen, if they came this time
        shot the house, perhaps a dog, indiscriminate
        as the circulating lists of marked individuals:

                radio announcers,
                teachers,
                the religious,
                students,
                so-and-so Jean Baptiste,
                followed by
                woman of so-and-so Jean Baptiste.

The woman and man laugh now at their fifty-eight-
and-nine-year-old daring, the old couple,
how at rooster's crow they crept into their station wagon

Through the hills of Plaisance, down the coast into Gonaives
where stood their old church (sign-of-the-cross)
through the Raboteau the army dared not enter,
where the people threw back the clothes the governors had brought,
threw foreign rice into canals.

They drove fast around the brown and green hills, like race car drivers,
like the drivers of country buses, like all the country's drivers,
this time not gunning for goats or stray street dogs,
but for the teaming capital, where anonymity would protect them.

Reversibility
Charlot Lucien
translated by Danielle Legros Georges

Look, said the flower,
At the passionate flame of my petals.
I gazed
And, adjusting my heel on it,
Crushed it against the earth.

Look, said the butterfly,
The rainbow mirrors itself in my wings.
I cast an eye, and
Lancing a deadly hand,
Crushed it between my fingers.

Look, sang the brook,
At my water's crystalline green.
I saw, then
Clearing my throat,
Spit passionately in its course.

Farther, a bird chattered on in space,
Mocking me with its cries,
Believing itself inaccessible.
I picked up a stone
And threw it.

The bird ceased to sing
And perched itself on a branch
Contemplating something below.
I saw it peck at sprigs, at flowers
Letting them drop to the tree's base...
I drew near,
and here,
Lying in mud
Head burst, bloody,
and petaled with flowers,
My son.
Dead.

Hoping for Lavalas
Patrick Sylvain

In the land where dictatorship is king,
          old rifles become
sub-machine guns and
handshakes turn into knives,
a Lavalas child has grown
into a priest,
a president,
a love,
he casts a shield of lungs
to help his country breathe
fresh and clean political air.

China

Sleeplessness
Tzu-yeh   [3 poems]
translated by Taylor Stoehr

Sleepless all night
        sleepless

full moon too bright
        too bright

I heard a voice
        my voice

answer the emptiness
        yes!

Toward Evening

Hot summer sky
        not a breeze
toward evening
        clouds.

Take my hand
        come amongst the leaves
cool melons float in the pool
        a red plum bobs.

Autumn

She opens her shutters
        to the autumn moon.

She blows out her candle
        silk stirs in the room.

She smiles to herself
        the last knot's undone.

Orchid blossoms fill
        the night with perfume.

Fragments of Shadow
Chen Dong Dong
translated by Yong Chin

I

The veins of the sun flew silent   In its shadow
Run mountains and a group of roofs
The coastal temples suddenly retreat   In the silence
I see Jin-wei's braids hanging all over the tree
Flakes of black birds are flying over here and then they fly away

The west wind disperses the sea and the midsummer
The fish are being taken
To the deserted city in the moon
On the first page of those music scores
Seven goats gather around Kua-fu dumbfounded
To observe his forest

I open the books and set the story of betrayal and revenge free
The seven goats bow at once
And calmly stride across the cliff overlooking the sea in the
              blazing sun

Now   Poetry
We escape death among the sharks

II

Singing a hymn to a Thought
Singing a hymn to a flatboat
Hearing the tides surge against the shore   Seeing the limbs weaving
I find
The verses are still under the reef

The overlooking sun has a wider vision
In the flower-filled harbor the lion is tender
And the maids run up to the dam of desire
Waiting to be stroked by us
Bronze butterflies are screaming their rustles

Which awaken Pan-gu and his language
Let us occassionally stroke the white salt
Let us occassionally recognize its direction
And let us understand the mumbling of the dead
Sunshine pours into the thick-bottomed vase
Midnight is singing
And we go drinking the midsummer in the sea

III

The sea is the painter of daytime
The high rocky wall with leaves dropping off is the painter of me
The sun raises storms and pushes the boat toward
The eyesight of Dusk
Now the calm broken-armed hymn flys far away from the Hall
And climbs up onto the black banner of the tower

I see alarmed birds rise over the sparse rocky beach and
The sea waters stretch out like a table cloth
Two mermaids
Whose spangled and slim bodies seem to be a fork-and-knife
A lunch within the white walls and two apples
And two sour oranges   Two adventures
To the lighthouse
Again I see so many alarmed birds rise
To search around the sun for freshwater and the flame's dreg

IV

Go into the dream to search out the west wind
Go onto the top of the lofty city wall
Split the memory
Make the sharks hop in joy with pebbles
And make the old voice surpass the sun in surprise
The black iron-horses hang high in the air
They neigh and gallop into eternity

Seven goats appear spontaneously
And ruthlessly leap in the crazy midsummer over the roofs and

the flag pole
On the breakwater a poplar is in high tide
Offering the chirping cicadas and music generously

The sea is at ebb   The sea pecked by parrots and glass
And the empty city behind me
Breaks into nine pieces now
Down with the stream
The west wind blossoms in full posture of the pomegranate
And makes Nu-wa discern me

V

River deers and kangaroos jumping
The maid in the red inn singing
Between mask and mask
The wine-soaked black dress is torn and dazzling
Her gaze is dry but warm

Side by side we are at the water's ford—
Her black hair attracts the wind
Off our lips the wounded birds fly away
The lost sun rains in torrents
And drenches Xin-tian, who is leading a dance on the beach

Each leaf is a running horse
And their breaths remind me of the cry of shoals
Opening the lid
Opening the glass vase in which the sound pierces the bubbles
I will witness the stars shedding blood
And the singing maid enters now
The shadow of the setting sun

I. line 4, Jin-wei: A legendary bird who tries to fill up the sea with twigs, because its human body was drowned in the sea. line 10, Kua-fu: A mythological hero who chased the sun until he died of thirst, and whose body became a forest. II. line 11, Pan-gu: The male creator of the earth and the heaven in Chinese myths. IV. line 18, Nu-wa: The female god who repaired the broken firmament in Chinese myths. V. line 10, Xin-tian: The rebellious hero against the god of heaven in Chinese myths.

City in Hibernation
Meng Lang
translated by Denis C. Mair

Go into a fallen leaf to follow after autumn
Down a long deserted street
Walk farther than a human being.

Sad days that hang from tall trees shed their leaves
But in whose heart do I hang painfully?

A long street dances in the breeze
What road could more resemble a bare tree trunk
Filled up inside with hollow cries?

Reach out to touch the sky's blue features
Pressed by her own strength into a curve
A lone leaf getting lower, approaching life's limit

I reach out my hand, raising a fallen leaf
As if at a burial, I offer it to a city's solemn sleep

No one awakens! No one awakens!
Like a human being, I'll walk this long empty street
            to the end!

Night
Bei Dao   [2 poems]
translated by Yanbing Chen and John Rosenwald

volleys of waves brimming with detail
light beyond us—
imagination arising from wounds
the moon: a nurse moving from bed to bed
winding a clock for every heart

we put on smiles
take off beards underwater
from three directions, we memorize the wind
and at the height of a cicada
watch a widow's world

more than all misfortunes, night
speaks with eloquence
night, under our feet
this lampshade for poetry
is already broken

Another

this sky, mediocre at chess
watches the sea change color
the ladder winds deep into the mirror
at the school for the blind, fingers
stroke the birds' extinction

this table idle in the winter
watches the lights flutter
memory, more than once, looks back
archers of freedom, in a foreign land
listen to the winds of history
some have long changed their names
or been suppressed by us
below the horizon
yet among us, another

Memory
Bei Ling   [2 poems]
translated by Tony Barnstone and Xi Chuan

You hear the sound of it peeling off
The sound of its fall to earth
Its old eyes are astigmatic
Reluctant to leave quietly
Like a solitary river
It makes these small noises

It's always behind us
Walking us forward on our feet
Ready to give us pain.

Silence
translated by Tang Chao and Lee Robinson

sunlight in layered beams
casts its slant on a page
hangs, like a clock
stretched into a labyrinth, a riddle and a
mystery

we watch each other across the wall
rain fictionalizes our windows
like weeking, like the secret codes of a harp
spreading words and
wounded silence

Ireland

A Nomad
Gregory O'Donaghue

Imagine a man
Who has mastered, along
With foreign currencies,
The inoffensive smirk.

Who comes and goes
As though he belonged;
As if to say that in
Any back-of-the-beyond

He is at least
As matter-of-fact as
Ticking red lights
Descending on runways.

He might never have imagined
Endless notes in bottles,
Or dreamed that love
Or some other miracle

Could tell him who he is:
On a picnic-chair.
At a lake's edge, a thin
Man with an open map.

Achill Island
Eithne Strong   [2 poems]

Do not speak now
because of the beauty.
And yet the day must not
pass before I bear witness.

No day has been like this day.

You could take my hand
strongly in yours
and with swift purpose
seek to speed me

past my failings; your voice
could tell me how to hold
when weakness drags
my traitor self.

But I must go alone
and put my head
low upon the heather
to find my strength.

Old druid hills
gird black the sunset sky.
Old, old strength of immemorial earth
lies quiet beneath my tangled heart.

Nigh midnight now
yet twilight holds the mystic time.
Heathered wind is light
about the ancient rocks.

Down the Street

Have you stood
and watched him go?
By a window have you?
And seen the sun
flood the day
where pain hung
at his going?

And have you waited long
long after he had left the sun,
not stirring because
of the coursing pain
beating hard
on the walls of your being
relentlessly?

And have you,
having stood
and waited
timelessly,
gathered carefully
your little shattered strengths
and without moving

and almost without hope,
tested their fragile weight
against the day
that must come
and go,
and come and go again
and he not there?

Astronauts
John F. Deane

They are tinfoil crayfish in free drift
through the underwater world of space;
they walk nonchalantly out on emptiness,
balance on fingertips a factory of steel;

what we miss are the bubbles
rising reassuringly above them and
tying them still to our breathing;
words emanate from them like the words we spoke

in childhood into resonating old tin cans;
further space is black beyond black
and the earth looms bigger and more beautiful
than we had remembered;

ah well, perhaps they will have learned something
and will come back to tell us if they can find the words.
Sometimes this is how I see it—death—
and I am turning slowly in an old-time waltz

outwards, away from camera, in silence;
I am a lexicon dispersed, debris
among debris or even, for a moment,
a shooting star in somebody's night sky.

Broken Arrow
Colm Breathnach

The air is fresh
after rain.

The sky is blue
with little white clouds

and things we never said to each other.

I shot an arrow into the ravine
when I thought I heard feathers rising.
Under a withered bush
I found it broken.
A small white feather
lying beside it

and there are things we haven't said to each other yet.

But who else will say
those things to you.

A large bright bird ascended to the skies,
and its wings hid the sun from my eyes.

And there are things that cannot be said even,

so I bring home to you in their place
this broken arrow
after the chase

and the things our hearts cannot express
rise through the sky on white wings.

Goddess
Fred Johnston

I will make myth out of a turn of phrase
your blue-green eye full of evening light

full-bellied, the boats come home
sails big-cheeked, gulls everywhere

with one hand's turn you've driven
the nail of love into the honeycomb heart

wind catches your dress, its shivering hem
new weather promised from the empty West

skin like monk's vellum, dig a cell
out of the scholar's skull, ransack

his eel's soul, that dark sinewy ripple
under the surface of his candlelit mind

his stone tower needs plundering—
your hand over mine, the river swelling.

To "the last good poem."

A Conversation with Eavan Boland   [1996]

c: Now that the woman is the author rather than the object of the Irish poem, you say such authorship re-opens questions of identity, issues of poetic motive, and ethical direction. "And since poetry is never local for long, that in turn widens out into further implications." Would you discuss what those implications may be?

EB: I think the movement from being the object to being the author of the Irish poem is very characteristic of women poets in Ireland. But it isn't unique to them. Not by any means. The new literatures of the minorities, the new voices within them, are also doing just that: they're testing out the relationship between authorship and the past. Between tradition and innovation. Between the margin and the center. So what I meant is that women poets in Ireland, just by inscribing their subject matter on the Irish poem, are opening questions which are wider than the local literature. On the other hand, I think Irish women poets are an interesting model at the moment of that relationship between margin and center. The truth is that, however daunting and established a literary tradition is, the history of language and literature has shown us over and over again that if the center defines the margin, the margin also defines the center. I came to feel this strongly as a woman poet in Ireland. Women poets began on the margins of the Irish poetic tradition, and I include myself in that. Twenty years ago they were perceived as writing from private lives which could not be fully political—as bringing subject matter into the Irish poem which was somehow not as fitted for its tradition as other subjects. And so there were tensions. Those tensions in turn opened an important dialogue between the margin and center of Irish poetry—as to just who was writing the so-called Irish poem. Who, if anyone, was setting the agenda for it. And even if the answers can't be found to those questions, the dialogue is challenging and refreshing. And has been, I think, good for Irish poetry.

c: Who is setting the agenda for poetry in Ireland and how is this done?

EB: That would be hard to say. Ideas of what poetry is, how it operates, should always, I suppose, come from the last good poem. So maybe the correct answer is that the poem in its time sets the agenda. Nothing more or less. But that isn't quite the complete answer either. There are other more subtle sides to that question. For a long time, for instance, I don't think Irish poetry set the agenda so much as it had an agenda set for it. I'm looking far back now, to the 19th and early 20th century. Then there were all kinds of national self-esteem, self-regard, self-discovery that made a subtle agenda for Irish poets. In my view, that was damaging. I think poets like Padraic Colum felt that kind of pressure and were injured by it. They were screen-tested for walk-on parts in an unfolding drama of Irish identity. Patrick Kavanagh lashes out against that in his wonderful "Self-Portrait," his prose piece, where he speaks about coming to Dublin and feeling under pressure from "the Irish thing." The truth is, of course, that poets shouldn't be part of those agendas, but of course in a small country like Ireland, with a powerful history, that's easier said than done. I suppose what all of this has taught me is that there's a real risk of being at the behest of another agenda than your own. Let me give an example. I think women's poetry in Ireland preexisted the critique for it. There was no critique in place in Irish poetry to consider their voices, their subject matter, the fact that both of these were calling into question the value system on which Irish poetry had operated for so long. So women poets there—I certainly felt this—often got reproached for failing to measure up to an agenda they had never set and didn't aspire to. That's one of the reasons I wrote *Object Lessons*. Apart from this, I've remained troubled about that whole relationship between poetry and the critique which greets it for several reasons. One of them is just my own location in Irish poetry, my sense of the richness and the narrowness of the tradition. But I'm also haunted in a small way by John Hewitt and his work, and the attitude to it at the time. I knew him a little bit. I reviewed him often. I once interviewed him for Irish television. I admired the edge and the outsider's darkness in his work. I even thought he was a defining perspective on some aspects of poetry in Ireland. But he was so often considered and dismissed with the critique which had been evolved for the mainstream national-poetic tradition that it was painful to watch. All that's changed since his death. But I also know for a fact—I spoke to him briefly a few weeks before he died—that he felt isolated and underappreciated. For me it was frustrating to see the poetic climate I lived in have such a dearth of vocabulary that it couldn't find the words to honour a valuable and challenging achievement. To get back to your question, the relation between poetry and agenda is never easy at any time.

c: What does the entry of the woman as an author in Irish poetry change, what does it add, what does it reveal about Ireland that wasn't evident before?

EB: Women poets in Ireland have broken silences, sometimes I think in quite modest ways, and often in more ambitious ones. Just being able to put a washing machine into a poem can seem a small thing. But when I was a young poet I felt these small things were signs for larger ones. I found it quite difficult to put the life I lived into the poem I wrote and also, of course, quite essential. It's only by doing these things, by insisting on their own reality in the poem, that poets in any tradition teach their poetry new human words. Just because it appears to be at a modest or domestic level, I don't think that act should be underestimated. It also re-writes the edges and limits of the possible subject matter of a contemporary lyric. That's important. And then of course these apparently small, domestic details widen and broaden to become part of the important political act of making a poetry more inclusive.

c: Juxtaposed with male poetry in Ireland, what do women's poems reveal about the differences between men and women in your country and universally? You argue that men treated women as objects in the Irish poem. Since then, how have women written about men or other loved ones. What does the object lesson teach the male poet for the 21st Century? How can or should the male poet discuss the woman, and love, in his poems? Are there examples that you can think of?

EB: Irish poetry has never really been a place where I look to find a fever chart of the differences between men and women, either in Ireland or beyond it. But I do see a considerable register of the relationship between the Irish poem and the literature of the past, with its compelling patterns of national subject matter and so on. And I think I need to be clear about the exact nature of this. I never, for instance—although your question might suggest this—merely argued that men treated women as objects in the Irish poem. That wouldn't make sense. What I did argue is that the confusion of the feminine with the national in some male poetry—the mixing of one set of images with another—made an icon of the feminine and an emblem of the national. That's the result of all those casual and customary usages of Cathleen ni Houlihan and the Shan van Vocht. And in the process I really do think a poetry can lose its heart and its hearing for the daily, complex, surprising lives of women—especially when they don't fit that iconography. Some of that may be changing now. Let me also take up a phrase you use in your question. "How can or should the male poet discuss" etc.? I don't feel I have, or should have, a view on that. Those are freedoms which properly belong to other poets. My problem was never with the ambiguous references of any male poet to an actual theme, or a woman, or any of that. If anything I think we need to recognize that the imaginative freedoms of all poets—men and women—are mirrors of one another. We need to support all poets in their search for those freedoms. My criticism was of a customary, conventional, and stifling iconography within the Irish poem, which I felt was closely linked to intolerance of women as actual makers of that poem. And I want to emphasize again, I think this may be changing.

c: You speak of the woman poet to have been outside history until recent times. Was women's poetry not a significant part of the Irish Literary Revival? What of Ethna Carbery, Katherine Tynan, Susan Mitchell and others? What similarities or differences are there between women's poetry during the Revival and the re-emergence of women's poetry during your generation? What might be their cumulative impact on future generations of Irish writing?

EB: Those writers you mention—Katherine Tynan especially—were poets I looked at with great respect when I was young. I still look at them with great respect. But no, I don't think they were considered—the ones who lived at the time of the Revival—to be ground-breaking Irish poets. The truth is their poems were always interesting, but often quite conventional. Sometimes they seem, sadly enough, just to be echoing the conventional Revival lyric rather than questioning, through a lens of womanhood, what was going on at that time. Certainly there's an anomaly in having women poets in Ireland writing anti-colonial poems when they themselves were members of a colonized constituency, and not using the second to refer to the first. It seems contradictory. If they could have brought together the two conditions, even through irony, it would have made their work more coherent and persuasive. Without that there's definitely some contradiction. Certainly, though it's painful to say it of talented and distinguished women, most of them—I remain very interested in Katharine Tynan—missed the opportunity to ask the radical questions of the connection between Irish poetry and the national tradition which I think an Irish woman poet needed to ask if she was going to find her own voice. I think it's important, by the way, to be truthful and direct about all this, even if it is difficult. Of course I want to read Irish women poets in recent 19th and early 20th century history. On the other hand, quite a lot of what they wrote is not good at all and wishful thinking won't change that. It doesn't—I think recent feminist history shows this—alter or undo exclusions or omissions to produce names and argue that those names change the contours of a literature, simply because the writers were women. That misses the point of the argument.

c: During the Irish Literary Revival, Irish myth and folklore became a major subject matter for poetry—and a political act. What kind of role does such matter play in contemporary Irish poetry?

EB: The search for subject-matter is always a part—maybe a somewhat self-conscious part—of a search for a national literature. There are very endearing and aspiring aspects of this in the literature of the Irish Revival, from Douglas Hyde to Lady Gregory. But it was self-conscious. It was very willed. Occasionally it had absurd characteristics. The best part of it—I'm thinking of the actual Cuchulain legends here—was the way it allowed a poet like Yeats to explore a line between invention and memory, between self-creation and self-mythologizing. There's something so big and spacious and interesting about those Cuchulain plays he wrote. And "Cuchulain Comforted" at the end of his life is a wonderful underworld elegy for all the heroisms he had finally discarded. So, what works, works. But I think that subject matter has long been replaced together with the intense self-consciousness that went with it.

c: What aspects of the Irish revival do you find endearing or inspiring?

EB: I think what's so impressive about the Irish Revival are the elements of individual courage and expression that managed to co-exist with a fairly onerous programme of national literary endeavour, which could really have been suppressive of imaginative enquiry. The writers didn't let themselves be suppressed. And that liberated all of us who came after. I think in the end these writers—I'm thinking especially of Yeats, Synge, O'Casey—did, as the saying goes, speak truth to power. Yeats, especially, managed to make out of a very fragmented series of commitments to theatre, and popular culture, and elite yearning and so on, a deeply coherent and demanding private vision. He told the truth as an artist. And of course it could have been so different. We could have had a carefully executed series of sentimental actions in poetry and prose and drama. Which would have reassured us of our Irishness and, in the process, made it synonomous with our humanity. Instead, through the best of the work in the Revival, the core of the Irish experience—its disaffection and endurance—was made the starting point for a profoundly improvisational study of language under duress, and identity which was never satisified with itself. It seems to me a wonderful redemption of history—that out of all that silence came this particularly challenging music.

I've never ceased to be grateful for it all.

c: In *Object Lessons* you write that poetry and "poetic images are not ornaments; they are truths." With this in mind, has the poetry that has been written by men with the woman as an ornament not been the truth of the times? And if these poems were in fact not truths, how could they have spoken to so many people? Isn't the lack of female representation an exact reflection of the times in a political sense?

EB: This is a complicated matter. Images are not ornaments. They are indeed signs for a truth. But I think the question also somewhat short-circuits the references to the arguments I've been making. I don't think that poems "with the woman as ornament" ever really were true in their time, in the sense of powerful poetic truth. There are good, persuasive, moving love poems in every time. Their truth—this certainly is the case of Donne and Shakespeare and Housman and Auden, all wonderful love poets—lies in the volatility, pain, and truth of the subject; that is, in the voice of the male speaker regretting his loss or celebrating his love. The more volatile the subject the more real and true the object. That I think is almost a law of language and poetry. But the subtle political and poetic question of whether the love poem is addressed to a silent object, or in fact is part of the silencing of the object, is a fascinating one. But asking whether the ornamental image isn't "a truth of the times" is like asking whether the absence of African-American poets isn't a truth of American poetry in the 19th century. These are facts, rather than truths. You never want to dignify omissions and distortions as truths.

c: Can we ask you the same question you asked Padraic Colum. What do you really think of Yeats?

EB: I love Yeats. I still remember the excitement, all those years ago, when I was in school, reading his work under the bedclothes with a torch. I remember buying his books on my weekends off in town. I still have some of those original books—the big, hardbacked Macmillan editions with green covers. Of course I'm not uncritical of him. There were inventions and distortions in his configuring of Irish poetry which were very costly for the poets who came immediately after him. I can clearly see how hard it was for a poet like Patrick Kavanagh to write himself into the foreground of Irish poetry when he'd been politicized—or his world had been politicized—and diminished in the background of Yeats's poetry. But Yeats is a fascinating, turbulent poet, always pushing the edges of the self within the poem. He's a wonderful, exciting formal writer. And he's a poet who in the end managed the paradox: he made a high poetic self out of a humiliated human one.

c: Your prose seems to critique the subjects and objects of the poem in Ireland. Your poetry introduces the poetry of the woman's life. However, it also seems that the tools that you use to tell your story are the conventional and traditional forms of meter and rhyme that were patented by and continually used by male poets. As women have important and different stories to tell, would they not have a different approach that could challenge or compliment the form of poetry as well?

EB: The question of the use of form in women's poetry is both interesting and has advocates on both sides. It's an important debate and both sides have strong arguments. I'm not actually sure I belong to any side. But, certainly, as it became plain over the last twenty or so years that women were going to be an ambitious and defining presence in contemporary poetry, there came to be a feeling by some women poets that women should be formal separatists. That is, they shouldn't use meter or rhyme. They shouldn't draw on the formal inheritance men had constructed. I make clear in *Object Lessons* that I don't agree, although I admire some of the women poets such as Adrienne Rich, who argued in this way. I'm inclined to the view that women should be formal subversives. That is, they should use the historic forms but bring to them such new experiences and voices that an immediate and luminous dialogue was opened in such poems between the new voice and the old form. I still hold that view.

c: You have translated, "After the Irish of Egan O'Rahilly," could you discuss that process and the issue of living in a country with traditional and inherited languages.

EB: I translated the Egan O'Rahilly poem when I was twenty-one. It went into my first book. I had no Irish and so the translation was helped—as often happens—by a friend's literal translation. It was all very studentish and hit-or-miss. But in some small way I touched something I might have missed otherwise: the fury and pain of a great European poem. I'm glad I did that.

c: Could you discuss how there is no contradiction between the way you make an assonance fit a line and the way you lift up a child?

EB: The actual phrase from the preface to *Object Lessons* is that "as a young woman and an uncertain poet" I wanted there to be "no contradiction" between the way I lifted a child or made an assonance. In other words, those two activities—both human and historic in their way—came from the one life and the one person. But those activities could easily split that life into two lives, because I lived in a country where the life of the woman and the life of the poet did, indeed, seem to be contradictory to one another. It was important to me to feel that the actions of love and language could be united in one life, one purpose, one intent. But to do that I had to dismantle the assumptions which I felt made the idea of poetry and the idea of womanhood in Ireland almost magnetically opposed to each other. *Object Lessons* is very much about that process.

c: What poets outside the English language do you read?

EB: Well of course, I don't think of myself as reading poetry outside the English language. I read versions. I have no Russian, no German, no French. So my interest in Baudelaire and Akhmatova and Paul Celan has to be satisfied by translations, through which I get the sense but never the nuance. Having said that, at Stanford I read a colleague's book—John Felstiner's splendid study *Paul Celan: Poet, Survivor, Jew*—and his discussion of "Todesfuge" really opened some doors for me and renewed my faith in what the translator can do for the reader.

c: What is the place and or role of the poet in the 21st Century?

EB: That's a big question, but I'll try. One of the things I like best in this new job at Stanford—and it's a wonderful place anyway—is that I get to teach the Stegner Fellows, who are fine poets and will be poets in the 21st century. Having said that neither in that workshop, nor here, do I have an easy answer—only a reflective one. But I'll give the reflection anyway in case it helps. One of the things this century didn't address enough—I'm speaking narrowly in terms of poetry—is the question of who the poet is. And it remains a very live question. Between Ireland and the United States for instance there are wide differences in the sense of the identity of the poet. In Ireland the poet is communal, sometimes public, with quite a bardic shadow about the whole thing. In America almost the opposite is true. Poets often seem to feel isolated. Having the privilege of travelling between the two countries I've come to think there are two sides to it. I love and admire American poetry and I've felt very enabled by its tradition, by poets like Robert Lowell and Adrienne Rich. Occasionally it has seemed to me—this is an enormous simplification that American poets feel too isolated and Irish poets not isolated enough. In America I think the isolation—the sundering of communal links and all the loneliness and self-questioning that results from that—has led to a glorious century of experiment. In Ireland I think we've kept the communal links, almost more than any other country in Europe. Our poets are still part of their community, are still informed by the communal sense. But there isn't as much experiment. There isn't as much self-questioning.

Mating with the Well
Medbh McGuckian   [2 poems]

I am Ireland-blind and stone-lined
and open to the purity of death, I am danced into form
by little crosses sewn on to a shirt,
and the mouth of the other world
holds me in the renewed earth as in a cup or skirt.

When a stone screams water gives itself
where it has coursed unwordily,
swamping the nothingness of the horizon,
the pooled indentation of your elbow,
your englobed-within-mountain blessed clay.

But the rhythm of war like a corrupt star
moon-dead, volcanic, others itself,
and does not leave when angered, mother-needs
the picked and leafy daffodil you are.

The Tamarind Tree

January 2, 1996

The lowest string of winter beggars my muse:
his mind is the moon that I am selling land on.
My crooked soul breathes its life air from his heels,
when it should worship the desireless horizon.

Like a bird sitting with another bird
within the same bodily tree, like the swan
who knows the art of sucking milk
out of a mixture of milk and water, the sun

decreasing fails to rob me, my steel-framed heart
leaves unprayed for the planets of his ankles,
the polished animals of his eyelids.

But soon, on the Sunday called Laetare, impure ghosts
wearing the skins of us almsgiving trees,
will pass like heraldic nettles into the unmixed sunray.

Old Spice
Catherine Phil MacCarthy

We stood together in the parlour
after all those years
you asking where was the youngest
girl, the small fat one
who used to plague you with questions.
I smiled back

giving you time to scan the room,
discover me a grown woman,
easily spotting the eldest
and there's the middle one
close to her husband.
That mole under the eye

on the side of your cheek
just the same, your face
all at once furrows and plains,
a felt geography in my hands
breaking open words,
foreign, tolerant, friend.

Though my eyes are level
with yours taking me in,
you ask innocently
how long it's been
since you swung me to the ceiling,
my fingers long

to touch of their own accord
your face warm and
cool at the same time,
find themselves checked
by a deep reserve
and the scent of aftershave.

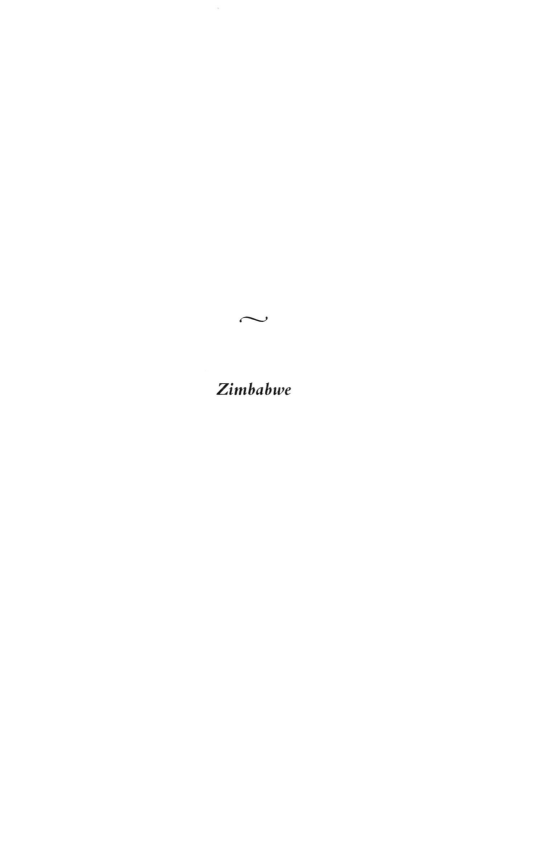

Zimbabwe

New Writing from Zimbabwe
Sue Standing

Since 1980, when the southern African nation of Zimbabwe gained independence from Ian Smith's repressive Rhodesian Front government, literature has flourished, though most of it is, unfortunately, not widely available outside of the country. (See bibliography for a list of recent works in English and addresses of presses in Zimbabwe.) While the selection that follows is necessarily only a small sampling of current writing, and unhappily does not include contemporary work in translation from the two main indigenous languages in Zimbabwe—Shona and Ndebele (which comprise a large proportion of both the oral and written literature of Zimbabwe)—it does illustrate some of the same thematic and aesthetic characteristics as other writing during and after what is known as the Second Chimurenga, particularly as it pertains to social and political engagement. (The original Chimurenga—"War of Liberation"—uprising in 1896-1897 inspired the 20th-century liberation struggle.)

Literature written in English as well as in Shona and Ndebele also draws from the oral traditions of these and other African languages. Traditional genres such as proverbs, folk tales, praise poems, love songs, lullabies, boasts, creation sagas, and narrative poetry inform current writing, along with the rise of other forms such as the novel, drama, and various types of poetry—and influences of Marxism, Surrealism, and Feminism.

While there isn't room in this brief introduction for a detailed examination of the history of Zimbabwean literature and its literary forms(1), I want to place the selection that follows in context by including a few examples of traditional poems and mentioning some notable contemporary writers. In the following traditional Shona poem, a praise poem in a series from a courtship cycle, we can see part of the reservoir from which contemporary writers have drawn, what K.Z. Muchemwa has called "a haunting sense of the spirit of place, of energies in particular places permeating and shaping the rhythm of people's lives"(2):

Mother of What-yet-is-to-be

Thank you, Guardian of orphans.
You have a heart generous as that of the honey-guide
Which cares for children other than its own.
You give as another might cast away out of pique.
Kernel of the nut,

While I am one of the shells.
My dear one of the long and graceful neck.
You have a neck that a louse may not climb without a rest,
You have a gait like the planting of ground-peas,
And running like the planting of ground-nuts.
You have round buttocks fit for grinding rice
As you walk abroad in your beauty.

translated from the Shona by Aaron C. Hodza (3)

Most poetry from the oral tradition, it should be recalled, would have been recited or sung to musical accompaniment—in Zimbabwe that would consist primarily of mbira (thumb piano), marimba, rattles, and drums—and improvised for a particular occasion. Some of the ways in which traditional and contemporary poetry intersect can be seen if we look at, for example, two poems written in the persona of a man in search of a bride. Here is "The Boastful Lover," another traditional Shona poem:

Swiftly I come!
I who can make a beehive and its owner drunk with sweetness.
I can captivate even those unborn.
Those who live, see me and say:
'That troublesome rascal is come again!
He shakes our self-possession,
A ruined village full of wild sweet mowa!
One who will not grow old!
Fresh as the succulent bowels of a porcupine.'
I am not to be tamed—
Except by him who gives me his daughter for a wife.
I am free, no-one can keep me where the white sadza is,
Not even where they make dembaremba do I stay.
I am like an eagle, if I miss my prey let me claw offal!
I am the rays of the sun!
A beautiful creature that will not permit its feathers to drop.
Other creatures spit out blood,
Others, like us, drop saliva.
Ah, yes! Give me beer my friend.

recorded by and translated from the Shona by
Aaron C. Hodza (4)

And here, from a similar point of view, but with a very different tone, is "Bring Me a Bride" by Eddison Zvobgo (b. 1935), a member of what has been called the "pioneer" generation of Zimbabwean writers:

> Bring me a bride, waning moon, on your return.
> You lie half-hid in the west
> Like a slice from a pumpkin.
>
> The young men's hut with its smoke stifles me.
> I gasp for breath as I sleep alone
> Like thirst before the rain.
>
> I am tired of grazing endlessly, like an ox, on new growth only,
> In all the stages of the night waiting for you to come
> As you lie upon your bed.
>
> Speak to me from the horizon over yonder,
> Shine upon this youth until she comes
> Do not waste time in sleep.
>
> Smile at me moon, waning moon.
> When you come back from where you go
> Come back with a wife for me!
>
> *written in Shona, translated by George Fortune* (5)

Less traditionally oriented, Musaemura Zimunya (b. 1949), one of Zimbabwe's most anthologized poets, has written lyrically about Zimbabwean landscape and history, as well as taking on political and urban issues. His brand of social satire and pithy style can be seen in this poem from *Perfect Poise*:

Benzocrats

> The benzocrats own the bushveld;
> see them charge on the squatters
> handguns blazing out of windows.
> See them charge on mudhuts
> the light of their torches a dawn of fire.
> The peugeotcrats are not far behind,
> for together they own the road and the land(6).

Freedom Nyamubaya, another well-known contemporary poet, was a Freedom Fighter during the war of liberation, having joined the Zimbabwe Liberation Army in Mozambique. After Zimbabwean independence, she founded MOTSRUD, an NGO that provides agro-services to rural farmers, and now works for the UN in Mozambique. Her poems reflect her experiences in the Chimurenga struggle as she endured the double burden of racism and sexism. This excerpt from "Journey and Half," in her most recent collection, *Dusk of Dawn*, shows the biting power of her poetry:

> Have you ever been ordered to strip
> In front of a thousand shouting eyes
> Forced to lie on your back
> With your feet astride
> Allowing your vagina to be inspected
> By somebody whom you have never seen before?
>
> Imagine lying on your back
> On an empty stomach
> On top of angry biting ants
> On hot dry African sand
> And asked to imitate making love.(7)

Another poet of note is Emmanuel Ngara, who is also a literary critic. Many of his poems also concentrate on political concerns—the liberation struggle, post-independence corruption, AIDS—as well as on recapturing the pre-colonial history of Zimbabwe by, in his words, "linking the distant past, the near past and the present, and overcoming the barriers of time and space."(8)

Kristina Rungano Masuwa (b. 1963), whose poem "The Rights of a Soldier" is included in this issue, was the first Zimbabwean woman to have a solo collection of her poems published. Her work embodies many of the conflicts women experience pulled between traditional expectations and modern realities.

This brief summary of the contemporary poetry scene would not be complete without at least mentioning the iconoclastic Dambudzo Marechera (1952-1987), whose influence continues to be widely-felt, particularly on the younger generation of Zimbabwean poets. Marechera's poems as well as his fiction raise questions of nationalism, pan-Africanism, and identity itself. "Identity is an act of faith impossible to verify," said Marechera. As can be seen in the following excerpt from "Fragments," Marechera moves swiftly between images, fusing the quotidian with the historical:

> the wind burns black in my nostrils
> the cinders of a tribe lie neglected in the ash-tray
> beneath the dark silent mask are stubs
> of burnt-out stars
> nascent gleams long since dead
> the black mask knotted over a dead cigarette
> mask of summer proverbs and seasonal poems
> never written, but scattered over seven hills
> like broken metal
> the scrap-iron of a lost empire. (9)

Marechera is perhaps best known for his 1978 novel, *The House of Hunger*, which portrayed the desperation of the generation of black intellectuals who came of age during the worst of the Ian Smith regime. Prior to Marechera, two important works of black Zimbabwean (then Rhodesian) literature in English are Stanlake Samkange's *On Trial for My Country* and Wilson Katiyo's *A Son of the Soil*. Stanley Nyamfukudza's *The Non-Believer's Journey* is also essential reading. Of the current generation of Zimbabwean prose writers, arguably the most important are Chenjerai Hove, Charles Mungoshi, Shimmer Chinodya, Tsitsi Dangarembga, and Yvonne Vera.

Chenjerai Hove (b. 1954) has written in both Shona and English. His work—he writes poetry as well as fiction—is concerned with, among other things, issues of powerlessness, the liberation struggle, and the lives of rural men and women. He uses the proverbs, idioms, and syntax of Shona in his English work to lyrical effect. His novel *Bones* (1991), which tells the story of Marita, an illiterate farm-worker, has an experimental narrative structure, and has been praised as a "milestone" in Zimbabwean literature.

Like Hove, Charles Mungoshi (b. 1947) writes bilingually and writes both poetry and prose. Mungoshi's most salient characteristic is his spare, understated style. In 1976, he received the top prizes in two sections of the PEN International Book Centre Awards—for the best work in an African language for his novel in Shona, *Ndiko kupindana kwamazuva* ("How Time Passes"), and his novel in English, *Waiting for the Rain*. In English, he is best known for his short stories, which often portray the anxieties of childhood and the social isolation of adults.

Harvest of Thorns (1989), the first novel in English by Shimmer Chinodya

(b. 1957), is set during the war of liberation from the perspective of a freedom fighter. Chinodya has said that in writing this novel "his interest was to explore the psychological reactions and development of a young man, still a boy really, who suddenly found himself in the situation of war."(10) Chinodya uses a stream-of-conscious narrative technique to move back and forth between past and present to powerful effect.

Tsitsi Dangarembga (b. 1959) has become internationally-known for her 1988 novel *Nervous Conditions*. *Nervous Conditions*, with its examination of gender roles and class struggles through the eyes of a young female narrator, has become an important work in the literary canon and the subject of numerous analyses. It is important for both its critique of colonialism and its examination of the constraints on the lives of Shona women as well as for its wrenching coming-of-age story.

The young writer Yvonne Vera is less well-known outside Zimbabwe than are Hove, Mungoshi, Chinodya, and Dangaremba, but her two novels and collection of short stories have received many literary honors, including the Commonwealth Writers' Prize for the Africa Region. I hope that her work will soon be more widely available outside Zimbabwe. This passage from her novel *Without a Name* demonstrates her lyrical prose style:

The City

Clothes hung on wooden figures, on women still, thin and unmoving. The figures offered no names, no memory. The past had vanished. Perhaps they offered beginnings from the outside in. One could begin with a flattering garment, work inwards to the soul.... So the dresses hung limp on the women, offering tangible illusions, clothed realities. These glassed and protected women had long brown hair and red lips and arms stretched, offering a purchasable kind of salvation.(11)

As can be seen from the brief overview above, the contemporary literary scene in Zimbabwe is very lively indeed. A large number of in-country presses (as opposed to branches of international publishers, such as Longman and Heinemann), which publish works in Shona and Ndebele, as well as in English, keep works widely available. (See addresses following)(12). In addition, numerous writers' organizations such as Zimbabwe Writers Union (ZIWU), Zimbabwe Women Writers (which has published anthologies of women's writing in English, Shona, and Ndebele), and the Budding Writers Association of Zimbabwe have aided both established and emerging writers.

Another boost to Zimbabwe's literary eminence is the annual presence of the Zimbabwe International Book Fair, held in early August each year since 1983 on the grounds of the National Gallery in Harare. ZIBF comprises the largest exhibition of books, magazines, and journals in sub-Saharan Africa, and is open to both the trade and the public. In conjunction with the book fair, panels and seminars highlighting themes such as Human Rights and Censorship take place, along with writers' workshops and authors' appearances. The year I attended ZIBF, 1995, a special symposium on Dambudzo Marechera was held. It was also at ZIBF where I encountered some of the writers included in this special literary supplement. What follows is a selection by some of those writers and by others who generously responded to my invitation.

To all those who submitted and to those who helped by contacting other writers, my thanks. My gratitude also to Wheaton College which helped to support my trip to Zimbabwe with a research stipend and to the editors of compost who suggested this venture. Here's to a wider readership for Zimbabwean literature in general and to the continued development of a new generation of Zimbabwean writers. Verengai zvakanaka!

1. See Colin Style's introduction to *Mambo Book of Zimbabwean Verse in English* (which contains a wide range of poets and translations from traditional and contemporary Shona and Ndebele writing, as well as poems written originally in English; K.Z. Muchemwa's introduction to *Zimbabwean Poetry in English*); and Flora Veit-Wild's critical studies, *Patterns of Poetry in Zimbabwe and Teachers, Preachers, Non-Believers: A Social History of Zimbabwean Literature.*
2. *Zimbabwean Poetry in English*, p. XVIII.
3. *Shona Praise Poetry*, p. 293.
4. *Mambo Book of Zimbabwean Verse*, pp. 27-28.
5. *Mambo Book of Zimbabwean Verse*, p. 367.
6. *Perfect Poise*, p. 30.
7. *Dusk of Dawn*, p. 31.
8. *Songs from the Temple*, p. xi.
9. *Mambo Book of Zimbabwean Verse*, p. 293.
10. *Teachers, Preachers, Non-Believers*, p. 322
11. *Without a Name*, p. 81.
12. Another good source of Zimbabwean and other African books is from African Books Collective Ltd (The Jam Factory, 27 Park End Street, Oxford OX1 1HU, U.K.; e-mail: abc@dial.pipex.com), which is collectively owned by a group of African publishers to promote their books in Europe, North America, and the Commonwealth Countries outside of Africa. Many of the titles mentioned in this essay and in the bibliography are available from either the individual presses or from ABC.

Messengers of Thieves
Albert Nyathi   [2 poems]

We have learnt to pray
With our eyes wide open
Where lies are a part of truth.
We screw our bitter eyes
To see the same old men in dear suits
And computerized briefcases.
Turning our fatigued ears
We hear the same meaningless old song
Sung in a foreign language
From a tongue that reads in papers!
No one text, dear brother,
But the way we live
Shall render us scholars.

Ngwanaka

If you do not listen
to the old mouths
whose teeth have ground
many cattle bones,
you will meet wild lion
who ravages travellers in the bush,
my son, my son.

If you don't ask
from the grey beard
in which forest wild buffalo resides,
you will deform your foresight
too early in life.

If your tongue fails you
and you throw it
carelessly everywhere anywhere,
be assured, my son,
you may be dumb forever.
My son, Ngwanaka,
Mntanami, o my son…

This Soil
Emmanuel Sigauke

This place
Was once the footing land
Of ancient warriors.
The same land
Was stampeded by writhing hunters
As the animals under pursuit
Fled a blazing fire…

This rock here
Was once Mambo's stool:
Mambo who ruled with Spear;
Mambo, whose warriors
Made cold the anger of Chauruka;
Mambo who reigned like Munhumutapa.

That kopje there
Glamoured today by colleges and lodges,
Was once the center
Of children's hide-and-seek
Yesterday
When cattle freely traversed
This Bonomgwe expanse:
The forest that echoed with abundance.

In that river there
Once Nehanda washed
And Kaguvi waited beyond that dome
As the virile fighters
Sharpened spears at that hill
Readying
For perpetual action
To reclaim
An endangered soil,
Their wealth.

The Identity Crisis
Stephen Alumenda

I totally refuse to be associated
  with the barren tawny fields of my homeland
Or grandmother's wrinkled face drawn tight
  like a neglected rhino hide,
Her vision marred by corrosive drought nightmares
And non-existent drought-relief trucks
Laden with grain to rival the feud
  of a persistent hunger tradition

They say we have to preserve
  the country's cultural image
  from the shame of torpid westernization
But I've chosen the neon, mini-skirt tainted
  box-cut lanes of the city
And its Castle-draught lisping throat
In place of the endless spoors of the bush warthog
And corn-glutted raucous cries of the guinea fowl

You see I can't take grandmother
  to the spacious Sheraton Hotel
  because she can't nose around
Or take uncle who still slurps his quick brew
  in tongue-smacking shame
Let alone Sekuru who is ignorant of modern politics
  even that of the common Middle East
Yet they say he was the backbone of our revolution

I've painted the country's image a scarlet
  to drown the old tradition
But my true identity is blurred in the shackles
  of insipid westernization.

Betrayal
Lindsay Pentolfe Aegerter

I am scared of the snake. The snake slithers and slides. The sound of the slow, sluggish shape is sibilant. It is the sound of the words I hear in my mind. I am scared of the snake. Don't be. Oh please take it away. Close your eyes do, I do. But when I close my eyes there's a snake. So I open them to take away the terror. And then the words slither instead and it's slippery. It's cold. It's heavy on my skin. I shudder oh God oh God. So I close my eyes, you see. And see another snake. Only this time bigger. Oh please, oh please, please take it away; take away the terror. And so I open my eyes you see, look up and see the moon silver behind the trees, the leaves of the msasa, and the wind slowly slides on to the gliding light of the moon on the leaves, and they silently whisper and wistfully they whimper and rustle, and in the sound of the leaves and the sound of the words is the sibilance of the snake, and I shudder and say softly, sadly, oh please, oh please stop. I close my eyes on salty tears and heave and my throat is throbbing; it is tight; it gets tighter; and my chin is dimpled; I can see my mother's dimpled chin; don't cry mum, my chin dimples too when I cry and my lips go numb and my mouth goes numb too; oh please God, take away the snakes. The salty tears spill over the edges of my eyes as I lie on the ground, dry ground of Africa, under the silent stars and silver moon and hear the sibilance of its sound on the tawny leaves of the msasa tree above me. The tears slither snake-like from my eyes into my mouth, tributaries of tears turn to my temples and weave their way into my hair, my ears. I am damp and tear-filled and my cheeks are aching with trying to stop the sobs but the tears are filling my mouth, my throat; my chokes become sobs and you hear. Don't cry my love. Ooh please take them away. I cry. You hold my heart and kiss the tears on my eyes, on my cheeks, from my mouth, from my ears, from the hollow in my throat. There are no snakes. There are snakes in Africa. There are snakes that slither and slide in the dry grass of Africa. There are snakes in the bush. We are sleeping on the hard dry ground of the African bush, the stars above us. It is beautiful my love. Oh yes, oh yes I sob with the joy of such sublime beauty, such African haunting beauty. Oh the taste of the tears in your mouth, oh my love you take away the snakes. I close my eyes under African skies and snakes slither away to their holes in the ground. They won't hurt you: just watch where you walk, where I walk in this wilderness of tawny fawns and russet red and tans and blacks and all that is the color of this country, this continent.

I wake to palest pinks at dawn. My eyes and cheeks and mouth feel crusted and caked with the salt of last night's fears. My wide eyes, wide-eyed, wake up, look up to the leaves of the trees and the moon has gone and the night has given way to first fleeting moments of day. I turn my head and look to the ground, dry ground beside my body, naked body. Ants, armies of big black Matabele ants march in spasms of industry, crawl over clods of earth, hump huge heavy weights on sturdy backs, maneuver through jungle-like blades of grass, dry grass, dry ground. I hear the sound of insects and birds chattering and clattering and creaking and squeaking and rustling in the trees on the ground in the grass. The breeze is warm on my face, my body turned up to the day's dawn. Pink fades and amber edges the clouds that whisper wisps of whimsy warmth thread through blue. Blue, blue, bright blue sky above and sounds and smells of Africa such, oh such, that I cannot find the words.

I turn to the other side and see your face, sleeping face, sleeping eyes, lips loose, a little dribble of moisture soft shimmers. You are pristine, perfect, like silver hoarfrost lying quiet on the early morning. I look and look at your lovely face, your sleeping softly eyes, closed, sleepy soft face, and I think you are my love, you take away the snakes. You sense my gaze and pretend not to but I see the rapid movement of your eye behind its thin disguise of sleeping closed lid. I do not want to wake you but to watch you as you lie in splendor beneath the light dark dapple light of a thousand leaves flirting upon you in darting, dancing movements. It's the breeze you see, there's a warm breeze that plays with the leaves of the trees, and, it's the light you see, that plays with your perfection. The sunlight catches the golden down, the tiny fine hairs that dust your golden chest. I don't mean to wake you. I'm glad you woke me; I want to see the day's beginning; I want to see it with you. You were so scared last night my love, scared of the snakes. Are you scared now? I'm not scared now. I'm safe awake; it's when I sleep that fear brings tears—it's the snakes in my dreams you see. Yes I see, but you can't live in Africa and be scared of snakes because there are snakes that slither and slide and slowly glide beneath the greens and browns and tawny tans of the grass and the leaves that have fallen from the trees. Why are you cold, why do you shudder? I am scared of the snake. It's daytime, there are no dreams. Yes but there are snakes in Africa. I'm not scared of lions. Or leopards. I would like to put my face into a lion's mane, a leopard's tummy, and rub my face into its fur; I would like to kiss the soft spots, the fur, the body of the cat, I would like to love the cat. I love lions and leopards; I know they are fierce more than the snake. I'm not scared of elephant or buffalo or rhino. I'm not even scared of crocodiles because crocodiles are hard, they're not soft, slimy, sinister. But we are wasting the day my love.

We walk along the sandy shores of the lake. The mountains of the Matusadona are vaguely blue-green reaching high into the blue of the mid-morning sky. The lake is flat and mirror-reflecting blue and the water laps lightly onto the sand in slow, rhythmic sounds. We climb across some rocks and there, quiet in the sun, is the imprint of a crocodile's belly sketched into the sand, perfect in its sunken scaled symmetry, the pattern of its belly indelible in my mind, not indelible in the sand, because the wind will sweep away the image, if not the water licking it liquid away.

The silhouettes of the slim bare branches on dead dried trees stand half-submerged in the water that flooded the plain many years ago to make the lake that is my favorite place, your favorite place, Kariba. We walk some more along the shore and we take off scant clothing. You slip off your brown leather belt and swing it slowly, snake-like, around my flesh. I laugh and scream and run from you. We softly splash our feet into the cool water, we swim and laugh and swim and you dive deep and come up behind me and I laugh delighted, scared, not really scared, and your hands, such hands, slide up my legs, my back, and to my neck. You kiss the back of my neck, the water in your mouth against my skin, and I turn to kiss your mouth but you are gone again beneath the water, through my legs. You entwine your winding body around mine and you are in front of me; your face glistens in the sun; the water is shimmering in the sunlight on your face.

We stalk silently through the dry grass, long, dry grass. You tell me in a whisper to watch the shadow beneath the great grey gnarled baobab and explain the elephant behind the home of African spirits, sacred, ancient, enormous. I look, entranced. It is so wild out here and we are so alone and this is all ours, this African wilderness. The elephant moves its mighty bulk backwards and look, it is high on its hind legs; its head is back; its trunk is touching the topmost leaves of the tree. He is oblivious to our intrusion. We don't mean to intrude, we will not linger any longer, don't worry, we will not disturb you, we are simply intrigued, enchanted. We walk more and the bush gets thick. It is very hot and the ground burns my bare feet. I am walking barefoot on ground upon which snakes have surely slid. There is a sable, do you see it? Oh yes, look at him, his horns so tall, so regal, arching back a straight sweep, his coat like coal gleaming, his eyes alert, his head pert and upturned, his nostrils flickering for smells of strangeness, his tail sweeping swiftly the sunsoaked air.

It is hot, are you hot, would you like to wash away the warmth? Yes:

I see there is a small stream, a river that nestles in the bush and lies deep beneath the trees. So again we swim softly, silently. I will never be able to fathom this feeling of liquid gold and blue that licks my body. I will never be able to grasp the fathomless secrets of hidden depths that darken as I dive deep, deep, and how cold it becomes, so I come up for breath and warmth and light and what is not strange.

And soon it is late and the sun is heavy in the sky and we have lived a lifetime in a day and it is wild out here and we are alone, so alone with it all and I will burst my heart is too small to hold it all. You take me through the hand through vast, vast tracts of land so seemingly untouched, untrammeled. You find a patch of grass; it is soft—so surprising—an oasis, if one has oases in this southern stretch of savanna, in this southern hemisphere, which is not a desert but dry and wild. You lie down, you stretch out, you pull me onto the grass beside you, and we lie looking up for a while, silent, not speaking, not disturbing the sounds. And from behind the silhouette of half-submerged trees standing stark and strange in the lake, from behind the full leafy foliage that is colored in khakis, the sun begins to drop and it lands low on the horizon, a big red ball in a scarlet sky. It glows and casts its iridescence onto the water and there is something stark and strange and still and I feel, you feel, suspended in time. It is slipping away, the day is going to fall beneath the watercolor horizon, and the moon is creeping up quietly behind us, behind the msasas and mopanies. Suddenly the shrill cry of a fish eagle pierces the stillness as it swoops from the sky; its claws skim the surface of the molten, liquid lake and it sweeps skyward, soaring away to some place of solitude to take its evening meal.

The sun has gone and still we sit and now the color is twilight, violet twilight. Stars appear, spangled starlit sky, close, scattered, star sky. You stand and stretch and slowly move away behind long, dry grass, dark, dry blades of grass. I sigh and smile at stars and sky and a sense of your strangeness; you are ever-elusive; you are ever-present. You are gone, you are gone from me. I feel you close by, where are you? It is quiet, it is dark, the sounds, the African sounds are soft, softly sinister, silent sounds.

There is a strange rustle, a rustle behind me, and I do not hear it really because there have been many strange rustles in the day's, dry day's delights, and I am happy, sublimely happy, happy sitting here with you here, you not here, in this place at this time. My flesh creeps coldly; it is the breeze, cool night breeze, and suddenly you are here; you stand before me hands outstretched. I reach out and take your hand; your hand is a snake; there is a snake coming from your arm; you are smiling; the snake lashes and I scream and I scream and the snake is around me, your arm is around me, the snake has wound its tail, snake tail body around me, I am choking, I am screaming, oh God oh God and the snake's head sways in front of my eyes, it stands up in front of my face, it sways, it sways while its long hard silver scales grey dusty soft slippery body clutches me; it is wound around me, its head at my face it sways and spits, it sways and slips and slithers and hisses and its sound of sibilance sears my soul my skin my flesh my blood my heart. I scream I am dying; I think I am dying. You stand before me smiling; your head swaying snake-like, you say, smiling, do not be scared my love, look at the beautiful snake; it will not hurt you; it is so beautiful, sensuous sliding; it wants to touch you, to get inside you. Your eyes are snakes, your eyes, your laughter is hissing, the snake is thrashing, it is lashing the stillness, my screams are tearing my throat. My heart has broken. You see you cannot live in Africa and be scared of snakes my love. I want to help you, to cure you of your fears, take away the tears, touch the snake, don't cry my love, kiss the snake, take the snake inside you. O my heart, my heart. You have torn, tattered my heart, shattered my soul. My throat has burst broken the dreams, the beauty. My screams are silent; my soul is splintered, cutting the edges of my being. I am tired. I will lie down now quietly. I will lie down on the ground, dry ground of Africa under silvery moon and star-strung sky and I will die while you kiss me smiling.

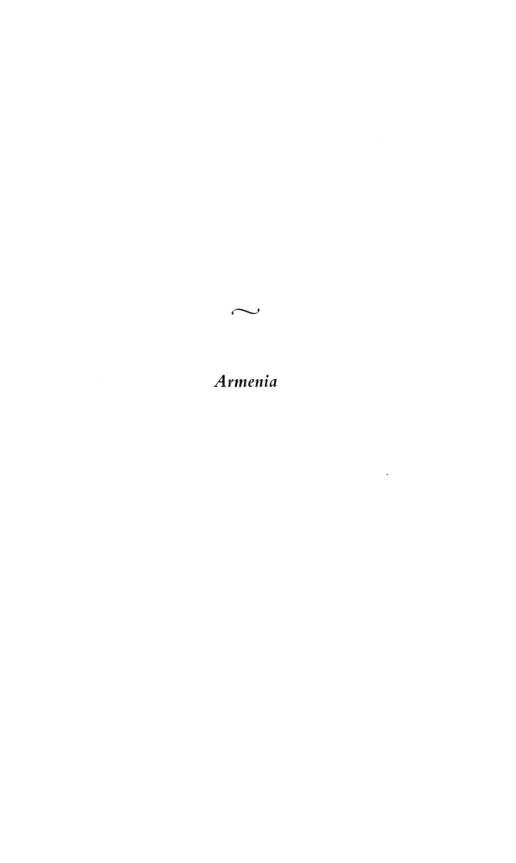

Armenia

From Foremost to Endangered: Armenian Poetry
Diana Der-Hovanessian

Just as in other eastern European countries, poetry in Armenia has long been a vital part of the arts scene. However in Armenia, poetry is the most important of the arts. In times of oppression and suppression, and during Turkish, tsarist and communist censorships, Armenian poetry with its oblique ways of telling truth, was not only entertainment but a way of restoring pride.

Today in the small area remaining to Armenia, the main stumbling blocks to publishing are economic. Due to the blockades enforced by Turkey and the Azerbaijani Turks, there is a great shortage of paper as well as electric power. And unlike the previous communist regime, the government no longer supports the arts.

Armenia, called the most stable country in the volatile Caucasus region of the former Soviet Union, has a long history of outsiders conquering their land. In fact, most of the land in historic Armenia now belongs to Turkey.

The people call themselves Hai (Hye) and their country Haiastan, after Haik, the legendary great-grandson of Noah. The language is Indo-European and the people are a blend of Indo-Europeans migrating eastward and indigenous Urartuans and Hittites, which Armenians claim as ancestors.

The written form of the language was developed in the fifth century when Mesrob Mashtots was commissioned to create an alphabet (406 A.D.) to keep the Armenian church separate from the Byzantines; Greek letters had been used previously. A network of schools developed to teach the written language; translations of the Bible and church writings were made; and a new literature began to flourish. Sahag, the head of the church who assigned Mesrob the task of creating the alphabet, and Mesrob Mashtots himself wrote hymns still sung to this day.

Armenia (except for dry periods during invasion and massacres) has a long chain of poetry for study ... from ancient inscriptions in cuneiform down to modern times. A reader can trace the uses of poetry as incantation, benediction, celebration, and political comment; and can observe how pagan chants to the sun evolve into praises for the light of Christ, then see these same rhythms in Eghishe Charents's youthful poems praising the red dawn of communism.

From the earliest times to the present day, poetry has been a vital part of everyday life. Everyone can and does quote and toast with poetry. In earlier ages, the poet had been the religious leader. In times of subjugation, he was both conscience and witness of his time; both prophet and political leader.

During the Soviet period, this high position for the poet was retained. What will happen now, during a market economy, remains to be seen.

The tiny country of modern Armenia contains only a fraction of its ancient lands—now part of Turkey, Azerbaijan, and Iran. Because it was at the crossroads of east and west, and a frequent battleground for foreign nations, Armenia's frontiers changed frequently with invasions of the region.

When it became the first Christian nation in 301 A.D., its ancient pagan poetry was destroyed. Only a few examples of poems that had been transmitted orally for millennia were preserved by historian Movses of Khorene in the 5th century. One fragment describes the birth of the fire god Vahkakn thus: Yercner yercin yev yercir/ Yercner yev tsirani tsov, etc.

> Earth was erupting,
> the skies contracting,
> and in labor the flame colored seas.
> From the reeds smoke bellowed,
> then fire followed
> and out ran a small fair boy.
> His bright hair ablaze,
> his red beard suns' rays
> and his eyes double suns aglow.

Folk poems and variations of the folk epics were also handed down orally for centuries. After Christianity was adopted, the folk epics began to acquire Christian overtones. The folk poems from the oral tradition and the ritual chants from pagan days (which became Christian chants), are two of the main influences on modern Armenian poetry. The third influence is the political oppression, which accounts for poems of protest and periods of absence of writing altogether, for instance, during the Mongol and Ottoman invasions or the Turkish massacres of 1886 and 1915. (The latter, which started with the extermination of 200 poets and other writers, also destroyed the reading public, stopping all literature for almost a generation.)

A typical folk poem is the "Song of the Crane" (Groung) written in quatrains called hyrens (meaning in the Armenian style).

Crane

Where do you come from crane?
I ache to hear your call,
to know you come from home.
Have you any news at all?

I bless your wings, your eyes.
My heart is torn in two,
the exile's soul all sighs,
waiting for bits of news.

The hymns of the church, which provide the second strong influence on the modern Armenian poem, the cascading religious chant called the sharagan (rows of jewels), with long, rhythmic Homeric listings and musical parallelisms are best illustrated in the work of Krikor Naregatsi or Gregory of Narek (951–1003)—who wrote a thousand years before Dante and Chaucer. His cadences are still a strong influence on Armenian poetry.

The first modern poet, the first to write purely personal poems and in the vernacular, was Bedros Tourian (1851–1872). He read contemporary French literature, Hugo, LaMartine, de Musset, and wrote lyrical verses that won a large audience of admirers.

The most prominent poets writing at the turn of the century in Istanbul were Siamanto (Adom Yarjanian, 1878-1915), Daniel Varoujan (1884-1915), and Roupen Sevag (1890–1915). All three were perfect examples of the poet as leader and hero. Daniel Varoujan has been called by modern critics (London Times Literary Supplement 1979.) as "one of the most lifefilled poets in western literature." All three were among the 200 writers executed at the onset of the Armenian genocide by the Ottoman Turks in 1915.

That genocide left a permanent mark, not only by removing the writers and readers, but by entering the psyche of every surviving writer.

The work of one poet, Vahan Tekeyan, who was in Jerusalem at the onset of the genocide, illustrates the pain and bitterness felt by Armenians in 1917 when they saw the Turks getting away with both crimes and gains.

We Shall Say to God

Should it happen we do not endure
this uneven fight and drained
of strength and agonized
we fall on death's door not to rise
and the great crime ends
with the last Armenian eyes
closing without seeing a victorious day,
let us swear that when we find
God in his paradise offering comfort
to make amends for our pain,

let us swear we will refuse
saying, "No! Send us to hell again.
We choose hell. You made us know it well.
Keep your paradise for the Turk."

Tekeyan did not always stay bitter, but wrote more visionary poems. He became one of the leading diaspora writers.

The father of Soviet Armenian poetry was Eghishe Charents, who gained fame at 20 with one of the strongest anti-violence poems written after the defense of Van, where he had gone as a 16-year-old soldier after the Turkish massacres had removed most of the population, including the nations' top writers Varoujan, Siamanto, Sevag, Krikor Zohrab, and others in Istanbul.

Charents, often called the Armenian Mayakovsky, became a stronger and more versatile writer. By imitating the lyricism of Vahan Derian, he developed his own dramatic style which varied from the polemic to subtle satire. He died in prison after being disillusioned with the system under Stalin.

The leading poets after Charents were Hovaness Shiraz (1915–1985), the most popular poet of his time, and Barouyr Sevag (1924–1972), whose work is widely admired on many levels (metaphysical, political, patriotic, as well as celebratory).

During the earthquake of 1988, several talented poets living in Leninakan, now Gumri, were killed. And during the hardship days of recent freedom, other prominent poets have died: Hamo Sahian; Vahakn Davtian, president of the Writers Union; Maro Markarian; Gevorg Emin; and Hrachia Hovanessian, all in the last two years. Only Sylvia Gaboudikian and Saghatel Haroutunian of the older generation remain. Younger poets, Arevshad Avakian, Razmig Davoyan, Davit Hovaness, Ardem Haroutunian, Yuri Sahakian, Hovaness, Krikorian, Armen Mardirossian, Ludvig Touryan, Anahid Barsamian, Medakse, and Henrik Edoyan are widely published. And among the younger and promising: Armen Shekoyan, Hrachia Saruchan, and Hrachia Tamrazian.

Their styles and subjects are similar to contemporary poetry worldwide, Grigorian and Haroutunian can be compared to the New York School. Aramais Sahagian is a clever satirist while Vahakn Davtian's work had been compared to Yeats in the past. But his later work was similar to the poetry of another Irish poet, Seamus Heaney. But the theme that is strongest in Armenian poetry is a genre of love poetry addressed to the land itself. Emin has a famous poem to Ararat, the sacred mountain of the Armenians which lies just across the border, like a taunt and a reminder of loss, "always in sight, always out of reach, like a great love."

There are diasporan Armenian poets writing in Beirut, Syria, Egypt, and Montreal, Canada. Best known among these is Zahrad (Zareh Yaldiciyan 1923–) in Istanbul who writes wry, whimsical, sharp verse. Vahe Oshagan, Krikor Bledian, Zulal Kazanjian, born in Beirut and doubly exiled to France, are the noted post-surrealists. Vahe Oshagan has also lived in the United States and Australia. Other Armenian poets of the diaspora write in the languages of the countries where they live.

The poems in the essay and in the following section are translated by Diana Der-Hovanessian. The Tekeyan poem is from Anthology of Armenian Poetry, *Columbia University Press, edited by Diana Der-Hovanessian and M. Margossian, and the folk poem from "Come Sit Beside Me and Listen to Koutchag," from* Medieval Armenian Poems, *translated by DDH, Ashod Press, N.Y.*

A Handful of Ash

*to the memory of Akn**

Siamanto

It was a like a mansion, spacious, sumptuous
and from its rooftop I could see
the roaring Euphrates bearing
the fallen stars of my dreams.

I heard of its ruins with tears, tears,
heard of its walls toppled, heard
of terror, massacre, blood running
over the lawn's neat flowered rim;

Of blue room, my room, grayed
with ashes, where walls and rugs
had warmed a happy childhood
nurturing my flying soul, its wings.

And was the gold framed mirror shattered,
splintering its airy store
of reflected resolutions,
musings, plans and childish hopes?

Did the garden's singing Spring die,
the mulberry and the willow trees?
And the brook between them dry
sinking then to disappear?

In dreams I still hear my caged bird
cooing at day's break to stir
us and the rose bushes awake
with its gentle partride cries.

Hyereni doon, native home, I will return,
I promise. After death, even as ash;
or come as the exiled dove comes
to weep its broken hearted sighs.

But who will bring, who will bring now
the handful of your sacred ash
to bury on the day I'm buried, mingling
singer with his ash-turned song?

*Siamanto's birthplace is on the banks of the Euphrates. He was in America when the news of the 1896 massacres reached him. His family and home were lost.

After a War
Aramais Sahagian

At the edge of the crowd

the man on crutches

swings over the land he saved

but never touches.

Ars Poetica
Arevshad Avakian

Let the light that wakes
in the sun's eye be
reflected in the boughs.

Let the childhood of
the waters remain in
the mountains but let the river

remember its source
when it reaches
the sea. And let the poem

remain the poet's
letter addressed
to the troubled but without

troubling words,
just petals marking
where birds walked.

Autobiography
Hamo Sahian

I won't list where I was born
nor where I went to school.
My whole life is in my poems.
My story is there.

That's the only place to look.
I am no where else.
I am a thousand people
and none of them is me.

Start with a baby, of course.
Then comes the obedient child;
the mischief maker follows.
And you multiply, multiply

into a thousand selves
but none of them is me.

Dusk
Maro Markarian

The wind stirs
the peach trees
velvet blossoms
into flight
delaying dusk
with petals
of falling light.

Few
Barouyr Sevag

We are few, we Armenians,
and we don't think of ourselves
as better than anyone else. But
we must admit we are the one
people with an Ararat and
the only people with a Sevan
that catches the true images
of the heavens.

And is it not true that our land
is where David fought
and Narek wrote? And were we not
the first to sculpt monasteries
from stone and fashion fish
from rock and birds from clay?

We are few and we are called
Hai; and don't think
of ourselves as superior
to others, but still our fate
has been different. Too much
blood has flowed from us.
However, even when we were many
and huge, even in our time of
strength, we did not destroy
any other race. Nor was any soul
struck down by the blow of our arm.

If any were enslaved
it was only by our books.
And if any were ruled
it was only by our riches. Evidently it was Death who loved
us although we never loved it
back nor gave ourselves to it.
Only when we were discouraged
did we abandon our lands to it.

Only when we were enslaved
did we leave and try to build
bridges, arches, tried to plow
other land, raise other crops,
sing other songs.

Now we are few. But we are Armenian
and we know how to weep from pain
of wounds that never heal. Yet
we also know how to celebrate
health with songs of praise.

We know how to fight back and
pierce the enemy's side
and how to befriend the friend
and to return his favor tenfold.

And for the sake of light
and justice we know
how to shape our lives.

However, should fire try to forge
us, change us into strange, new
shapes, we know how to tame the flame.

If the world is dark, darkness
taught us how to mold candles, to
know the worth of warmth and love,
passion and respect.
We also know that although, not
superior, we are Armenians and proud.
We exist. We stand. We are few
but we shall grow.

Earth
Arevshad Avakian

I am shouting your name
in the dark
at the top of my voice.
Listen. Hear me before
the metal worms eat
your entrails.
Listen while blood
is still red and your nerves
still unravelled by the daily
crash and crush of the tides.

I am shouting your name
in broad daylight.
My hands are not strong
enough to stop you. So, please
hear the unpronounced words
rising like terror.

In the light, in the dark
with hope fading
I shout your name. Look
with compassion at the stars
spread in an unending road before you.

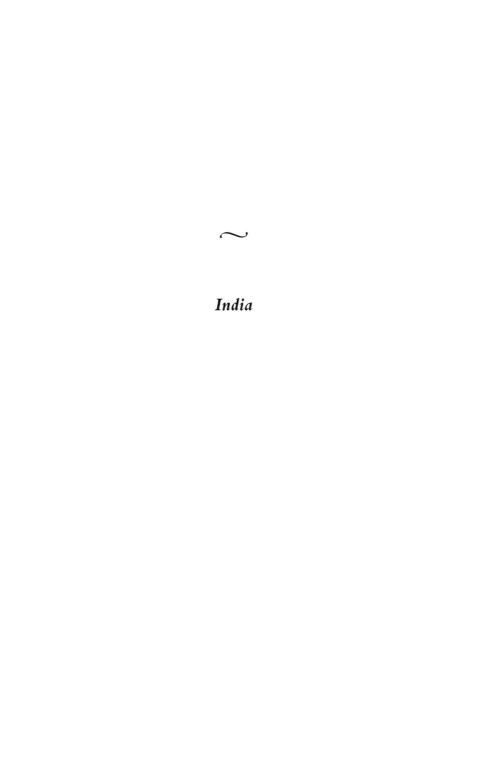

India

Women Poets from Calcutta
Carolyne Wright

Despite its all-too-well-known urban problems, Calcutta is, in terms of the arts, a world-class city. Every evening there are recitals of Indian classical music and dance, theater productions (in Bengali, Hindi, or English), films, poetry readings, lectures, and other cultural events at spacious, modern theaters such as Rabindra Sadan, Nandan, or Kala Mandir. There are foreign films and visiting writers, professors, and media figures at the foreign cultural missions—the Alliance Française, British Council, Max Müller Bhavan, United States Information Service (U.S.I.S.), and even Gorky Sadan, the Russian (formerly Soviet) cultural house. There are innumerable private performances in middle- and upper-class homes, as well as street events—*pujas* at corner temples or thatched *pandal* booths, wedding and funeral processions, political demonstrations, and street theater. It is appropriate that the third goddess who presides over this city (after the fearsome crusader Durga and the terrible bloodthirsty Kali) is Saraswati, patroness of learning and the arts, whose festival is celebrated in late January or early February, at the height of the cultural season.

A survey of Calcutta's literary life begins with a visit to College Street, the publishers' and booksellers' district that grew up among the crumbling nineteenth-century mansions near the original main campus of Calcutta University. All the principal publishers (Bengali, English, Hindi, and Sanskrit) maintain editorial offices and retail outlets here, in the cramped, bookshelf-lined rooms of dilapidated Victorian buildings. Their entrances are barely visible from sidewalks crowded with jerry-built bookstalls and obstructed by pavement book and magazine vendors. This is the mecca for students in search of scarce and all-too-often out-of-print college textbooks, and also for the serious literary browser, who may be invited by the salesclerks to see additional stock in the godown (a warehouse, from the Bengali word *gudam*)—which usually means climbing up a shaky, iron shipboard-style circular staircase to more floors of shelf-lined rooms. The famous Calcutta Coffee House is here, too, where Bengali writers and intellectuals have traditionally met for hours of *adda*, literary discussions and gossip.

The biggest literary events of the year, however, occur when College Street moves downtown to the Maidan exhibition grounds in January and February, for the book fairs of West Bengal and Calcutta. The West Bengal Book Fair is geared to librarians, who make their year's purchases there with funds provided by state and central governments. The world-renowned

Calcutta Book Fair, which lasts for some ten days in late January-early February, will celebrate its quarter century next year; it is now Asia's largest bookselling fair, and a bookbuyer's paradise. Over 400 booksellers—commercial and institutional publishers, as well as a growing number of foreign publishers, mostly from the U.K., the U.S., and a number of European countries—display and sell there. There is a large contingent of home-grown English-language publishers—Manohar, Rupa, Seagull, and Writers Workshop—as well as the Indian branches of multinational houses such as Longmans, Oxford University Press, and Penguin Books. A nation that publishes literature in at least sixteen regional languages (each with its own script), India is also the world's third largest publisher of books in English, after the U.K. and the U.S.

Despite its increasing international presence, the Calcutta Book Fair retains a distinctly Bengali ambience, evident in the Bengali script on signboards and book jackets, the women in saris and men in *dhotis* or *kurta-pajama*, and the songs of Rabindranath Tagore and Nazrul Islam played over the public address system. Nor is the vitality of Bengali literature diminished in any way, judging from the crowds in the exhibits of Ananda, Dey's, M.C. Sarkar, and other prestigious editorial houses. These publishers time the appearance of new titles for the book fair, and sometimes two or three printings of a popular author's book will sell out in the fair's ten-day course.

No doubt, then, that Bengali as a literary culture is flourishing. According to the latest census (one writer friend quipped), there were 3,957,486 poets in Bengal! Little magazines abound, each supported by its group of devoted writer-members, who often pay production costs from their own pockets. The dozen or so "established" newspapers and magazines—such as *Ananda Bazar Patrika*, *Bartaman*, *Desh*, and *Jugantar*—regularly print poems and stories, and also a special "Puja Number" issue for the Durga Puja season each September-October. These are hefty, telephone directory-sized tomes that keep Bengal's better-known writers scribbling feverishly for months every year, turning out poems, stories, essays, and even full-length novels to meet the deadlines. The small magazines publish their contributors' books, and young writers often come to the attention of the larger journals thereby. Publishing's biggest plum is *Desh*, the *New Yorker* of Bengali magazines. To have the poetry editor ask to see a few poems is, for the young poet, to behold vistas of untold glory—or at least a guaranteed literary future. Yet there is also a sizable "anti-establishment" contingent in Calcutta's literary community, opposed to the commercialism and patronage of the big-name writers. Members of these groups often refuse to send their work to the mainstream publishers, and thus keep some of the most vigorous new writing out of the reach of the larger reading public.

In addition to the annual book fairs, Calcutta hosts other large-scale literary events—among them the Kabita Utsav, the All-India Poetry Festival held in January, which features talks, seminars, exhibits, and readings by renowned poets in most of the major languages, including English. These take place in different venues—Nandan (the West Bengal Film Society auditorium), the National Library, and Viswa Bharati, the university started by Rabindranath Tagore in his ancestral village of Shantiniketan, two hours north of Calcutta by train. In the second week of every May, the birth anniversary of this Nobel laureate and giant of Bengali letters, state and local governments, as well as various Tagore-inspired private foundations, sponsor lectures, performances of his plays, exhibits of his paintings, and concerts of the ever-popular *Rabindra-sangeet*, the songs for which Tagore composed both lyrics and music. These functions are held at Calcutta's many literary and cultural institutions, which maintain libraries, sponsor research and much-needed translation projects from various regional languages into others, and publish literary and academic books, filling vital needs in a city with overcrowded universities and colleges and no free public library system.

The Bharatiya Bhasha Parishad (Society of Indian Languages) and Sahitya Akademi (Academy of Literature) confer some of the most prestigious national book awards. The West Bengal government gives the coveted Rabindra Puraskar, the Rabindranath Tagore Prize—roughly the equivalent of the Pulitzer Prize—for the year's best books, in several categories, written in Bengali or on a Bengali subject. While I was in Calcutta, the Sahitya Akademi held a week-long conference on literary translation at the Salt Lake Stadium, inviting writers, translators, Indologists, and literary scholars from several countries to speak on the subject, an inescapable issue in a nation with so many regional literatures. The Bengali book lover on a budget, however, does not have to attend literary festivals and conferences, or make the arduous expedition (in overcrowded busses and trams with triple-digit temperatures in the hot season) to the publishers' bookshops of College Street, in order to find reading material. Chain superstores have not yet extended their predatory reach to Bengal's most literary city, and on main thoroughfares throughout South Calcutta—Lower Circular Road, Ballygunge Road, Landsdowne Road, Rash Behari Avenue, Gariahat Road—small neighborhood bookshops and open-air bookstalls carry good selections of a wide range of Bengali titles, literary and academic volumes among them, as well as school primers and texts, notebooks, and writing supplies.

Short-term visitors to Calcutta may not be aware of all these Bengali-language literary resources. Most book-seeking visitors will find their way, duly following the directions in their Lonely Planet, Fodor's, or other traveller's guides, to the mainly English-language Oxford and Cambridge Bookstores on genteelly dilapidated Park Street, in the Chowringhee area downtown where most tourists tend to congregate. A few intrepid souls will venture around the corner to Free School (now Mirza Ghalib) Street, to Seagull Books, an alternative publisher with its bookstore outlet housed on the third floor of an industrial office building above a Dunlop Tyre showroom. Such serendipitous customers will be well rewarded by their visit—if they happen to notice the inconspicuous Seagull hoarding (signboard) on the wall by the stairwell entrance as they step gingerly, heckled by rickshaw pullers and troupes of Rajasthani women beggars, along with the narrow, rubble-strewn footpath between trenches dug for telephone cable repair.

Notwithstanding the challenges to its commercial visibility, Seagull's small, blessedly air-conditioned shop contains the city's best selection of English-language books on a variety of subjects. (One disgruntled Calcutta journalist dubbed it a "specialty shop [that] has built up a highbrow clientele by importing books on such subjects as feminism, sociology and semiotics.") In actuality, Seagull Press has for over a decade brought out innovative, attractively produced works on theater and film, including a series of film scripts translated into English of noted directors Satyajit Ray, Shyam Benegal, and others. Seagull serves as Indian distributor for books by a number of British publishers, and the U.S. visitor will be pleased to note copies of titles from independent presses such as Graywolf, Persea, and Black Sparrow on the shelves.

Another alternative shop on a shoestring budget is Classic Books, set back on a large grassy plot on Middleton Street, overshadowed by highrise office towers and decaying mansions. Their application for a stall at the book fair denied year after year, Classic's owners decided in 1988 to hold their own alternative book fair, which ran for a week in January and featured poetry readings, short plays, and concerts of the *bauls*, Bengal's renowned sect of devotional folk musicians.

No overview of Calcutta's literary life would be complete without a visit to the suburban Lake Gardens residence of Professor P. Lal, poet, teacher, translator, publisher, and founder of the forty-year-old Writers Workshop, featured some years ago in the BBC's "The Story of English" series seen on PBS. Begun in 1958 to provide a forum and publication outlet for Indian poetry (and some fiction, drama, and criticism) written in English, the workshop has weathered criticism from various quarters for being too eclectic, for publishing anyone with a manuscript, and even for aiding and abetting literary expression in English in post-colonial India. But the urbane and gentlemanly Lal asserts that none of these ungenerous comments matters. To date, the workshop has brought out nearly a thousand titles on local, "Gutenberg-era" hand presses, giving employment to whole families of printers and bookbinders. These volumes are distinctive for their covers, made from bright handloom saris ("You can recognize a Writers Workshop book a mile off," says Lal), and they have found their way to bookstores, libraries, and even university classrooms around the world.

Although many Calcutta poets and writers have visited the U. S. and acquired books here, awareness among most Calcuttans of poetry in English is awareness of English poetry, and most of that none too contemporary. Bengali poets with whom I have worked list Shakespeare, the Romantics, Tennyson, Browning, and sometimes Yeats among their influences. They also name Tolstoy, Chekhov, and Dostoyevsky: until recently, the Russian classics have been widely available in Calcutta, in inexpensive Soviet-printed English translations. Fewer Bengalis list Dickinson or Whitman as influences; almost none cites any influence more recent than Eliot. One of my translators, Paramita Banerjee, keeps the *Collected Poems* of Sylvia Plath and a selection of Pablo Neruda in English translation by her bedside. Another translator, Jyotirmoy Datta, who spent several months in the late 1960s at the University of Iowa's International Writing Program, knows Allen Ginsberg's work; Ginsberg even stayed at his house when he visited Calcutta several years ago. As she says in her interview, poet Kabita Sinha came to know the work of Alice Walker during her residency in 1980-1981 at Iowa's International Writing Program, and she continues to acquire books by Gwendolyn Brooks, Toni Morrison, Gloria Naylor, and other African-American women writers for her research. A friend at the American Library of the U.S.I.S. (the most heavily used of all U.S.I.S. libraries worldwide) reports that anthologies of younger contemporary American poets are almost constantly checked out. Collections by American poets are almost unobtainable in bookstores; American publishers don't seem to distribute to India. Whatever is available (I've seen Wallace Stevens, Plath, and Eliot, but these last two are also claimed by the British as their own) comes in a U.K. edition. British publishers rarely publish editions of any but the most well-established contemporary (Merwin, Wilbur), or the recently-made-modern (Ashbery, Ginsberg) American figures; but even these titles are rarely seen here. Imported books, with prices translated into rupees from their pound or dollar prices, are beyond the budgets of most Calcutta readers anyway.

Bengali Women Writers
Carolyne Wright

Though they write in the highly nuanced and musical language of Rabindranath Tagore, winner of the Nobel Prize for Literature in 1913, and though their language is as old as English, not many Bengali writers have been translated. Bengali literature is under-represented in English in part because its script is non-Roman, in part because it is difficult to study outside of West Bengal and Bangladesh: only a few universities in the West offer even elementary courses. Non-Bengalis learning the language are generally scholars of South Asian religions, anthropologists studying folk culture, or aid-agency and development consultants. The handful of non-Bengali literary translators usually concentrate on one major writer—almost always male.

Bengali women poets and writers were not significantly represented in English translation until the mid-1980s, yet women have participated in literary activities in Bengal since the latter half of the ninetenth century, when, as part of the widespread social reforms of the "Bengal Renaissance" movement, young upper-caste and upper-class Bengali men began to demand brides who were educated, and families began sending their daughters to newly created girls' schools or hiring home tutors. As privileged women learned to read and write, they started to question many of the socially sanctioned customs that had restricted their activities and participation in their society: *purdah* (the seclusion of women), child marriage, *sati* (the immolation of Hindu widows on their husbands' funeral pyres), prohibitions against any career but marriage and family. Educated housewives wrote diary-like life narratives; some of these were of high literary quality and were serially published in newspapers and magazines—often under pseudonyms so as not to violate *purdah*'s dictates of public anonymity for women.

By the early twentieth century, Bengali women ventured to publish under their own names; some became so popular that a few male writers took female pen names to increase their own readership! One of the first works available in English was, in fact, written in English by Begum Rokeya Sakhawat Hossain (1880-1932), essayist, educator, and pioneering Bengali Muslim feminist. "Sultana's Dream," a short story first published in 1905 in a Madras-based English periodical, *The Indian Ladies' Magazine*, is a fantasy satire about a utopian "Ladyland" in which men are in *purdah*—relegated to menial tasks and childrearing—while wise and powerful women govern the peaceful, prosperous nation. In her lifelong campaign for women's education and autonomy and against *purdah*, Begum Rokeya started the Sakhawat

Memorial Girls' School in Calcutta, still functioning to this day. She wrote many essays and articles in Bengali, chiefly *The Secluded Ones*, a series of reports about the indignities and excesses of women's seclusion. She is very highly regarded in Bangladesh, her essays are part of the school curriculum, and schoolchildren are grateful to her for possessing a lively prose style—so different from the dull didacticism of much of their assigned reading!

Another woman who began writing in *purdah* was Jyotirmoyee Devi (1894-1988). Tutored at home, married at age 11, and widowed with six children at 25, she moved from Rajasthan to her in-laws' house in Calcutta after her husband died. Her *River Churning: A Partition Novel*, dealing with the violence and social upheaval in North India after the 1947 Partition, has recently been translated to English. Calcutta-born Shudha Mazumdar (1899-1994) received an English-medium convent-school education and a thorough training in traditional Bengali culture before marriage at age 12 to an Indian Civil Service officer twice her age. Wherever her husband was posted, she organized efforts to improve women's health and welfare, joined the struggle for Indian independence, and wrote prose reminiscences of Bengali life. The first volume of her *Memoirs of an Indian Woman* (1989), written in English, recalls her life up to the early 1930s, against the backdrop of the Indian nationalist movement and the changing roles of women in colonial Bengal.

In 1930, sixteen-year-old poet Maitreyi Devi (1914-1990), daughter of a renowned Indian philosopher, fell in love with a Romanian student who had come to Calcutta to study with her father. When the mutual attraction was discovered, the student, future Indologist Mircea Eliade, was thrown out of the house and eventually returned to Europe to write *Maitreyi*, a fictionalized romance about which the real Maitreyi learned with shock and consternation nearly forty years later. Her own "reply" to Eliade's novel was *It Does Not Die* ("*Na Hanyate*"), first published in Bengali in 1974, and in English in the author's own translation by the Writers Workshop, Calcutta, in 1976. It was an immediate and longstanding bestseller in Bengali. The two books, Eliade's (now titled *Bengal Nights* after the French translation of the Romanian original) and Devi's (a reprint of the first Writers Workshop edition), were published together in 1994 by the University of Chicago. Even in the fast-paced and overly sensationalized American market, these books created a stir among readers for the conflicting depictions of a love affair and the cultural notions—and misreadings, especially Eliade's—upon which it was based.

Most of these earlier writers wrote in English, translated their Bengali originals themselves, or employed other Bengali native speakers to translate their work. Part of the British colonial legacy in Bengal is the enduring presence of English: many educated people in the subcontinent have at least basic fluency. Even now, most translations from Bengali to English are by English-educated Bengalis for Indian or Bangladeshi publishers. Such translations too often read like translations: the English is frequently awkward—demonstrating the perils of translating from one's native language to a second language studied from books, without experience of current usage or idiomatic and colloquial nuances only native or near-native speakers could distinguish. Vocabulary in English reflects not the twentieth-century usages of the original Bengali, for example, but the British Victorian terminology the translator learned in school. Dialogue may be similarly stiff, bookish, overly formal. Whatever grace or colloquial ease the original work possessed is not carried over into English. (There is also the post-colonial, subaltern position that the various English usages of the subcontinent are not "deviations" from some distant norm, but legitimate variants. "Indian English" is indeed a rich idiomatic variation; but many who hold such views make their points with perfect fluency in the Oxbridge or Ivy League accents in which they have been educated. Such critiques ultimately sidestep the issue: the need for faithful and graceful translations, no matter what variant of English the target language may be.)

Collaborative translation would seem to be the best option when there are so few native English speakers (whether of Indian or European origin) both committed to literary translation and fluent enough in a language of the subcontinent to do these translations independently. Unfortunately there is not much financial incentive for either independent or collaborative translation, unless one receives a fellowship (not many of which are available within India) or is commissioned by a publisher for a specific assignment—usually a novel. Thus, most of the best modern or contemporary work from Bengali, or any other of the regional languages, has yet to appear in good English translation.

Notable translators whose work is available in the West are Berkeley-based Kalpana Bardhan and renowned post-colonial subaltern scholar Gayatri Chakravorty Spivak: both of these women are native speakers of Bengali residing for many years in the U. S. Both have made substantial contributions, particularly of stories of Mahasweta Devi (b. 1926), one of West Bengal's leading fiction writers, winner of the Neustadt Prize and the Magsaysay Award, and an energetic social activist for the rights of India's indigenous pre-Aryan tribal peoples. As far as I am aware, there are precisely three non-Bengali native English speakers sufficiently fluent in *bangla* to translate on their own: all are university professors who teach intensive *bangla* language courses, and all happen to focus on the work of deceased male poets. One is William Radice of the School of Oriental and African Studies in London, who has translated a *Selected Poems* and a *Selected Short Stories of Rabindranath Tagore* (1861-1941), both volumes published by Penguin Books. The University of Chicago's Clinton B. Seely has written a seminal literary biography of modernist poet Jibanananda Das (1899-1954), *A Poet Apart*, with translations of several of Das's most important poems. Carol Salomon of the University of Washington is preparing translations of the songs of the nineteenth-century *baul* (devotional folk poet and singer), the extremely long-lived—if traditional lore about his life may be believed—Lalan Fakir (c. 1780-1890).

Some Bengali "expatriate" women writers are settled in the West but contribute actively to Bengali literary publishing in their home countries. Like Calcutta-born poet, translator, and literary scholar Ketaki Kushari Dyson (b. 1940), who has resided near Oxford since her graduate school days, such writers self-translate and also write original work in English for non-Bengali readers. Others, like poet and popular fiction writer Nabaneeta Dev Sen (b. 1938), prepare preliminary versions for other translators to work from. Another rapidly evolving subgenre consists of work by women writers of Bengali origin, settled in the West, fluent in Bengali but writing in English, chiefly about the immigrant's or cultural hybrid's experience. Such writers, including Bharati Mukherjee (b. 1942) and Chitra Banerjee Divakaruni (b. 1956), who have major North American and U.K. publishers, are not themselves subjects for translation. Divakaruni does occasional poetry translations, however, for anthologies. A few other young Bengali women, raised and educated in the West, but accustomed from infancy to speak—and also trained to read and write—in their parents' first language, have begun translating: theirs is the ideal balance of fluency in both source and target languages. One such translator is novelist and short story writer Jhumpa Lahiri, who is preparing a collection of short stories by Ashapurna Devi (b. 1909), one of West Bengal's most popular fiction writers.

My own translation efforts have been collaborative, since my knowledge of Bengali was limited at the start of my project. Though my *bangla* has improved—thanks in large part to the opportunities provided by fellowships to live and speak the language for a total of four years in Calcutta and Dhaka—I am acutely aware that many subtleties still elude my grasp. Working with a number of co-translators, and in many cases with the writers themselves, is painstaking and time-consuming, but it is satisfying to produce English versions that meet with the approval of both the original writer and non-Bengali readers: translations that sound natural in English, and remain faithful to the Bengali as well. Of the work completed, much of the poetry has appeared in literary magazines, and two individual poetry collections—by Bangladeshi dissident writer Taslima Nasrin (b. 1962) and by Calcutta-based poet and urban development worker Anuradha Mahapatra (b. 1957)—have been published. In preparation are *A Bouquet of Roses on the Burning Ground: Poetry by Bengali Women*, a comprehensive anthology of poetry in translation; and *Crossing the Seasonal River: Stories of Bengal by Women*, an anthology of prose in translation (short stories, memoir, and novel excerpts) by about fifty of the leading twentieth-century Bengali (West Bengali as well as Bangladeshi) women poets and writers, including the poets featured here. Several other notable Calcutta poets whom I have translated are not represented here, due to space limitations, but their work is important and has been featured elsewhere, including the original feature in compost #10 (1998). Among them are Radharani Devi (1904-1989), her daughter Nabaneeta Dev Sen (b. 1938), Ketaki Kushari Dyson (b. 1940), Gita Chattopadhyay (b. 1941), Pratima Ray (b. 1942), Rama Ghosh (b. 1944), Debarati Kitra (b. 1946), Sanjukta Bandyopadhyay (b. 1958), and Mallika Sengupta (b. 1960).

Truth Is God
An Interview with Kabita Sinha   [1997]

c: Your name is Kabita, which means poetry in Bengali. Was it your fate to become a poet?

KS: No, my grandfather gave that name to me. I had no idea I would become a poet. My grandfather was a writer. My mother used to write poems, my grandmother also used to write poems, so there was a literary atmosphere in our house. We had a library of about 10,000 books. I spent most of my childhood in the library reading. When I was four years old I could read Bengali very well, and Sanskrit, and other Sanskrit scriptures.

c: What was your poetry like before you were published? Would you say you changed in any way after you were published?

KS: Actually I began to write pleasure poetry—sweet poetry—but later on when I came to know more about the world my writing changed. I was born into a very rich family. My grandfather used to be called Rajah (King). I did not know what poverty was. But after I got married everything changed. I became very, very poor. We had to struggle, constantly. I was always strug-gling, writing, and producing children. So I came to know what the real world was like. Then I started researching backward and forward, that means my grandfather, ancestors, everyone. I discovered what they were doing, what they were suffering. I found the suffering of women everywhere. Even in the literary world. People would say of me, "She is a poet—no—she writes poetry. She is a sort of poet." Anger started growing inside me. Before I had no anger. My life changed and my poetry changed.

c: Do you see yourself as having a particular project or mission in terms of writing about Bengali women and culture? How do you approach that through your art?

KS: I have two projects in my mind. One is to discover the inner world of women and how women have changed since the Second World War.
 After the Second World War there was a radical change in the situation of Indian women. After the Second World War women started coming out of their homes. Before the Second World War, the only job for women was teaching. But office work and factory work, and other various labors of life,

began to put women side-by-side with men. This became the case because of the evils of war and famine. These two occurrences in our culture completely changed women in India. Especially Bengal because Bengal was struck hard by the famine and then by the political division of Bengal into Bangladesh and West Bengal. So, one after another, sadness descended.

When I went to Iowa in 1980-81, I was exposed to the writers of the world: African writers, German writers, Hungarian writers, Swedish writers, men, and women. It was there I became interested in reading black female writers. I was very much moved by Alice Walker's *The Color Purple*. I found similarities between African American female writers and Bengali women. The situations these characters face are very similar to the situations Bengali women encounter, especially the untouchables. In the United States the problem is between colored and white. In India the problem is between untouchables and touchables. It is the same problem. I have written a poem about it. For example, in India, if an untouchable and a touchable are walking down—if even the untouchable's shadow touches you (you being a Brahmin or upper class) you have to bathe. Untouchables are untouchable. With the exception of raping or other bad things—untouchables are not untouchable. There is an untouchable caste called Humbe. If a Humbe woman is raped, during the rape she finds that she can be touched. This is the man's world.

c: We heard you were doing research on African American poets. Who are some of the people you are researching?

KS: I am researching African American poets and novelists. In India some tribes are untouchables—Kol, Santal, Munda, and others near the south coast of Madras. Their skin is very similar to the Negroid color. It is written in the older scriptures that they arrived in India on a big swan.

Perhaps some African Aborigines came to India and formed the untouchable groups there. I want to do a comparative study between these African American writers whose origin is also Africa, and these tribes. Their totems and their gods all are very similar to the African totems and gods. I found that in *The Color Purple*, Celie used to write letters to God. One day she decided: God I won't write to you. Next time I will not write to you, I will write to my sister (who is doing some missionary work somewhere in Africa). Why? Because you are white, you are a man.

So, Celie is in search of a black God. She is in search of a, not a white God, but a God, something similar to her. And a woman. Not a man. Not a man—not a white person. A woman goddess. In India there are goddesses as well. One goddess is the goddess of will. She is very fair looking, very well clad with lots of ornaments. She is our goddess of education. She's Saraswati, she is very fair, very beautiful, very white, and very prim. Durga, the ten-armed goddess, is the goddess of strength. They are all yellow or golden yellow or something like that. But there is only one goddess who is completely different from all the goddesses of India. She is black. Her name is Kali. And this Kali is standing on a white [fair] man, Shiva, her husband . . . she's standing one foot on Shiva's body—chest. She is the goddess of destruction. Her hair is black. She is black and is holding human heads and is wearing human hands as a skirt. She is standing on the white man. That image of Kali is worshipped, especially in Bengal and various parts of India, but especially in Bengal. This is a very strange thing: old Bengalis, they used to hate their wives. They tried to repress their wives, but they used to worship Kali. Kali is the symbol of Shakti (power), and Kali is the symbol of activeness—activity. That means something in our religion. It is said that when the snakes lie motionless, she is *Prakriti*—a man, and when the snakes move, she is Shakti—god. To you, *prakriti* means "nature," but we think that prakriti has its own life. Whereas Purush means doing completely nothing—being inert. It also means "man," "male," etc. You see, while prakriti is doing everything—she is doing everything. Man is inert, but woman is doing the work. Actually, in our religion, it is said that man and woman are the same. Inside a person there is a man and a woman. The man is inert, the woman is active. That is the final argument … in our religion…

c: Is it important for women to be bilingual to reach other cultures?

KS: In India the problem is that we have 22 very strong languages. It is not possible to know all 22 languages plus English? We cannot do that, but Hindi is the official language of India. So people learn Hindi. Most women learn a little bit of workable Hindi and those who are educated learn English.

c: Bengali is characterized as being very symbolic and phonetic, having a lot of very rich sounds and is highly imagistic. Those are not some of the words people would use to explain English. When literature is being translated from Bengali to English, do you feel a lot is lost in translation when people read your poetry and other forms of Bengali literature in English? Do they miss out on something?

KS: Yes. Yes. I noticed that when I was in England in a literary group they asked me the same question. So I read a poem to them, a very small poem of mine called "Immersion." I read that poem. I then said that I have read this poem to you and you could not understand anything. Still I read that poem. Then I described "Immersion" to them—it means you put something underwater. There is a Goddess called Durga, the goddess with ten arms. We worship her with the same importance as you celebrate Christmas—we worship during Durga Puja. Once a year, people wait for the coming of the Durga Puja. We worship her for five days. After the fifth day, we put out a big bowl of water. In the bowl we place a mirror and wait for her reflection to come. When the goddess appears—when her reflection comes into the mirror—we slowly immerse the mirror into the water. After her immersion, we see the goddess—her hands floating out, her eyes floating out, and her ornaments floating out. Having explained this, I could now read the poem and you could follow everything.

What I'm saying is that you cannot translate something from Bengali to English or English to Bengali unless you know the culture. My poem, "Eve Speaks to God," is untranslatable. You have to know something about the culture. There is a part in the poem, "Eve Speaks to God," in which Eve says that, "In the Garden of Eden I was dead." She is speaking to God, she is giving God a piece of her mind. She is telling God, "I am the first to rebel. I rebelled and I made Adam eat the apple. I lured him to eat that apple, because I know that knowledge is good, not bad." You don't have to be happy, but you must be truthful in order to become an independent person. While you're God's child, you're still a dependent child and you must live in the Garden of Eden eating only fruit, never knowing what happiness really is. Until one day, you are shown what sorrow is—until that day, you can't be complete.

It is then that Eve says, "I first discovered grace and I made the Heaven and Hell differentiation between nudity and dressing up. I changed your curse into blessing. You cursed me. You said that I must endure deep pain to bear a child, but I saw your face in my child's face." As you know, the Bible says that man is made after God. It is with this in mind that Eve explains how she first rebelled, then went home and met a new God, one that does not think that she is just a doll or a yo-yo, like Adam, but knows that she is an individual person. This poem, "Eve Speaks to God," is understood by everyone. When I went to the Frankfurt book fair, they translated my poem into German and it was greatly appreciated.

c: What would you want people to understand as Bengali culture? What differentiates Bengal and Calcutta from the rest?

KS: Actually in India there was a great political leader whose name was Tilak. He said, "What Bengal thinks today, India thinks tomorrow." Up to 1912, Calcutta was the capital of India and Bengal was the capital region. Later, the capital shifted to Delhi. So, we came into first contact with the English, the colony of English people. At that time the Bengalis learned English with their heart and soul. Because they had to serve under the English people—as clerks, as translators, or this and that. After two generations the other states of India started to learn English. But we learned English earlier than they did—and English culture, English books, and English novels. So our novelists read early English writers. We are not very familiar with American writers but we are more familiar with English writers. By that time, Bengal had already been exposed to the modern world—Bengal was a coastal country and at that time, the most interesting thing was not only the English people, but also the Portuguese, and the other coastal Pirates—the Mag (the Bengali name for the Arakan or Burmese people, who are regarded in old lore as lawless brigands, since some of them used to be pirates along the Burmese coast. Bengalis tend to pronounce this word as if it were spelled "Mogue"—which rhymes with "rogue"—which they were). The Mag used to come, and Morgues. You don't know the Morgues. Morgue means the African people who stayed in the Far East. You see lots of mixed blood in Bengal. In Bengal you can find a Negroid, you can find an English-like person, very fair and very beautiful with golden hair, you can find Portuguese, you can find Spaniards. In that way Bengal is very different.

c: Calcutta has experienced both positive and negative contact with many other cultures over time: Greek, Portuguese, Japan, China. We understand that the Bengali word Baba, for father, is actually Turkish. What other influences have the cultures had on the language and literature of the region?

KS: Lots of foreign words have entered our language. In our grammar books we wanted to mix words so our language would be rich. However, we cannot be flexible. That is the thing. We used to call a table, *tabin*—not table—we do not know what the Bengali word is for table. We know the English word—table. There is a Bengali word for chair and table. Table means *mage* and chair means *kedera*, but we never use them. In all of our vocabularies we often use foreign words. We think in that way we are rich. I'll give you an example. "She is going to the garden to have some flowers." We say exactly the same thing. We find a lot of similarities with the English people. And as I was saying, when I was explaining about translation, we know their culture, as we know the British culture because we have gone through their works. In addition, we know London. A lot of Bengali people, who are literate people, went from Calcutta to London. And when they came back they kept journals and diaries. So London is almost in our palm, we know every road, every street of London, we know Big Ben, we know everything. We know the London Bridge. We have to read British histories, the whole of the British history. We know Byron, Shelley, and definitely Shakespeare. Shakespeare is a favorite. He is the writer of all writers.

c: India is said to be opening its doors to international globalization. We've heard that the magazine DESH has photos of Cindy Crawford in its pages. How will this influence Bengali, the language and the literature?

KS: India is opening its doors. Our household people, my children, my grandchildren, they are very familiar with "The Bold and Beautiful," "The Young and The Restless," "The Price Is Right." These evil things are coming. My last novel is about this. The name of my last novel is *Rakta Gambuj*. That means the Bloody Pillar. In that book I dealt with the communication problem, that India is now facing. India is facing great cultural problems. People are not showing channel 39 where women are making beautiful gardens, beautiful homes, and decorating. They are not showing that, they are only showing "The Price Is Right," "Oprah," "The Maury Povich Show." And everybody is glued to the TV— "Oh, what is happening to the characters? What is happening to Richard? What is happening to Chris?" But this is not real. We are not connected with these things. We are not connected with this culture. It's taking the place of all the old stories. My grandchildren are glued to the TV, watching "The Young and The Restless." That is the last program on TV at night…it's a great problem….

c: Much of the West's contact with Indian cultures is from the influx of engineers, computer programmers, etc., from your continent. But they are from different regions. Both Calcutta and Kerala (where Arundhati Roy, author of *The God of Small Things*, is from) are more known for their artistic and cultural contributions. Both of these states have a long history of Marxism. Is there a correlation between the political ideology and the reason why there is so much emphasis on art and literature?

KS: Politics has no relation to literature in India. I am a resident of Bengal which has a certain type of communism. There are communist journals in

India but they are not very well known. One writer, Mahasweta Devi, is a communist but writes very well. She is five years older than I, and she lives that life. She lives among the tribal people and visits their villages. I wrote a poem for her once, it's titled, "Mahasweta." I compared her to fire. In the blast furnace when a fire goes to its ultimate heat, it becomes white. I compared her to that. You are not only fire, you are the ultimate fire, and you are way before your time. You are so modern, so visionary. It would almost be better if you were to come along 300 years from now.

c: In addition to culture, many religions have graced the soils of Calcutta: Islam, Christianity, and Hinduism. How has this influenced the art and literature in India?

KS: Religion influences me very much, from the beginning, right from my heart. Not so much in the sense of worshipping goddesses or anything like that. I practice the religion of truth. I think truth is god.

c: Is there a difference between the poetry of the different states in India? Bengal being the most artistic?

KS: You see, other states have their flickers of greatness. But it is Bengali poetry that is at par with world poetry. There are some very good Urdu poems and poets in other states, but not too many. In Bengal, when our children are 14 years old they are already practicing their poetry.

c: Why do you think there is a resurgence in Bengali literature in the world, more specifically, the U.S. these days?

KS: Do you see a resurgence? Hmm. Max Müller and other great philosophers were very interested in Bengali culture. They translated many of the Upanishads and other works a long time ago. Since then there has been a long history of exchange of literature and religion. It has been going on for a long time, and it has been continuous. So, I don't really see a resurgence. I remember when I was in Iowa at the International Writing Program. I was wearing the central red dot on my forehead and somebody asked me what the meaning of it was. I said that the dot means that we have a third eye. It opens when we gain more consciousness, more intelligence. The person was amazed! She thought it was ornamental, some kind of make-up or something. But she never knew the deep meaning of the central dot. Likewise, when you come to my house I will not shake your hand, I will clasp my hands like this (palms together, fingers and thumbs melded together in prayer), to *namaskar*. *Namaskar* means worshipping the soul inside you. This is a symbol. There are a lot of symbols in India and they reveal to the world what our heritage is. My grandchildren may not know all of our rich meanings within our culture … I will try to teach them but they are too busy watching TV, but I will try.

c: Like many of the other countries that we have featured in compost there is a long oral tradition of poetry in Calcutta. Has women's poetry been on a similar trajectory or is it more of a written poetry?

KS: Of course you know the work of Rabindranath Tagore? Let me translate for you one of his poems. In India the Aryans came, the non-Aryans came, the Chinese came, the Chukkas came (bandit types), Pathan (Afghan), Mongol (Mongolia), and assembled in one body. Now the West is opening its door and it has also come. We all come together and mingle but we stay India. That is Tagore's poem.

c: Toru Dutt and Maitreyee Devi are considered some of the earliest modern female poets who wrote in Bengali. Are they of historical importance or do they have a lasting influence on Bengali women's poetry today?

KS: Neither have a lasting impact. Although Maitreyee Devi is famous for her autobiography, *Na Hanyate*, ("It Does Not Die"). When she was very young, she had a love affair with a young scholar, Mircea Eliade; he used to teach at Chicago. [See Carolyne Wright's brief summary of this story in her introductory essay.] This novel was very good; it won the Rabindra Puraskar (The Tagore Prize) in Calcutta. But she was a better novelist, not really a poet of world standard. She was a favorite disciple of Tagore. Sarojini Naidu is okay, we read one or two of her poems, but she is a bit too political.

c: Contemporary Bengali literature is always characterized as being under the shadow of Tagore. What is his legacy in terms of contemporary women's poetry in Calcutta?

KS: Bengali literature has completely come out of the shadow of Tagore. Tagore has enriched our roots. But with all respect, we have gone beyond Tagore. After Tagore a very important poet was Jibanananda Das. He was a very powerful poet. Since him we have left Tagore's shadow. He was our door to modernism. If you go through his poems today you will find it very modern. Like the one I just quoted, it is very old but transcends time.

c: How do you think that male/female poetry differs in India?

KS: Female poems are very personal and are in their own language. Whether it is weak or strong they never care, they just want to say something very personal. A woman's torture is not only within her life, but also in previous lives. So when a woman wants to speak, she speaks many truths. The truth is sometimes very bitter. It is a strange thing that most of our female poets write "nude" poems, they are never covered. They are just there.

c: Is there a male bias in acknowledging women in the literary canon in India?

KS: Men seldom recognize women poets. Early on I was not recognized. Early on I was invited to read my poems at a prestigious literary conference. After the renowned poets read their works I was called up and introduced as a female poet of Bengal. I went up to the stage and said that if the person did not withdraw the "woman" thing that I would withdraw from the reading. I am a poet, just a poet. Not a female poet. That was my way of protesting. Once I refused the Lila Prize, a prestigious prize offered only to female writers. When it was offered to me I refused because it was only for women. But my husband told me that I should take it. When one story is returned other female writers often stop writing. With me, when one was returned I would keep on sending them more and more poems. I worked and earned my name.

c: What is revealed through the female poet that wouldn't be evident to the outsider?

KS: The pain is what is revealed through female poets. There is an interesting poet, Miti, who used to say that there was a female writer who used to get her door spit on because she wrote poems. Another story of a woman I was told about wrote in the 19th century. After 50 years a researcher went to her house to find out about the woman who wrote those poems. She went to the door and a very old lady came to the door. The lady at the door said that the poet had died. That means she is mentally dead. Once upon a time she was alive, but now she no longer writes poems. It is difficult to go on giving, giving, giving—when you are not given back anything, you can vanish.

c: Do female writers tend to write about nature, to enter into a world of myth and wonder to escape their lives? Or, do they tend to write politically, to express their social entanglements and afflictions?

KS: Politics come, but never directly. If the poem permits, then the politics come. Early on in one of my poems I objected to the division of Bengal into West Bengal and Bangladesh. But they were not political poems that I wrote. I used this to show that I could not accept a divided Bengali like East Germany and West Germany. In that way politics can come in, but often not.

c: India is rich with metaphor and color. You say you attempt to express truth in your poems. Where do you find it when things are not so good?

KS: One uses everything, their past, their present, their future, and their dreams in their poems. Even children's fairy tales.

c: How are you and other liberated, intellectual poets seen by more traditional women in Calcutta?

KS: If I don't communicate with all women it is useless to write. When I recite my poems I always watch the faces to see how my poems are taken. When I see their faces, they seem to be with me.

c: Western literature has the legacy of Sappho in its older literature. Is there a similar figure in the Mahabarat and the Upanishads? If not, how are women presented in these texts?

KS: Our literature has very strong women in it, but not a lesbian, like Sappho. Mallataree is a very strong woman. Ram's wife Sita in the *Ramayana*. She stayed in a demon's house, the demon (Ravana) put her in a burning fire, but Sita came out of the fire clean. After that Rama came back with Sita to their kingdom but the people demanded another test of her. She said she was the daughter of the earth. She said, "Oh earth you open and close, I do not want to be tested again." That was her strength, her protest. Draupadi in the Mahabharata had five husbands. Once her sari was taken away. She prayed to lord Krishna for a sari and many came. These stories are the pillars of our culture. They have become folklore and are transmitted in our children.

c: What do you think the role of the poet in the twenty-first century will be?

KS: In our Vedas it is said that our road is on a razor's edge, that we are walking on a razor's edge. The road is very far away, but what the poet does is see the road. The poet can see the way beyond the horizon. The poet has foresight and we will need that. When poetry is strong, our direction is strong. When you go to a play or painting, over time, what remains is a sense of liking it. The sense of liking it, is poetry. Everything comes to poetry. It is the ultimate. My second book is called *Kabita Parameshwari*; it means "poetry is the supreme goddess."

Friends Nowadays
Kabita Sinha   [3 poems]
translated by Carolyne Wright with Swapna Mitra-Banerjee
and the author

Hey look at us, a few friends walking side by side
You know we've kissed the mouth of the same bottle

                                                    the six of us!

So who's got bad teeth?   We didn't care, the cigarette
passing from mouth to mouth   Finger to finger
we swapped rings.   From one body to the other
our trousers   favorite women   leather belts passed around.

Why all this,   as if there were detectives' electronic
eyes or tape recorders, concealed on all sides.

Keeping this in mind, however,
to tell the truth, just between the two of us, mind you,
I still go to visit these friends nowadays
                        pounding loudly on the door
a clear unmistakable notice

So he has time to slip back behind the flower vase
                                        his sharp dagger
which he secretly sharpens everyday

for me.

Poetry Has No God but a Goddess
translated by Carolyne Wright with the author

Before You can abandon me
God, I am abandoning You.
Halfway through the Sabbath service
           the Black woman, the wet nurse
           walked out of church.

For three hundred years the Black woman
        was a neutered drudge,
with America wrung the white milk
from her black breasts!
Her head lowered, muffled in a kerchief, her eyes
         like hard-boiled eggs,
         she was a beast of burden.

But now, no more, no more, Amen!
Tearing off her kerchief, she let
      her black hair cascade down.
As soon as she stood up straight, her breast swelled,
         she raised her chin, her whole demeanor changed.
Rumba! Rumba! The curves of her waist, her shapely thighs
and hips emerged.

At the mouth of the East River, a woman stands
         clumsy, padded with clothes,
the bloodless white Statue of Liberty
         bereft of eyeballs.
The Black woman called to her—Liberty?—Do you know
        what freedom is?
If you knew you'd throw off the load of clothing

Like me.

Right now, I want to keep a leukoderma-stricken
      male god under my feet.

Kali is drawing me instinctively from the East.

Turning
translated by Carolyne Wright with Enakshi Chatterjee

Who breaks in her own way from within,
who breaks step by step the vast expanse
               of sky from the sapphire.
Incessant showers go on breaking from the clouds,
buds break ceaselessly into flower,
               the night's heart cracks open in a morning
                      burning like an open wound.

The subject is breakage, yet all these breakings
               and fallings-down
                     are the essential mortar.

If mountains break down into sand, sand little by little turns
                   to silt, crushed by

the sea's incessant waves, waves crashing on the shore.
Like winding lanes, they all come running
           from separate directions
                  to the central, turning,   point.

Escalator
Rajlakshmi Devi
translated by Carolyne Wright and Swapna Mitra-Banerjee

You aren't moving, neither am I.
Global organizations, Nature, the processes
              of life, are all moving.
As if by some inexorable circulatory system,
Moment by moment, slowly, slowly—
I'm coming closer to you.

As if by some inexorable circulatory system
All the planet's automations
Are moving away from us.

You aren't moving, neither am I.
But what a powerful will—
What a fetter of unbounded force—
That, moment by moment, slowly, slowly,
Is pulling me closer to you.

Long-lived and Blessed with Sons
Vijaya Mukhopadhyay
translated by Carolyne Wright with Sunil B. Ray

A battered aluminum bowl,
an oil-begrimed cane beside her,
the mother lies there on the footpath.
Countless wrinkles score her face—
milestones along her own road.
How many sons does she have,
                and what are they doing?
Freight-car robbers, pimps
or cripples, honest beggars?
The mother lies there on the footpath,
needing some sort of shelter like Nirmal Hriday;
or, having turned it down,
she goes on lying there, surviving there
only through sheer will to survive,
the long-lived mother, blessed with sons.

The Hub of the Universe: Celebrating Boston

So I woke up with the taste of Old Milwakee's on my toes because they say the money trickles down from trees of telephones and coffee, copper mines and used canals; but in the foreign student stores it seems Marx never holds the gun and la gente would have won if the gringos trees were fallen and the leaves had never come; but I want to rejoice in the youth of my soul and the souls of our youth; yet I can't because my best friend got wasted last night—I found him lying naked in his own shit. On my seventeenth birthday, staring into the mirror at my naked, skinny body, I became suddenly conscious of myself—one still moment like a drop of water: mirror of the water of the time; a reflection of my shadowy face breaking into pieces. My spirit is purple and it comes from all sides straight through to your chest carrying the power of the living and surviving the power of those who have struggled before us feeding our souls, and when we rough but beautiful beasts march skipping to Bethlehem or Boston or "anywhere out of this world," including everywhere on this earth similar jewels will be laid around the hearth ... compost!

King
Mary Louise Sullivan

As a boy he used to wear an old scarf around his head
like a diadem and my mother, my sisters and I would call him
King. A king is not a king without an entourage,

So all of us would march behind him rattling on
pots and pans with wooden spoons, in celebration of the King
of our house, a small brown shoe box at the end of a long street

in Nowhere.
        When no one was home, he would sit on the edge of his bed
rolling tears fat as pennies down his face in streams,
making rivers run silently through the house where he
was King.
          Now his mother washes the dishes
with a view that hasn't changed in all these years—
it's still the same pine tree and rhododendron bush

which blooms faster some springs than others. She is waiting
for him to call and when he does, his voice shakes
when he asks her for money, for who ever heard

Of a prodigal king? No doubt, he is King, he wears
a crown of scars, pink, amber and gold scars,
threading circles in circles in circles
                    around his regal head.

Reflections
Arindam Banerji

At times a moment comes still as a drop of water,
when you don't want to go anywhere,
when you want to wait patiently
by the side of a solitary Krishnachura tree
in a lonely railway station sitting meditatively.

While flying towards the heaven
a Sankacheel offers me a darting glance!
I don't know why. I don't know why.
Alas, you haven't learned any lessons from the history.
Perhaps the bird wanted to say that!

Our mistakes keep on growing in numbers....
One still moment like a drop of water:
mirror of the water or of the time;
a reflection of my shadowy face breaking into pieces.

An Interview with Robert Pinsky

c: What's ahead? What's the idea? How is it expressed today? How should, could and will it evolve into the future of the new millennium? And how will it be dealt with through language, or how will it be expressed? And, how do you do it in your work? When we talk about this thing called the "New World Order" there's obviously a politics and economics that are around the changing of the millennium. Do you think the "New World Order" is sort of a solidification of a national and an international oligarchy?

RP: I'll try not to be a jerk by talking about things I don't know too much about. I'll try to bring everything back to what I do know about in my own art of poetry. I practice this inherently traditional, ancient art in a country famous for being fluid, changing, involved in speed and shifting surfaces. It is the country that invented jazz, rock and roll, Hollywood movies. In it, I practice this non-technological, even in a way primitive and historical art, based on the sounds of English words spoken by one voice.

And I'm a product, myself, of that kind of change, that kind of contrast—change and contrast that will probably accelerate in the future. My family illustrates this in a characteristic American way. Most of my great-grandparents didn't even speak this language, my parents didn't go to college. I'm considered, I think, among writers, relatively high-brow, rather well educated in things of the past: I'm crazy about Renaissance poetry, I know something about other things that are not modern. But, compared to the time of Keats and maybe even to the time of Eliot, compared to, say, an educated average person, a business person or medical doctor, I am in certain respects an ignoramus: I read Latin, which they took for granted, only very haltingly with a dictionary at my side. I have vague ideas which Greek roots are in English words. My French isn't too hot. I represent knowledge that is only *relatively* stable or continuous with the past, in these ways. This makes me, not inferior to that literate doctor or business man of the past, but quite different—a product of accelerating changes.

Immigration and the influence of other cultures in this country seem likely to accelerate more, we are in for a lot of rapid transition. Our genius as a country, the explosive genius of our art, has been able to subsume that kind of change: in exchange for Latin or for Renaissance poetry, some vital new mix. We make art out of unlikely ingredients and almost out of loss itself. A book like [Willa Cather's] *My Antonia* is, in a way, about the loss of European culture, the loss of almost everything, out in the plains. All the immigrant novels of writers like Henry Roth, all the stories of American immigrants are in a way stories of the loss of some European thing or Asian thing. And all the great writing of African-Americans has to do, too, with the loss of a culture, and the invention from loss of something new. And in this country, aside from the past, there is always the "nativistic," right-wing anxiety of the loss of something in the present, something that isn't stable enough because of new immigrants who come in and bring change. So, it is a culture that creates things, driven by loss and readjustment, things like our movies and songs and, indeed, our literature. William Faulkner is so elegiac and at a sense of tremendous speed, almost bewildering speed of change and attrition amid the elegy, so that one generation has trouble speaking to the next, sometimes literally. We invent from fragments.

I taught a lot of kids of Asian immigrants at Berkeley [California]. There, you can see the southeast Asian version or Chinese version of this same phenomenon in these students. It is something to be patriotic about, because at the same time that it is sad, a movement from generation to generation that involves conflict and pain, it also has this great, unpredictable vigor, an unpredictable quality where nobody can say what any given one of "those" people is going to write, or paint, or see, or how they are going to see. To think of any generation as "those" people, or one kind of person, is mixed-up and mistaken, too. More and more of my children's friends are, say, half Hawaiian, half Jewish, half Black, and those three "halves" actually do go into some people. So, when I think about what I do in the art of poetry and how it is in some way, I hope, connected to what George Herbert did, or John Keats did, or Emily Dickinson did, I'm also aware of all the ways in which it is completely disconnected, formally, in idiom, in what you assume your audience knows, in what you yourself know. I assume that someone practicing my art 50 years from now or 100 years from now will be at least as different from me as I am from those people. This is dizzy-making and intimidating, but also exciting. I think that any terms we use for a "New Order" are going to seem antiquated in maybe as little as five years.

c: In America, from what we see, all these different ethnic influences have been lost to mainstream "pop" culture, instead of holding on and having pride in one's traditional roots and culture. We guess it's all really coming back much more now in a sort of cultural sensitivity.

RP: It is just very hard to predict. This or that kid could become a classical musician, or another kind, and it is hard to say if even the term "classical" has any stability. It is the unpredictability, to me, that is very much the American part of it. We have social classes, but we don't have them in as oppressive or rigid a way as the English do. We have standard curricula and canons, but we don't have them with the rigidity of the French. Without being chauvinistic about it, whatever virtues those European social or educational systems have, our own virtues traditionally have been the ones that go with all bets being off, everything suspended, not being able to tell or determine, not knowing. The fact that it is an option to feel quite mainstream and normal for that person of "halves" or fragments distinguishes this country from, say, Japan or Romania.

For all our imperfections, in a way our very ignorance or what used to be known as our innocence, our unanchored quality, historically, though it has catastrophic effects, too—our optimism that has tangled us in wars or dangerous technologies—our sunny relative disregard for what the past might indicate, traditionally has been linked to our genius, has been desirable. When I think about what kind of poem I want to write, I believe I think like an American, so I try to think what that means. What does all that downside and upside of that readiness to change or experiment mean? What do I have to say of that, what do I know of it?

c: Do you think we're going to carry all of that optimism into the next century, as at the turn of this century when everyone was saying "let's go!", "everything is wide open!"

RP: I would say that if we do it probably will come from immigrant sources, in a large measure. Apparently, it will come from people who have Spanish-speaking parents and grandparents, and people who have parents and grandparents who speak Asian languages. That kind of pure, or relatively pure, eagerness for what we do here. It probably will come from sources like that, it traditionally has. Traditionally, it has been the Italians, the Irish, or the Jews or somebody who just grins and says, "This looks great, I can open a grocery store on the corner." Like the Koreans now. In a rather crude model, one generation starts a grocery store and the next generation starts examining eyes and writing free verse.

c: In *Situation of Poetry* you say that because of this optimism that modern ideas have a moral detachment. Do you think that is the after effect of all this optimism?

RP: I think Modernism, if by Modernism we mean more or less Pound and Eliot for poetry, I think it looked toward Europe, was a Europewardlooking, reactionary movement in many ways. That they aspired to restore some pre-Romantic idea of Europe, along with the moral detachment and the emphasis on craft and on vividness. They were in some ways like the English pre-Raphaelites. They had an implausible idea of immediacy and directness, simplicity. "The image is always the adequate symbol" and so forth. And moral detachment or impersonality is associated with them and scholarship for years used to relate that to revulsion at the horror of World War I. I think that Modernism may also, in the case of those two writers, have had a self-loathing component, a feeling that American provinciality was extremely hampering both as a set of manners, and as a way of being an artist or writer. They both tried to react against a soft or soppy late-Romantic quality in art, but they probably were also reacting against a cloying provinciality, or limiting provinciality, that they found in the American culture of their time, which we haven't lived through: it probably was truly boring. To sympathize with them, there was doubtless a justifiable, youthful insistence upon excellence on their part. In retrospect, this shades off into snobbery, an anti-democratic feeling, and they were both to some extent political reactionaries too, as was Yeats.

c: What do you think today's poetry is trying to do? Or what is the idea of today's poetry compared to what Pound and Eliot were doing?

RP: Well, there's been a lot of water under the bridge. The living poets I read with most pleasure tend to emphasize that poetry is continuous with other uses of language. The Modernist idea refreshed poetry partly by calling attention to its essence, which is to say ways in which poetry is not continuous with other kinds of language, but different. Both Pound and Eliot like technological or theoretical metaphors for what the poem does: it is a kind of catalyst in a chemical reaction, or whatever. The critical rhetoric of Modernism emphasized the way poetry represented an alternative to the rest of life. And we inherit that: when I read a new poem by poets younger than me, say Tom Sleigh or Mark Halliday, I do see a sophisticated awareness of all that Modernist view of poetry's distinct nature. But the rhetoric in these young poets, the applied aesthetic, seems to seek the overlap between poetry and all other language, as though exploring the idea that your theory of poetry doesn't necessarily have to be different than your theory of speech or your theory of journalism or your theory of political discourse. The question is not to find out how poetry is different, but how poetry is continuous with other uses of its medium.

c: How do you think that is going to evolve? Octavio Paz says that, "Words and myths are metaphors for the unexplainable" and there was an anxiety at the coming of the 20th century. Do you see this anxiety in anybody's art today or do you see this idea of the millennium coming at all?

RP: I suppose that our own zeitgeist seems to be a terrific reaction, a kind of hangover from a period of believing in explanations—and I don't mean only Marxism. I mean for example social expertise. As recently as Johnson's Great Society we were ready to assume, as a nation, that there were experts in human behavior, human communities. And if we heeded such people who told us how, we could better educate our children, integrate our cities, restore our neighborhoods. The idea was that there were people who had gone to school and studied the organizing of human life the same way you might study aerodynamics or isotopes, or the way you study archeology. These experts were going to help us out.

I think people have grown skeptical about that, and we're in a period that I suppose could be rather frightening politically, could be reactionary in a bad way. But for good and ill we appear to be in a mood to respect mystery more than we did. I can be optimistic about that in some ways, welcome it as reaffirming poetry, as that provocative Paz statement implies. Poetry has to do with asserting the power of the mysterious and the unexplained in human behavior, but so does fashion. The history of the irrational exaltation of the 20th century, and the history of following great mass impulses, or individual impulses even, is not a glorious history. It is bloody—even worse than the history of experts, which is bad enough. I wouldn't be overly sunny about it. (Now I do feel that I have fallen into talking like a jerk, as I said I wouldn't, because I am not talking about poetry.)

A convenient instance is Robert Bly's popular appeal. I consider him a friend, but for twelve or fifteen years I have had misgivings about his innocent, to me unquestioning attachment to the "shadow" part of people, his essays that talk about the forest being more important than any tree, and what part of your body do you think with. All that is easy, maybe, for an upper-middle-class Lutheran from Minnesota. But the same ideas might have spooky, raising-the-hair-on-the-back-of-your-neck overtones for somebody of different social, religious, ethnic origins. At times I have tried to discuss this with Robert. He sort of nods but has seemed to me not to get the idea. Now, he has written a best-seller that he emphatically does not view as a reaction against the women's movement, a book about how valuable it is for men to experience their primitive male warrior feelings.

138

It seems to me a revival of something I'm not particularly crazy about, a certain vein, in American Protestantism. Maybe there are guys of Southeast Asian descent out there banging drums and wearing face paint, but it is not my impression. My impression is that these people are in one manner or another frustrated would-be Viking raiders.

c: Paz talks about that in his Nobel Prize acceptance speech, not only in the case of Robert Bly, but also with the individual and spirituality. He talks about poetry and spirituality: the institutionalized religions are being shifted and there is a move back toward mother-earth-ism, towards new age religions, and there's a lot of people going into them and into these Bly-movements, but then there are all these other people who are totally disenchanted with all that and so their only religion is poetry. Their poems are their own personal prayers, to be able to figure out their own spirituality.

RP: I may be a congenitally timid person or it may be part of my own view of history, what comes out of me in history, but when people start putting aside their conventional forms of behavior and saying we're going to be a little more like maenads, or now we're going to put on the masks and run screeching for a while, part of me wrings its hands a bit. I become rather anxious. Part of this feeling is intuitive, and part of it comes from thinking about European history.

c: *An explanation of America*, which you wrote in the 70s, was published during the Jimmy Carter years. How would you write it today? Does your daughter ever ask you questions about it?

RP: She doesn't much ask me about it. She has said she's a little tired of people who say to her, "Are you 'you'?" Because she's that formal, nominal 'you' in the book. In a way, maybe I am still stuck in the mood of that book, because what I am saying to you now is not unlike what I say in the section called "Bad Dreams," in which I imagine a man out in the prairie falling in love with his "shadow." At that point, mine is a kind of a rationalist, moderate viewpoint. My hero in an unspoken way in that book among the so-called Modernists was James Joyce, who unlike D.H. Lawrence, unlike W.B. Yeats, unlike Ezra Pound, unlike T.S. Eliot, unlike lesser figures like Wyndham Lewis or e. e. cummings, never had a flirtation with fascist ideas. Joyce in this respect was a good Catholic humanist. Joyce's experimentation as an artist did not lead him in the direction of believing in crazy ideas about authority or race, as it did so many of the others. This fact embodies, in my opinion, one of the great unwritten-about subjects of its kind. Joyce had plenty of rage, but it didn't express itself in right-wing politics or anti-Semitism. His hero was a wanderer. He didn't identify with some mass-consciousness or nationalism or racialism. He was an ex-Catholic, humanist individualist. In that sense he's a kind of human hero to me, compared to my other literary heros.

c: In contrast, what do you think is represented in the generation of poets after Eliot, Pound and Joyce?

RP: I guess you mean the generation of poets who include Robert Lowell, Robert Duncan, Elizabeth Bishop? It has been a long time since anyone has been as grandiose as Eliot. If you think of the writers who just sprang into my mind—Lowell's breakthrough book was one very much about personal experience. Later in his career, he wrote a book called *History*, and it is very much not a grand theory of history. Bishop—how do we read her? As a poet of loneliness and selfhood. I suppose it's been a complaint against *History*: I guess it's not as global or doesn't embody a kind of ambitious worldview as the Modernists. But maybe that's part of our complaint with them, maybe it explains the ascent of Stevens.

When I was in college and graduate school, Wallace Stevens, if he was considered a great poet, wasn't as great a poet as Pound and Eliot. I don't think that is the literary critical fashion anymore. I think the professors now view Stevens as very great indeed. People paying attention to these things, in general, decided that if you read Eliot and Pound as sages, or as people with large worldviews, they didn't come off well. So now we read "The Waste Land" much less as being about Europe and much more as being about Eliot. We don't necessarily value Eliot the way we did, compared to Stevens, as being so much greater. Pound had a compelling idea of the epic—as a poem containing history, about whole communities. But it's not satisfying to read our poets as people who will tell us a lot about any specific history.

Personally, I certainly don't read them as prophets—when I read my favorite poets of that generation—including Robert Frost and William Carlos Williams—I read them thinking about my own historical circumstance and theirs and the time in between. I find I'm most interested in the sort of things we have been talking about. I'm interested in American syncretism, and how you might mix classical myth, street language and hi-low culture. How all this mix and swirling processes itself and how carefully it's attended to and how well it's sorted out. I suppose that's my hobby horse for this decade, so when I read the great Moderns I'm thinking about that. It's largely a matter of how the idiom is used, how language is used. Williams loves abstractions. In school, you are taught that he was very interested in wheelbarrows and chickens. When you read his work, you notice that he loves to begin a poem saying "It's the anarchy of poverty that delights me." He likes formality in language. And I think he likes it because of contrast, the way it gets mixed in. I'm interested in the way that Stevens makes you feel the Latin and the English in a title like "An Ordinary Evening in New Haven," he slows you down, you think about every one of those words and the mix of all of them.

c: The image in "Braveries" [I of Part Three: Its Everlasting Possibilities, in *An explanation of America*]: you talk about this child coming out into the horrors of war, retreating. Is that an image of America seeing its horrors that it has created? Trying to bury itself or retreating?

RP: I thought it was an incredibly rich image. It occurs at the beginning of a poem by Ben Jonson. The "Brave Infant of Saguntum" is born in the middle of a horrible battle and the myth was that the infant comes out, looks around, and then goes back in. Physical impossibility. The combination of the physical impossibility of going backwards and the fact it could be attractive to go backwards seem to me very appropriate to the history we were talking about before. Kevin says his town was destroyed by developers. My own town—the beautiful oceanfront—it's now all either slums or condos. The downtown is destroyed. Something in me feels as if I want it to go back, I want it to be 1954 again. But you can't, and what is more you shouldn't. Though you should remember it. You can't undo your own history, which is life, it is you.

It's the character in Ellison's *Invisible Man* who carries around a link from a slave chain. That link is now part of you and you can't go back into the womb. You must begin in the present, you suddenly can't go back, though in some imaginative way you go back because you carry that link around with you.

c: Is that what you have in mind when you talk about limits in "Braveries"?

RP: That's one of the main limits at stake in the poem. If the poem had anything as grandiose as a political theory it would be this moderate, limit-conscious, not particularly exalted idea. You might almost say a conservative idea, literally conservative in the sense of hanging onto anything that's good. Not being easily willing to say, "Well, let's raze the neighborhood and build a new better one." And the old neighborhood had very frequent cross-streets, and corners are nice—why didn't someone at least say, let's keep the corners. Which I believe is a newly-recognized principle in city planning. People are frightened, and there's more crime when blocks are very long than when they are short—with short blocks, it is more likely that people can see one another. It will be more comforting, and you can have more corner stores, more corner activity. And it's a basic principle related to mixing: people like to come together. If you say, "Let's build a great block where everything is in one place, we can air-condition the whole thing, and etc.," as experts have done, then eventually things can begin to fall apart for the lack of the reassurance of those lower buildings, and the frequent street corners.

c: Those images that were utopian: those ideas seemed the ultimate.

RP: And they were Modernist. They were Bauhaus ideas, that go back to the idealistic, maybe fatally idealistic European thinkers who intended to make things new. They were tired of history, they wanted to invent something better. The sort of bastard descendant of that impulse is some disastrous housing project in America.

c: In "Serpent Knowledge" of *An explanation of America* you say one generation is different from the next in what it needs and knows. What do you think is different in between our generation and what it needs and what it knows compared to your generation?

RP: That should appear in your poem rather than mine. I have one orientation that I try to describe—a rather optimistic, I hope all-but-sentimental orientation—toward American immigration. So that if I try to say what I think would be good for the country, I think we need lots of new immigrants. It's a hopeful thought, to me. I'm afraid I would slip into cliches, if I tried literally to imagine rather than just mention the fact that I'm not the end of the story. That you inherit this story.

I said a while ago that though I'm fairly well-educated as a poet goes, in my generation, a few generations earlier what I know of the past would make me not especially well-educated in a literary way, for a business man or doctor, if only because I can't much read Latin. There were too many cultural strands coming into me, perhaps, for me to absorb *Paradise Lost*, as deeply as the townspeople who used to attend Fourth of July speeches in this country. All through the 19th century what families did on the Fourth of July, more than fireworks, was go to the center of town, village green or whatever, and listen to patriotic speeches. And the most quoted author in those speeches was John Milton. So it was when this was a solidly protestant, solidly Anglophone country. Well, we are not there anymore, we are somewhere else, and that is where we begin. I might suppose—but I certainly can't assume—that I am more attached to the English poetry of the 16th and 17th centuries than my counterpart in your generation would likely be. But I'm not sure. It's as I say in the America poem, it makes you a little dizzy to try to imagine, actually imagine, fifty years after your likely lifetime, and probably you wouldn't want to have to look at that world. You might go mad. It might be that Walt Whitman would go mad if he saw us hurtling through the air wearing headphones that pipe music into our brains, and the rest of it. Even he with his appetite might not be able to bear looking at so much change and difference, and I assume you and I might feel the same confronted by whatever is going to come along 150 or 200 years from now.

The Swan
Catherine A. Salmons

> *This poem is in response to a Boston Globe article*
> *describing a woman who tried to remove her breast*
> *implants herself, without anaesthesia ...*

The pain she said was all
in that white moment she could see
its wings the flapping sound inside her
filled her ears the clear swan throat and beak
      control and not this animal
she wanted, and to be someone
to tear away the vestige she had bought
this time her hands
and with a sweep of one small knife
as she had seen it done in pictures
drain this heresy ripe sky
why don't you rain? but she had not imagined
pain could so consume
and for a second on the edge of sleep
the air around her fluttered
and the wind was full of muscle and she knew
a power was there but she
had not yet found a way to grasp
her body as her own without
      destroying
as the blackness beckoned nature
never half so cruel her fingers
dropped the blade because her hands
could not go on
she bowed in silence to the frenzied creature
always, always some invasion knowing she had pushed
to where the lake would overturn
if she dove pulling back the mountain of its skin.

The Tulips Dream
Cindy Schuster

The tulips dream green dreams.
Hooves of rain corrode their sleep

and the dreams freeze bicycle
chains stranded at the edge

of spring. The light is strange.
The boy with the bicycle joins

the girl poking lizards on the bridge.
He veils her in a yellowed gown

and photographs her dozing on the tracks
of an abandoned train. The nightmares

of the tulips are obscene; they dream
of me. The tulips stick their necks out,

and I am stuck in their sticky dreams
where boys de-wing exotic butterflies

and delicately pluck the tongues
from geckoes.

A Conical Hat
Kevin Bowen   [5 poems]

for Le Cao Dai and Vu Giang Huong

A moment of awkwardness
as he bends to lift the gift
to the table, not as if
he could hide it, the broad
.conical shape of the non la
stared up at us all through dinner,
the girl who served us
stepping around it
as if to draw attention all the more.

Across the table all night
I watch the stories
come alive in his eyes.
I can almost see the bulb burning.
A man pedals a bicycle underground.
In the shadows of the bunker
he makes power for lights and suction
in the operating room.
Lungs burn, he inhales
fine red bits of earth.
They are digging to expand the tunnels,
make more room for the wounded.

A figure in white
draws a suture through
last bits of skin,
prays his sight holds.
One day he walks
straight off the earth,
right into the brown, wrinkled
hide of an elephant,
carves meat for a starving platoon,
takes machete and scalpel,
makes cut after cut

until he's covered
in blood and muscle,
fighting for air.

1970. A break in the fighting.
A game of volleyball, interrupted.
A gunship sprays the pitch.
Two nurses killed, he drags
their bodies down, heavy
and smoking, into the tunnels.

Ten years his wife
slept in mountain caves,
after bombs, repaired roads,
made posters, paintings
to record each detail.

"Ham Rong Bridge, 1970," he shows me.
A woodcut made on rice paper.
Two women in conical hats
load rocks along a road.

In the background trucks
grow wings of camouflage,
rattle across the bridge
heading south.

His eyes burn as he looks
through the woodcut.
I thank him. I will need this hat,
the cool circle of its shade.

Temple at Quan Loi, 1969

Outside the gate
the old woman
walks up the hill
from the temple.
Her pace
deliberate as a procession.
From the corner of an eye
she stares.
She must wish our deaths.
Beneath the white silk band
breasts ache for a husband.
She passes in mourning,
counting each step.
Her prayers rain down like rockets.

Late Word in the City of Memory: West End

for F.X. J.

When the derricks
move in single file up the street
and the garbage burns blue
under your window,
know: soon it will be time to leave.

In the days that remain
memorize names,
house by house, block by block.
The Burke's here, the Fitzgerald's there.
The Capadalupo's and the Pasqua's.

And in the procession to the church
who played John the Baptist,
who spat in whose eye,
and what politician
swore at whose mother
simply for raising her fist
to the man who tore down her house,
and every house around it,
left a vacant lot of rubble
forty acres wide, only
the streetlights still standing.

Pier Launching

Teach me the songs
That make a man raise
His glass at dusk
Until a star dances in it.
             Charles Simic, "White"

1.Keeraunmore

Land where the bog runs out.
Beside Brendan's house,
the way the light bends,
the way the walls curve,
cut like knives the green stubs
of the hills. That beadwork
of stone, black rock face,
he climbed home at night.

Dusk. A farmer shoos his cows in for milking.

Inside the house, Colm packing for Boston.
Oona home from the city.
Everyone preparing for the wedding tomorrow.
Rooms filled with smells of smoke and drink and cooking,
clatter of knife and fork, hands cutting into soft flesh
of potato and bacon.
The scent of whiskey seeping through the darkness.
In a solemn corner, the television set, bearing
the weight of a dozen framed photographs.
The fire hissing at the grate.

Down the road: the old house.
The green world taking it back.

2. *Ionad na bféileacáin*: The Museum of Tropical Butterflies, Carraroe

Saturday, mid-afternoon. Everyone off to the wedding.
Tourists lean their hungry thirsty bodies
down the path to O'Flaherty's back garden,

garden of flowers rolling off to the sea,
garden of pints set out on white wrought-iron tables
a small rock promontory,
miniature thatched shed for lovers.

Across the road, the Museum of Tropical Butterflies,
just opened. Inside, 'The Hats of Ireland' on display.
The snack shop and concession, paintings of wildlife.

Open and the heat of Asia and Africa descends.

Along the walls from cages, rows of pupa hanging
down long wooden spools,
here and there, the blue and yellow
of a wing just breaking out.

They shed their skins many times before
entering this final phase of chrysalis.

Trails lace past the narrow beds of flowers.
Some so familiar. The flamingo,
its deep purple leaves; the Passiflora,
 Passion Flower; Goosefoot, Winter Jasmine,
 Rose of China, Buddhlia and Umbrella Trees.

Five days old and still alive,
the Great Atlas Moth of Colombia,
hangs from the ceiling,
wings gently waving.

Overhead, the Peacocks,
the iachis io; eyes on their wings
like the others to see. The Zephyrs,
White Tree Nymphs, The Great Purple Emperor,
the Indian Moon Moth, like the one
we found on a path once
on another island,
folded gently into a bag
—that night its mate beating wildly at the screen—

Left and right, we move
through the house of passing souls.

3. Pier Launching

Peadar, Joe Colman, the two Sean's and Andrew
down at the pier from the wedding.
Joe Colman jacking the boat slowly
off the braces; so carefully, one by one,

he settles the hard crooked pins
under the keel, checks the balance
fore and aft. All back work from here,
pushing, leaning, heaving to move her

the hundred feet down into the tide.
Five feet maybe six at a time
we push and pull, feel her slide
like a slow child forward under our arms.

With each small progress someone
picks the pins up from under the keel
as the boat lifts and sets them free;
then walks round to the bow, sets

them down again. Hands thick
with paint and tar, palms map
the lapped contours of the jagged
black hillsides. Soon, the Martello

tower across the bay swallowed
in a soft yellow light that falls
and takes the brown golden slopes
of Roseveel. At the new French factory,

a trawler cuts its engine, rolls in
on the tide. Fifty feet down the pier,
The Christine, smooth polished planks
cut from the lush rainforests. Beside her,

the blue black skin, red furled sail
of an old hooker. Each time the boat
moves forward now, someone cracks
a joke in Irish,—will she float?—one

last heave, and she slips down the runway,
settles into the water. A moment, as everyone
looks. Joe Colman leaps his sixty years
out across the blue white bow, wobbles

for just a second before he gets his bearings
—the boat lighter now, so long out of the sea.
But then he rights himself, steps down, lifts
up a floorboard to check for water, takes

long rusted spikes in his hands, sets them
in the sprockets; last, the long thin oars he loops
and slides through them, like rings on a lover's
fingers. So gentle the way the boat cuts

through the water. Peadar, the two Sean's and Andrew
gaze down from the pier, nod their approval, as first one,
then the other, he dips the oars into the blue seas,
slowly begins to move the boat out into the bay.

A thin silver sliver of moon rises above him.
The first evening star settles across the beam.
One last look before sons turn back to the road,
their cars, the short drive back to the wedding.

The Children's Tet

Crowds so thick on Tran Hung Dao
they must pass their bicycles over their heads
to get close to the student troupe
acting the old story.
The figure in black unmasked,
the dragon slain, fireworks
light the river,
traffic moves again.
Tonight the children rule.
In torch-lit packs
hunch-backed dragons
snake down streets,
chasing drums follow.
Who is head or tail
will change as they charge
into the world of their elders.
Parents watch, not yet sure to be afraid.
One boy's eyes search the crowd,
he beats his chest in confusion,
but has no need for worry,
tonight the city is filled with dragons.

Untitled
Michelle Joyner

When my boy Ronnie
died
I felt a
pain like a
knife plunging
into my vein
and then Nothing.

Goods
Martha Collins   [2 poems]

Looks, books, a night's rest, time,
news, food, who could ask for anything
more and yet we do and it's a good
thing too, we're told: goods are good.
And Good, if not for good, seems good
for nothing—merely law, it's what we do
not do, and deeds are woman's work: she
was made for doing good, he was made
for making. But we're all good for all
we're worth, and better to be one
whose earthly goods are small comforts
than to strip the least to get the most
of all. And best is one who's good without
a blessed end in sight. Who's good for life.

Ills

Knees creak belly back head aches age
adds loss less hair hearing color muscle,
messengers of All gone, That's it, ill-
fated natured timed to stop for good
or ill. But who's to blame for the meat-
less bones that ridge the children's skin,
the cardboard houses, concrete beds, the less
blest who rage against the least, the evil
one, good God, or just ourselves? Some
one falls, we think we're safe: we're
the crows on the graveyard fence. And does
it matter anyway? All the doctor did
was name the ill she couldn't cure. Death
is being ill all over. Ill all over and done.

Catechizing the Dandelion
Jennifer Rose

Catechizing the dandelion, I kneel in the grass
though I lack the Catholic tourist's portable sign
of faith, that quick cross.

I have no way to worship at this white cathedral
detaching its prisms.
I have not memorized its Latin epithets.

For one franc, lights illuminate its transepts ten minutes.
Still I cannot decipher the frescoes of dust.
Still the icons are hidden.

But all afternoon, the wind has been proselytizing,
converting the dandelion, bead by bead—
Brittle reliquary! Dimmed nimbus!

Its tonsured head
now bows like mine, bent to appraise
the mysteries of faith. . . .
I think of the ruined church
that sits in the fields near Cuise-la-Motte.
Its bricks are scattered like the trepanned skull

of an anchorite left to rot.
But faith germinates in the burst pod of its skeleton
and tapers of yellow dandelions flicker near the altar.

Uncles
Sam Cornish

for Herbert and Eddie

lord take away
the weather in his bones so
all of them teeth can make a smile
he is a Baptist and can almost
break your heart
in the living room at the kitchen table
life is hard and the living
is where he finds it
uncle has a spittoon and ash tray
has arms where I can hide and smile and cry
smokes a fine big cigar almost a father
(and to some he is) uncles brothers of mothers
and fathers and friend of mine uncles black
and brown (some are yeller) married to sisters
men of the family strong as a big coal truck
at ballgames and barber
shops work in factories, grocery stores and liquor
stores takes the elevator up faster
than young feet on the stair
uncle was a sharecropper from Alabama Mississippi
Virginia Rising Sun Maryland has paychecks and
Superman comic books comes equipped
with walks (and hugs) thick pork chops from the butcher
shop and pints of Pikesville Whiskey for himself
and Kosher wine sweet for Grandmother
because it's Jewish is good
dark and thick Shapiro concord grape
Uncle carries a pistol
and his friends call him Jim
say he sings like the Inkspots
with their ringed fingers and deep
southern voices not wanting
to set the world on fire
he just makes a woman's heart

smoke (a little) and cuss
the winter and the lonely life
my uncle with a strap put the fear
of God into my behind and nasty mouth
because I talked back to my mother
his sister his friend
he teaches first grade
in summer softball
now rides the rails serving
sandwiches and coffee
and shines shoes so black
they shine and say sugar daddy
cause he pays
the rent brings soul food on Sunday
and a dime for me
before dinner bowing his head to lead
the table in thanks
in Jesus Name Amen
uncles smell of smoke
and soap and work dancing and laughing
away trouble uncles
voices (is a drum) like thunder
laughter like lightly falling rain
thick fingers
and hands like
hunks of meat they are
family
when the father is dead
or walked away
all the men we want our fathers to be
all the men (I hope) we are

A Conversation with Rosanna Warren

c: What do you think it will mean to be an American in the twenty-first century, and how may that be manifest in literature?

RW: I think it will probably have to do with being a citizen of a declining empire presiding over a world that looks as if it's going to be increasingly slaughterous and insane. I think our country will be like a giant that's half asleep; tossing and turning and crushing many small creatures as he tosses and turns, even unwittingly.

We are the remaining superpower. However, our super powers are not in very good shape. We saw the crumbling of the British empire one hundred years ago; I think that we will soon find ourselves in the same position. We will have the discomfort and conceptual readjustments of being members of a crumbling empire.

c: In response to this "crumbling" that you speak of, you have said that the art of translation "guarantees our shared survival." How will it, as you also say, "engender our future"?

RW: I think it is hard to predict because art is always inventing a future that we cannot yet imagine. Thank goodness, because if we could imagine it, we would be doomed to it. I'm glad to say that's our hope. We don't know what windows of the human imagination will open, what cracks it will find.

Translation is crucial in a world where almost no one is listening to anybody else. Even people who speak the same nominal language are not listening to each other. As a postscript for this I want to put in a plug for an organization that is called Cultural Survival. Their work is an extension of the kind of work that we will want to be doing to remain humane in the next century, that is to understand in their terms cultures that are foreign to us. To fight against this sinister, global, multi-corporate image of successful adaptation that is being forced on the whole world. On the whole, human history is at best tragedy and at worst mindless horror.

Although there have been few pockets of time when more enlightened understandings have occurred, I guess I have to hope that those small events will continue to occur and that violence, both personal and institutional, will be somewhat restrained by conscience.

It is possible that the arts can contribute quite practically and materially to small processes of healing. I've seen this in the prisons where I have participated in poetry readings. That has given me a model to believe that an esoteric art like poetry can work quite directly in a social way to help people find a voice and rethink their lives.

c: How can translation help us look at ourselves?

RW: When you look at any time or place of cultural vitality you see a lot of translation going on. At such a time there is just spontaneous combustion going on. People become excited about each other's work.

The artistic contacts are much more private and idiosyncratic, resistant to corporate structures. One can't sentimentalize the relations between the material base of a society and the type of art it can afford. Look at the Italian Renaissance, there we saw double entry book keeping and new technologies for spinning and weaving. Banking was also invented then, but then there were all those Madonnas!

America is linguistically an odd country. Some citizens are now bilingual by the accidents of history and in some sense, birth. By and large however, I think American education produces fairly mono-lingual people. It is a rarity to have a young person who knows four different languages. You can't count on Americans to be able to read Chinese, Japanese, Hungarian, German, French, and Romanian. I wish that everyone in the state department would spend some time reading novels, plays, poems, and watching the movies of a culture before they went there.

At very deep cultural levels, if you don't have some understanding of the culture you are trying to deal with, you are going to make some terrible mistakes. Art could have a quite practical effect there, helping one discover common humanity.

c: Much of the translation that is done in America is by writers who have never been part of the culture that they are translating. This is the same America where people are beginning to hear statements like "you can't speak to that, you don't know my experience." That experience could be any number of things; gender, race, class, or any form of difference that one can think of on the planet.

RW: I don't want to make a dogmatic statement, almost anything is possible. It is clear that we have examples of very talented literary people who have a kind of intuition about a foreign culture, without knowledge of the language at all, like Ezra Pound. You do have to be a fairly remarkable mind to be able to intuit.

Speaking from my own experience of translating a play from the ancient Greek of Euripides, I know some Greek and I have read and studied it over the years, but I still wouldn't consider that I have the intuitive feel for it that I have for French or Italian, and to some extent Latin poetry. This project, in which I collaborated with my husband, the classical scholar Stephen Scully, was torture for me because all of my synapses were not activated immediately by the Greek, it was all mediated. It took me years to try to recreate an imaginative wholeness of the play. I can't imagine how one would sit down and translate a poem from a language that you just don't know. Some of the results I've seen are quite satisfying, but I know I couldn't work that way.

c: One of the essays in *The Art of Translation*, that you edited, says that some people do translation in cases where the poet from the "other" culture portrays the mime of a work, and the poet here tries to best represent the poem in the host language.

RW: I know this is done commonly. I don't think that William Merwin knows Russian; I think his translations of Mandelstam were collaborative. I know Joseph Brodsky's early poems were translated by English and Americans who clearly had tremendous help from Russian scholars. I find Merwin's translations very moving, but I say this without knowing the Russian, so my opinion isn't worth very much.

I consider myself a philologist in the old sense, a word lover. I don't really know how you can say you know a poem unless you can recite it in its original language and understand every tiny inflection of grammar. The notion of having the poem mediated through an "ambassador" troubles me personally.

c: You said that on the whole Americans are monolingual, because of this would you say that our understanding of the body of world literature is not complete?

RW: To speak of America as one whole subject is difficult. America is probably too diverse of a country to have a "we" that holds up in any kind of argument. Many reading Americans have a quite passionate connection with other literatures. The Spanish surrealists were everywhere! Or the influence of Japanese poetry on many North American writers, especially in California but emanating out from there. I don't think we are that parochial. Again, we can see passionate connections that were made. One of the appealing things about the United States is that we are so heterogenic and look out in so many directions. Elizabeth Bishop was reading Baudelaire, Horace and Virgil! The people with real curiosity will always look for what they can't find at home.

c: What is one curious of in the literature?

RW: That depends on the vitamin deficiency that the receiving country needs to take care of. Italy under fascism is an interesting case. Fascism closed Italy down mentally and spiritually. The activity of the great Italian poet Cesare Pavese was crucial to maintain life. He went to American literature. Here he found what he imagined to be direct contact with reality, an anti-rhetorical freedom, a sort of existential relation both to language and lived experience. He translated Melville; I read *Moby-Dick* in his Italian. He helped recreate Italian literature by doing that. He gave Italian novelists hope about what it was possible to write. There are times when translation is a very powerful act of resistance and transmission of a set of possibilities.

c: You were first a painter and then a poet, what brought about this change?

RW: That question strikes very deeply for me. Leaving painting causes me the same pain as the break-up of a great love affair, the love of one's life, in a sense. It wasn't consecutive though, it wasn't that I painted or wrote; all of my life, from my early childhood, I was painting *and* writing. In my early twenties I just slowly came to the rather tortured recognition that my painting wasn't developing. I wasn't pushing the art enough. I wasn't putting a lot of myself into it. Why wasn't I, I don't know. I guess writing had taken more of the upper hand, and my energy. But I had put many years into painting, and thinking of the world in visual terms. I feel very grateful for it, even though I hardly paint at all now, although I draw a little bit, just to keep my eye working. I never forget that words are already a translation of a primal experience that is beyond the bounds of my consciousness, and it is another area of visual cognition. I am first pre-conscious, or on the road to consciousness, to formal consciousness structured by language. To me that's the source of life. That is the source of my life, a preverbal reality. That is why as an undergraduate I reacted with such hostility to what was then becoming the very fashionable post-structuralist literary theory. It was the heyday of deconstruction and its post posts and these were theories giving a primacy to logos, to language as structuring all reality, which—even though I was only 18 or 19 years old—I just couldn't accept. My experience as a painter and as a person inside of a physical body who has many experiences that are non-verbal kept me from deconstruction.

c: In your poem "Echo" you write "—as light/ pools gold in olive oil left on the plates/ and Midas-like touches the pale green globes/ of grapes and gleaming ellipse/ at the rim of the glass." Is this an example of combining a visual eye with your language?

RW: I'm probably not the best person to analyze my poetry. Pre-metaphorically I feel poetry as clusters of cadences, certain vowels and consonants intertwining. This has to do with preconscious reality, preconscious cognition. It's what I find is lacking in so many theorists of literature. They have divorced themselves from that primal corporeality, the dance sense, the song sense. If that isn't carried into the written language, you have lost the soul of it. Then there is the great phenomenon of the human mind which creates complicated symbol systems, abstruse and allusive structures, and abstract thought. All of that crystallizes from those preverbal urgencies. I don't mean to denigrate them. They are there and they should be there and I love their complexity, but I yearn for an art and a criticism of art that reflects that kind of fullness of both cognition and representation.

c: Could you speak of this in the context of your new book on Max Jacob?

RW: This book on Max Jacob is a biography which has turned into a long pilgrimage for me. I didn't realize how long it would be when I started. I first thought "oh, this will just take a few years. I will get some dates, slap them down, then say 'so and so met so and so at a cafe.'" It hasn't turned out to be that way at all. I am meshed in this person's life now. Max Jacob knew practically everybody in twentieth century France. More deeply than that, his being as an artist is so complicated. It has taken me years to live into his life. I couldn't be so arrogant as I was in the beginning, thinking that I understood him. I won't claim ever to have understood him. I do hope that I will have followed the grain more closely by the time this book ever gets finished.

c: When he was at the monastery at the end of his life, in a letter to a young poet, Jacob was trying to sum up his art to foster something in the young poet. In the letter Jacob said two things, he said that you have to find your pearl. Strip the rhetoric, and find out what your humanness is all about. Secondly, Jacob said that you have to be striving to find out what real beauty is. He ends by saying that suffering and pain have to be your central motivation and an inspiration for this art.

RW: I don't know if Max Jacob read Keats' letters, but Keats said something similar after having nursed his brother through the tuberculosis that later killed the brother. Then writing to the living brother in America, he wrote the famous letter where he said "the world is a valley of soul making, it takes pain to school and intelligence to make it a soul." I think that Max Jacob was putting his perception of that to this young man. When you are young you don't think that pain has anything to do with life, or art. For some it doesn't. Clearly for Matisse, an artist of joy and sensuality, it was excluded from what the canvass recognized. Max Jacob, it must be remembered, was a Christian Jew, a deeply mystical person.

He believed that the mystery of sacrifice is at the heart of reality, or art. He was setting down his deepest convictions. The young man didn't prove to be much of a poet by the way. Many other French writers who (so to speak) "went to school" with him, did carry his lessons on for the rest of their life. Michel Leiris, the great post-surrealist writer, took tremendously from Max Jacob. He said in one of his memoirs that if he thought that sleeping with Max Jacob would grant him some of Max Jacob's wisdom and talent, that he would have done it!

c: When did Jacob and Picasso meet?

RW: Jacob saw Picasso's first exhibit in Paris when Picasso was nineteen in 1901. He was bowled over by it, and left Picasso a note in the gallery. They got together a few days later. They could hardly speak, not knowing each other's languages. They spent the whole evening together communicating by sign language and bits of language. At the end of this Max Jacob, who at the time was extremely poor, living sometimes as a secretary, sometimes as a janitor, gave Picasso a valuable etching and they became spiritual compatriots.

They lived together two years later when Picasso had come back to Paris, very poor. He was living in a horrible downtown hotel on the left bank. Max Jacob was living as a tutor to some rich family, and had a room on the right bank. He invited Pablo to share the room. Pablo was so desperate and poor that he did. They had a single bed that they shared sequentially, Picasso painted at night and Jacob slept and then they would switch. This only lasted for two months.

c: When does Apollinaire enter the picture?

RW: Jacob and Picasso met in 1901, Apollinaire doesn't come in until 1904. He was living in Germany, also working as a tutor, and writing the "Rhenanes," rhymed, symbolist poetry. Apollinaire's contact with Max Jacob helped Apollinaire get rid of some of his symbolist tricks. Then a fervent community formed around Picasso's studio, the Bateau-Lavoir. Juan Gris, Braque, André Salmon, were all there at different times.

c: When each artist would finish a day they would peek into the other's studio to see what the other was up to.

RW: Yes, there was tremendous competition, tremendous malice, tremendous energy, tremendous fraternity. The book is filled with this type of gossip. I am trying to figure out how to weave this with poetry criticism and with mystical speculation—not an easy formula!

c: You have a new book of poems, *Stained Glass*. Not having seen it we can't really ask about or critique it. Could you tell us a little bit about it?

RW: Sure, the book is poems that have accumulated over nine years. It is an intensely elegiac book, just because of life's circumstances. Its hard for me to talk about my own poems. I meant the book to be tough and sad and people who read it said it is tough and sad. I hope the next one will be cheerier.

c: You recently read a poem where one is overlooking the ocean and watches someone on a cliff bow down, looking like a "question mark." Is that poem in *Stained Glass*?

RW: Yes, that poem is "Tide Pickers," which is a poem from Brittany, I spent a summer there doing research on Max Jacob. I would see the people overlooking the ocean, picking out the periwinkles or whatever else they might find. I write slowly and somewhat tortuously. For me writing is a set of elaborate resistances. First is the resistance of the material itself, what I'm trying to discover to be said through me. Then I try to find a set of formal resistances that will make it come out as tautly as possible. That could be a formal stanza structure, or a certain meter or rhyme scheme; discovering the right resistance to test my strength.

c: Are their more poems of form in *Stained Glass* than in *Each Leaf Shines Separate*?

RW: There is quite a range of poems in *Stained Glass*. Some of them are sonnets, and a number of them are in rhyming quatrains. I translated a poem of Max Jacob's in rhyming couplets; that was fun. I don't really have an instinct for rhyming couplets on my own. There are also poems that are quite shattering and shattered in their form. Formally I am eclectic.

In *Each Leaf Shines Separate* you see a lot of Keats or Hart Crane, and even Catullus and Wallace Stevens. There I often have rhymes within the lines of the poem. In the new book Milton has been a very strong presence. I guess I was taking a sterner look at life. Another presence in this book that is not in the earlier book is Greek poetry. I have been studying Greek more vigorously now. Whereas the earlier book had a translation of Catullus' translation of one of Sappho's poems, this book has my translation of the Greek poet Alcman. The concluding poem is a meditation of book 24 of the *Iliad*.

When I was 15, 16 years old, Latin poetry was, for me, poetry. I had memorized Catullus and Virgil. After that it was French poetry; Baudelaire, Verlaine. I didn't begin to bring English and American poetry into my psyche until a few years later. I am now struggling with Greek. For me it is a very hard language. One of my rewards for finishing the Max Jacob book will be to study Greek poetry in a way I really want to do it. I want to be intimate with those poems.

c: What is your methodology for a project like that?

RW: Very simple pedagogic methodology. Greek is so hard I find that I need a teacher. There have been periods in my life when I try to read ten lines of Greek each day. I read a lot of book 24 of the *Iliad* that way. I just kept plugging away with my dictionary and going to my scholarly husband with questions. Donald Carne-Ross has been a great mentor for me of Greek poetry; the Alkman that I have understood is really thanks to Donald. He holds the Aurelio chair in the classics department (at Boston University). He is a superb Greek scholar, and is very generous with his time. When anyone wants to go read Pindar, or Sophocles, or Aesychlus, or Sappho, he is so delighted that someone would like to do that, he greets you with open arms.

In a way this all goes back to what we were talking about before; translations, and one's world view. These are all very personal motivations. I think the one thing that is general is that it takes a tremendous amount of work to identify your own personal civilization. Everyone has a compass, and you have to follow true north. If you haven't done it with labor and love you will not really get it.

Immigrants
Diana Der-Hovanessian   [2 poems]

Many endangered Mexican birds enter
the U.S. illegally   news item

"No, they do not fly at night
over the border," you inform me,
"or slither through the dark
water of the Rio Grande.
They come in burlap bags smuggled
by dealers of exotic fauna."

But I prefer my version of
the news: colorful parrots
flying back and forth
over borders shouting "Ola."

Widow

In an age of arranged marriages
they chose each other. And chose badly.
She first saw him at a picnic.
He was the soldier-hero-speaker.
She was the local beauty, Worcester born,
light haired, soft voice.
She had put down her kodak. And saw him
pick it up. Or at least she thought
it was hers. But it turned out to be
his own. "Do you want me to show you
how to use it?" she asked trying to
get back her camera. He was amused
as they settled whose was whose.
Later, his cousin who was in love
with her sent him to propose.
But luckily for me, their child,
they married each other instead.
From two distant worlds and mismatched
she ended by hating him until he died.
Then she remembered only the good days,
how handsome he was. How everyone
admired him. And the beginning:
"I was so bold. Like Priscilla Alden
I said. Speak for yourself, John."

Alma
Joseph DeRoche   [3 poems]

Dressed in red, my aunt looks through her sliding door.
Outside the balcony, the world glares green,
Floridian. The sun blares down a howl of yellow ore.
She looks unmoved upon the seething ferment of the scene.
The rot and riot which means growth will come unseen.
If she's not here to see it, what matter that growth goes
Or comes? The present is the presence that she knows.

In granite Maine, a gray, less complex shore,
She married, conceived her children. Into that mean,
Cold evergreen, she bore necessities she hungered for.
The winter Atlantic kept her conscience lean.
The snow, the ice, made any cutting edge of love more keen,
More clear. Then cancer cam. Inside that flow,
Her cells divide: the pain her watch keeps turning to.

Meanwhile Northeast turns August to the core.
Up North the summer's lust does not admit decline,
Diminishment, or to smooth flesh gone wounded raw.
What means a place where she's no longer fleshly seen?
High in the tree, the leaf first touched by frost can screen
Away all summers: one alarmist blood-red leaf can glow
The glory of the fall to come, the grip and rip of undertow.

The Mandarin's Recitation

What we are to learn are
Details: the sun rises at 6:34,
Sets at 4:23, High Tide, 8:35 a.m.,
Low, 2:31 a.m. There's only one
of the one but two of the others.
Be sure you know this. The heart's
But a beating muscle, enthusiasm
A vapor I cannot construct again.
When the transport is over what you
Need is a ticket, diploma, degree
In engineering. The concrete can be
Absolutely manipulated, like shame or
Guilt of failure. Only the almanac
Has a tight memory. Like the heart.
No need the half moon rising on
Your thumbnail. No need 29 1/2 days
Menstruation and the tide pulling
And pushing between zero and this
Place. No need at all. The stocks
Rise and fall: 8/52, 2/31, 29/5,
Numbers are all, the language of
Much of it, of God the pundits say,
The E=MC, too, and what of that when
Language or goodness or love terminally
Has nothing to do but deconstruct
What mother and father anciently
Said quite clearly was: No
Thing at all. Now. Let's be
Quite clear. Clinical. What's done
Is done. I give you the vein.
Construct. Put blood in it.

The Juke Box

The man who lives
in the juke box
juggles his past.

At night he replays
the songs he's collected
in differing order.

Each night,
a new opera.
Over and over,
he swims in surprise.
Over and over,
the stuff
that suffocates him
sings a fresh story.

The combinations,
at last, drive him to tears.
Nothing new here.
Whatever changes
but the order of things?
And he knows it.

He knows the heart looks.
He knows the heart locks.
He presses a button.
'Is that all there is?'
rolls out the juke box.
Under the voice of a song
he well knows
and a singer,
slowly he swings out a note,
pulls out a phrase
of his own.

He lays sound like carpets,
like bedding, like pillows,
adding a polish
that softens the bare ground
he sleeps on
and varnishes stone.

These songs I picked,
he seems to be crooning.
These songs are mine now.

All that's unchanging
he changes by joining.
All that he'll change
changes only by tone,
high note or low.

Silver blue lyrics,
note by note climbing,
tenor and torch song,
he chases the pain.

Just before sleeping,
louder, insistent,
his voice fills the room
with the stretch of his lyrics,
the reach of his range.

Out of the juke box
of songs he's collected
comes the clutch
of the music,
which makes up
to add up to all
that is static
and cannot be broke up,
the calculate
frozen sum of his name.

The Good Life
Sue Standing

seems to include lots of fake animals
scattered around the yard.

Somewhere (I know where) American families
are still dining in their cars:

a carhop on rollerskates brings the food
and attaches it to a tray on the window.

The news is frivolous today—
some guy who wants his antlers back,

and a religious freedom case:
"God and the Internal Revenue Service

have nothing in common with each other
and don't really understand each other."

The good life breezes by the grafted tree
without looking back, and the suburbanites

put up their Malthus wallpaper, a soothing
pattern of peas and bunnies multiplying.

Some people would be perfectly happy
in a universe where things had no names.

The good life lives in the past
because there's no future there.

At the Fruit Stand
Doug Holder

"Flip her the bird," he told the young man,
with the green assertion of a cigar,
clenched between his stained teeth.

The boy held the melon
like he was cupping a breast,
his hands in fluid movement,
through the wet jungle of grapes,
his fingers emerging glistening,
from the exploration.

"She thinks she's a class act."
He clenched harder on the cigar,
halting the smoke's circulation,
a limp appendage,
hanging from his brown mouth…
"Dump her."

The boy packed the bananas,
letting his hands,
slide down the yellow, unblemished skin,
wanting to peel it,
to have its fruit in his mouth.
"I'll give her another call."

As Timber in a Shallow Rain
J. Wright-Ryan

From farthest things commingle
Hunger, hatred, the unbearable resilience
Of being. Breaking like pheasants
By beaters flushed, a ricochet, a stray
Cock full of vengance or self;
A long slow bullet and the will to pull it,
Would my desire be any different?
The last to be consumed, you, who
No man would touch, I approach open.
Played as a crowd who I had left,
Not having left me, tears shy to leave
Those eyes. Once lit, what weight ashes burnt
In dry cisterns? An ambiguous answer
From an oracle sought of our own making
From a borrowed past reeking of must.

Dreams of Hands and Metamorphoses
Judit Flora

On sleepless nights I have been dreaming
that you tenderly stroke my hair.
Your gentle hands heal me.

I kiss the sweet ravines between your finger-peaks,
caress the pink palm's hillocks and lines, with my lips:
on sleepless nights I have been dreaming.

Tracking the scars (the trademark of your scalpel—my souvenir)
on my chest with my fingertips, I caress the path of
your gentle hands that heal me.

Lying in bed, I imagine that I enter your skin
and live in you—glorious existence—.
On sleepless nights I have been dreaming:
I see with your eyes and hear with your ears,
and we dream the same dreams.
(Your gentle hands heal me.)

Your thoughts would be mine and my laughter your thrill.
(But then, how could you stroke my hair?)
On sleepless nights, I have been dreaming
that your gentle hands heal me.

Staple
Wayne Sullins   [6 poems]

       Some people waited in line for as long as a week, only
to buy a gram or two because they had so little money. One
woman, with three children already, gave birth to a fourth,
a girl, just yards from the door of the shop. She was lucky,
she was able to buy enough for the whole family. And the
look on their faces—rapturous!
       Instances of those leaving the shop being attacked by
those less fortunate increased as time went on. Yet from
far and wide the hoards continued to storm the shop which had
become the talk of the continent, the shop whose sign read:
Undying devotion, by the pound.
       The supply came and went.
       The newspeople came and went.
       No one knows what became of the shopkeeper.

I did not mean to swallow
So many stars

I had only meant to sample
Their brilliance
When the expansion of light
Threatened
To dissuade my curiosity
Once

She spreads
Her lips
And says
It's all yours

Take care
She does not
Swallow you

No light
To read by
Down there

Ordered to wait until nightfall, he works by lamplight. His wife is embarrassed, watching him clean his weapon; he is so attentive to each and every part of the rifle.

His pleasure with her he takes in the full light of day, when he needn't worry about coming under fire. But it's over in a flash and she wishes she were made of metal—cold and useful.

Uniform

A stamen gets carried away,
And the world is overgrown
With one flower.

Trying Times

Word came that her head was still in the tree, and that
moss was growing from where her eyes had been.

We packed some things and went to see.

On the morning of the fourth day on the road we sighted
the tree, still far enough away that it didn't give much of
an impression. Some of us even talked of turning back be-
cause it looked fake—pressed flat against the sky.

But the tree was real and the moss hung all the way to
the ground. Each of us went and touched it. Each of us
went away crying.

The Couple
Michael B. Zack

He is by her bedside,
a candle, near,
on this side of death,

smoothing wrinkled bed sheet,
into an unfurrowed brow,
passing her the paper in the way

he had always gathered things
to watch her hold them.
Restless after so many days

in the ache of it,
numb from so much vigilance.
He frets around the hospital room

putting scrap into trash,
like a gardener dead-heading
to strengthen his plant.

As she speaks he knows,
at the end of so many years,
that her words are his,

and melt like ice into forlorn drops
which he pours half-full into
a water cup she might need later

in a night he stays awake,
sharing her illness
as best he can.

William Corbett

25 August '94

Dear Marni:

      Seventeen, Mary on my arm,
dinner and "West Side Story."
We were eight or ten,
boys and our dates, and spent
down to our last dimes
pissing off the white aproned
Cavanaugh's waiter who flung
the silver change at my back.
That night the Jets let
us down. "Krup you!" they
sang as they did just now
on the radio celebrating Leonard
Bernstein's birthday and, Marni,
your birthday too.
      I'm driving home over the back
road through Calais where we saw
the bear and around Greenwood
Lake with its tiny island where
sits a tinier cabin, thinking of you.
The ferns are rusty: we've had
some fall days but today, muggy,
mare's tails overhead, it's summer
and the city is far away.
I can't remember where you were
last here at this time of year
but you are everywhere today.
      "Somewhere a place" New York?
You loved it as a child. I see you
stride across 2nd Avenue in your
dungaree skirt. And then NYU
and now? Well, why not?
If it doesn't work out in New York
is still the other Vermont
as much there there as there is here.

When I came up to court
your mother, I left a New York
downpour and drove all night
through the small towns where,
the farther north I got, only
a few lights, kitchen lights
or the one above the gas station,
still burned. The radio faced
away: it was late August.
I smoked then, great mouthfuls
of smoke and rushing pine drenched
air from the open window to keep
me awake. You know I made it
but of that a.m. arrival
I remember nothing, only and now
the fine anticipation all the way.

Eddie and Juliet
Victor Howes

She vows, "I'll never speak to him again."
He only wanted one thing, as Mama
warned her, but, breathless, she breathes, "When?"
when he suggests they meet. She is so far
gone in the tragic love that turns to grief
now that he's dropped her. Meeting, now, he says
"So long. Let's keep it brief.
I'm heading off to college in six days."
He wants them to be friends, old friends. Just that.
He wants his frat pin back, and all those notes
he passed to her in math. "You are a rat,"
she moans thru tears, hating him with a hate
that will not die. Her turn to play her ace:
she says, "I'm pregnant," just to watch his face.

Immigrant Home Movie, 1963
Mariette Lippo

Without sound
there is no thunder to send her
crouching on the cellar step, no broken English,
no curse or prayer
in Italian, no husband calling her crazy
or worse, trying to
pinpoint the storm's distance
by counting seconds
between lightning and thunder,
while her son pans through the house
with his instruction book, tripod
and new 8mm Bell and Howell,
checking the light as he shoots her from behind,
shadowy, slightly out of focus,
the zipper of her black dress glinting, the apron
knotted at her neck, his presence
uncalled-for as she turns, stunned,
into the close-up, her face overexposed,
her lips voicelessly moving.

Ed Bullins Alive! [1996]

c: What is it about the theater that inspired you to be a playwright?

EB: The theater is where the action is for me. Theater works for me. I have written fiction, and I tried journalism and poetry. But, when I wrote my first play, I said that's it! Drama is what I am best at; it is a lean and intense form, but not as lean or intense as poetry. A play tells a story in a way that makes sense to me. I began to write for an audience and not a reader when I discovered that I could write plays, and I began to hear voices, not my own voice. This is how drama became my medium.

c: How is reading a play different from actually seeing a play?

EB: Reading a play is quite different than seeing a play, yet not that different at all. Reading a play is done by reading in a chair. Allow me to tell you a story about an experience I had early in my playwriting career. I was new to the theater in 1965 when my first play was produced at the Firehouse Repertory Theater in San Francisco. I had written several plays, and I had managed to interest some people in three of them. I was working with Robert Hartman, who was directing the plays. I was invited to the theater for one of the early auditions. I had been writing for five years and had written a couple of novels, which I threw away because they were trash. I walked into the theater, and it was like walking into a dark hallway. Yet, it happened to be a sunny summer day in California. I heard these voices as I was walking into the theater. These voices were speaking my words, and I almost fainted. The impact of hearing those voices was like hearing the disembodied voices of ghosts. After having my hands get all sweaty, my getting dizzy, and having a queasy stomach, I realized that it was not the excitement of my work being produced, but thinking—and even subconsciously—that this was spooky. Ghosts were speaking. What I realized then was that I had been listening to my own voice all this time as I had been writing for those previous four-to-five years. I had not been listening to characters, other presences, other people, and the other things that make up the story. Consequently it all clicked for me: this was a new type of writing, this was not completely me. I had to write for characters that were very different. This was a revelation!

c: Another interesting aspect of reading a play is that one can imagine what it looks like on a stage, and this envisioning can really open up one's imagination. With your plays it appears that one of the most important aspects is the affect the play has on the attending audience. Would you talk about this aspect of being in attendance at the theater rather than reading your plays at home?

EB: One of the best moments for me in the theater is when the play is running, and it is a successful run. Two or three weeks into the run, I can go into the theater after the curtain has gone up and listen to the audience while the play is being performed. The audience might laugh, it might be quiet, and it might hang on every word. This makes me realize again and again that that is why I am a playwright. Being in the audience, getting caught up in the excitement of it, the curtain coming down, the audience filing out, their talking about the play—even arguing about different points of view—and I can walk among them. They do not recognize me. I dig that!

c: Let's talk about how audiences react to particular plays. One of the more striking plays that you have written audience participation into is *It Bees That Way*. How did the audience react to that play?

EB: I do not think I saw a production of that. It was staged in London. It might be one of the few of my plays that I have never seen staged. It was more of a happening. Think of Richard Schechner, the head of The Drama Review; I think his theater group was called the Garage Theater Group. He would fill an empty room with found objects—tires or something—put people in the room and then throw some action into the room. This would cause people to act very strangely. They would come out of it saying, "Woooo, that was way out!" That is what *It Bees That Way* was; it put people into a semi-dark room with a simulated Harlem street corner and several Harlem underclass types—drunkards and junkies, today they would be crack addicts. The play mixed all these variables together improvisationally with a certain scenario that the actors had in mind, and their aim was to agitate the audience. Yes, this involves audience participation—short of lawsuits.

c: What about *A Short Play for a Small Theater*?

EB: What play was that?

c: It is the play where three-quarters of the audience has to be black, a quiet mood is created, incense is burning, and a man is sitting down painting his face. He then pulls out a gun and shoots at all the white folks in the audience until they are all dead.

EB: That was in my agit-prop phase. Those were the types of plays I was doing during the Black Power/Black Arts agenda. They were blanks, not real bullets! My play, *The American Flag Ritual,* is still playing. It was performed in New York City this past fall. In the play, a man comes out and urinates on the American flag, wipes his feet, and that is the play. I never thought it would be done again. The director, John Silber, made a point of doing it in a way that had something to do with race relations. That was interesting, but I didn't see it. I asked him, "why would you do it now?" When I wrote it, I was angry at the United States' involvement in Vietnam. I was angry that my friends had to go to Canada, at the race problem here, and other things like civil rights, etc. I asked him what purpose would it have now? He convinced me that he would do it tastefully, if there is such a thing. It is in-your-face theater.

c: What were Silber's reasons for doing the play today, in 1996?

EB: He wanted to show alternate theater that had been done in the 50s and 60s and make a statement about something going on today. I am not quite sure what the statement was he was trying to make, but I know that I will never get a National Endowment for the Arts grant for it to be performed.

c: Do you think that a playwright has a responsibility, and what is the role of the playwright today?

EB: Whatever role the playwright decides to take on. There is a wide spectrum to choose from—from the arts-for-arts-sake to a very committed advocacy theater. I could be very political now if I wished, but I do not know if I would achieve the same impact the theater had in the 60s. Alternate theater, Off Broadway Theater, Theater of the Absurd, Post-Absurdist Theater, Black Theater had immediacy. It was treated seriously; more seriously than today. But these are wonderful political times to do political plays. Look at the Republican circus, economics, society—but if you want to do political plays, my advice is to do it to the maximum. Do not do it half-way. Some of my most effective plays have been very simple story plays that have more universality and more far reaching results, like the play I am doing tomorrow, *A Son Come Home*. My most successful plays to date are little four-character plays. Some of the plays that I have spent years on with twelve to fifteen characters do not do as well as that little play, *A Son Come Home*, that I wrote instead of having taken a nap. I wrote it in about two or three hours on a summer afternoon.

c: In your novel, *The Reluctant Rapist*, which some say is autobiographical, rape is a central theme in the book and one which you use throughout your work. Can you talk about this?

EB: I like to consider *The Reluctant Rapist* more of a put-on than anything else. It is a parody. Eldridge Cleaver used to say that sex was a political weapon. I also consider it a parody of the *On the Road* type of novel. Some of it is parody, but everyone took it dead serious.

c: You have spoken on how action is one of the ways in which you convey your messages through your work. Is the act of rape a central metaphor in all of your work?

EB: When Gloria Steinam reviewed *The Reluctant Rapist*, she said in the review that after the book I could only write about cannibalism. I know that there is a repugnance toward the subject of rape. To answer candidly, we humans love spectacle. In *Othello* one waits through the entire play to see him, Othello, strangle Desdemona. The drama, the spectacle of this act speaks so voluminously. It is terrifying, horrible, and this is part of it. The other part of it has to do with power relationships—S&M. Murder is secondary to a good rape scene. Just the suggestion of rape: the screams, the sounds, the terror of it are going to get someone's attention. I know this sounds terrible, but this is what you take on with this territory. I am not advocating rape.

c: What is it that is imbued in the rape scene in your new play *Snickers?*" How does it differ from what is manifest in rapes in *The Reluctant Rapist*, *The Taking of Miss Janie*, *The Duplex*?

EB: The obvious past rape of "Ghost" by "Animal" is a male rape. Of course, it is a rape but a male same-sex rape in a confined space. It has some additional implications being a male rape—I believe—than the male-female, female-male, or female-female rape. The reports are that AIDS is transmitted faster through male-to-male intercourse. The act itself is a brutal, sadistic power trip—not that females do not experience victimization from similar male motivations and vices. The rapes in *The Reluctant Rapist*, *The Taking of Miss*

Janie, and *The Duplex* are mainly done through the guise or misconception of love-making. In prison, I am sure that many men have met their deaths for even using the word "love."

c: Why did you join the Navy?

EB: For upward mobility. I tried to join on my sixteenth birthday, but I was too young. I went back on my seventeenth birthday and joined. I loved most of my time in the Navy, especially when I was at sea, when we would go from port to port.

c: In *The Duplex*, the term "winespodeyodey" from an old Lightning Hopkins' song is used. How much does music play in your work?

EB: Quite a lot, especially in *The Duplex*. There are four movements, ballads—music was playing a lot in the play. *Goin' a Buffalo* has music playing another type of role. Metaphorically, the music leads the action of the play. Structurally, the play is like a piece of music, (rather than a beginning, middle, rising, falling action, and climax etc.) but music on a visceral level pushing the action forward, and riding on the action and vice versa. The music is what makes the composition.

c: In *The Taking of Miss Janie*, the voices of the characters perform solos, and *In the Wine Time* you have duets written into the play similar to John Coltrane and Ornette Coleman's harmolodics. Are you consciously influenced by the jazz of the 60s?

EB: I was influenced by the music, and then I let it slip into my subconscious. It became my creative model. When I was writing, I did not want to keep and use European models, and not much new American idiom or African-Diaspora idiom had been developed. I had to reach inside and find a way to tell a story in a different way, yet in recognizable manner. I was supposed to be a musician, according to my mother. However, music never took, until I became a writer.

c: What instrument were you supposed to play?

EB: Piano or any of the horns. My mom used to take me to see Count Basie and the Duke Ellington Band.

c: You said that new American idiom or African-Diaspora idiom had not yet been defined in the late 60s, so you developed a form by using jazz structures as a way to tell a story. But, in the late 60s when Black Radical Theater was making a large statement in America, you decided to split the movement into the Black Radical Theater and the Black Experience Movement when you guest edited The Drama Review's issue devoted to black theater in 1968. Did you know what you were getting yourself into?

EB: I wanted to create flack. I wanted to jolt people. The people I left out howled. The people I left out did not want to be called black, even though they were legitimate artists like Langston Hughes and all of the people who had come before us. There was a new consciousness and expression coming out of the consequences of Malcolm X and the Nation of Islam, Third World Revolutionary Politics, and the African Nation Movement. The political stuff caused the Black Radical Theater. The new type of black existential thinking, black nihilism, and the stuff that came out of post-Absurdist theater, I called Black Experience type of theater. The other theater group, Colored Theater, Negro Theater, conceded that it was trying to emulate Broadway and the historical past. I left that type of drama where it was located. This caused a lot of howling. I was considered the bad black boy of dramatic graffiti. I consciously did that, so much so that I managed to antagonize almost every group, black and white, at least once. There is a story going around in New York now that I am currently reinventing myself. Some say that I am writing nice plays now, while others scowl and say that it is not possible.

c: From Philadelphia to California, from New York to Boston, what has been your most significant experience?

EB: I would have to reflect on that for a long time. There have been many experiences. One experience that I think about is going back to California this last time. While I was out in California, people said that I had died out there—and I have been around so much death since the 80s. I was swept away by all of that death. I guess that this is significant for me, because people actually thought of me as dead, or if not dead, then passed over. But, I'm still here! This is a revelation. In coming back to the East Coast, I am asking myself the question, are things still like I remember them? In a way they are the same. There is still a regard for theater; it still means something. I believe this is very significant.

c: You could call this a Second Coming!

EB: I do not know about that. I hate to get messianic. You know what happens to messianic statements and martyrs. I have been around for a long time, but I do not want to die yet.

c: In your later plays you write about heroes and their lives. Who do you consider heroes that you have not written about yet?

EB: There are many, Malcolm X. Of course, he is getting criticism now, but I do not know why. I suppose each new generation has to put down the past generation. There is Thurgood Marshall, Alice Childress, not just African-American, there are many heroes.

C: Do you think there are many people out there today who are heroes and can lend hope to all?

EB: If they can set their sights that high there are many heroes out there. There is a lot of ground fog, and getting one's head above the fog to see what is out there is difficult. It has been difficult for me, and it has been difficult for youngsters. Sure, there is hope for the moment. Whether there will be a time, and whether it will be apparent as to what history needs is another question. Some will see it, and some will not. I was listening to a program this morning on C-SPAN. The man who heads the United Negro College Fund was talking about a program the Fund has created. The fund has taken about 39 black youths from places like Roxbury, Mattapan, Newark, Camden, North Philadelphia, South Central Los Angeles with grade point averages at about 1.5. The UNF has raised the money to give these kids the support they need, and the Fund has found them tutors, mentors, and leaders. They have bought the children some clothes, tickets to get home on holidays, and are sending them to black colleges around the country. A phenomenal number have become incredible students. I think that three of them have become their class presidents. I think that there were six in the whole program that dropped out, but the rest have been very successful. Now, these students will not recognize their role models for years, even though they have benefited heavily from them. I was really impressed by the program. This should be done in other areas of society, not only with minorities but with low-esteem individuals, too. I do not know if I believe totally in role models. For instance, Charles Barkley, who drives a BMW, in my day would be viewed as a phony.

c: Do you think a teacher can convey to a student that there are traditions that the students may not have been taught yet?

EB: It is a lot better today than in my day. I was rapped on my psychological fingers with a psychological ruler and had to hear, "THERE ARE NO BLACK WRITERS!!!! DON'T SAY THAT! THERE IS NO BLACK LITERATURE. DON'T SAY THAT!!" It was like that up until my college days.

c: Do you think it will change even more?

EB: I do not know. Is it going to change? Of course it is going to change, but how will it change? Will we march into the great millennium hand-in-hand like Martin Luther King, Jr., singing "We shall overcome." I don't know. It has changed in the 60s, the 70s, and the 80s. It might change another way. It might go back to segregation. They might roll back the clock; they might bring in machine guns. I do not want to get alarmist. I am working in my small way so that it does not happen. You see what is happening in these Republican primaries. We have to see where these corporations keep going. We have to keep our eye out on the police forces. They are building prisons at a pace of one per week in California. The great thing about theater is that it is do-able. One does not need a $500,000 camera or $5 million deduction. It is do-able, less scope of course, but it is do-able. One can do it and get it done, and I always liked that.

c: You said you write to make the world a better place. Has that dream been realized since you have been writing?

EB: YES! My life has improved. My family's life has improved. I think in these times we should take the high road. We should be mission-oriented. Some of us have gone into education to teach, to save the world, or if not save the world to preserve the world. We must have the expectations to demand the consciousness, the ability of excellence. We need to take it to a higher level, the consciousness of the students that I can reach out to, not only a minority but any student. I should reach out to them by doing the plays, showing them which way the library is, by challenging them to new thinking. There are many areas that we must now take to a new level. This challenge inspires me because with drama I have an art and religion wrapped up into one—not quite a religion. We must be creative, be challenged, and challenge other people.

c: When completed what will the *20th Century Cycle* plays say to the 21st Century?

EB: I do not know. It might be completed now, but I have another story for the cycle. It is called *Madame Marlow*, and it is set in the 1930s. But, now I am thinking of changing the way I operate in the cycle. Instead of doing stories on people-groups or family-groups, I may begin to identify people on an economic or professional level. Perhaps, I will tell their story—a lawyer, a doctor, or a garment worker. But, I waver on how to decide on which plays should be included.

c: The prologue of *In the Wine Time* is repeated in *The Duplex*. This prologue has two voices in it: one is a voice of one who sounds naive, eager, and confused, and the second voice is one of a mature, weary seeker. Do you see this as a defining framework for the cycle?

EB: I do not think so. When I was beginning to write plays, I wrote a number of one-act plays. Then I said to myself that it was time to write a full-length play. My first full-length play was *Goin' a Buffalo*. Then, I tried to write another full-length play. Some years before these plays were written, I had written some fiction or poetic prose. This writing had resulted in a number of vignettes—*In the Wine Time* and *In New England Winter*. I had planned to complete a book of vignettes, but it did not turn out that way. Since I had the vignette, I used it for a prologue, and I decided to write a play to follow it. So, I did and that was *In the Wine Time*. I was so happy with the play, I set out to write twenty of them, and I decided to call the series the *20th Century Cycle*. Even though I had written *Goin' a Buffalo*, it was outside of these plays, but only in my mind. In my mind, *Goin' a Buffalo* came before the concept of the cycle. Consequently, it was outside this cycle which includes: *In the Wine Time*, *In New England Winter*, and *The Duplex*. The next play is *Homeboys*, but I am not as happy with *Homeboys* as I am with the others. Some things happened in my life, and I have slowed down. I have only finished seven of these plays. But, I have to go back to *Homeboys* because it is not as good of a play or as good as I want it. The cycle concerns African-Americans in the 20th Century in modern America, or then modern America. But, I have not decided on it yet; it might be too traditional or too corny.

c: You have said that you are trying to make things more universal. Maybe this is the cause for your indecision?

194

EB: Some of my early stuff was universal right from the beginning. While some of it was more socially and politically specific, like *The American Flag Ritual*. This play was making a very poignant statement. But *A Son Come Home*, which I wrote very early on, has a very broad appeal.

c: You mentioned earlier that when you were writing plays in the 60s, an African-American idiom had not been defined, yet. What are the idioms of today or common idioms of the theater today? And, what are you trying to do with the idiom?

EB: The theater I started in was inspired by the political and social movements of the late-50s and 60s. The Civil Rights Movement started in 1955 to 1960, and I started writing my plays in 1965, learning from the previous decade. What then came out of this period was the Black Revolution, or the so-called Black Revolution. It did not last very long—from 1965 to the early 1970s. I wrote through this time when there was a big explosion of Black Theater. Then the Black Women playwrights movement came into prominence and Black Women's fiction. So things altered from the mid-1970s to mid-1980s.

c: What were the various idioms of the time, and how did they change?

EB: Women like Ntozake Shange and her *For Colored Girls Who Have Considered Suicide/When the Rainbow Is Enuf*, inspired many women playwrights. *Mississippi Delta*, by Ida Mae Enzesha Holland, is a play about a black woman living in the urban South going through that experience and other plays of that ilk—Sisterhood plays. Then it sort of reached a plateau in the mid-80s, and it is now waiting to take off into something else, I believe.

c: Is Suzan Lori-Parks helping this to move along? I see commonality in your work and hers.

EB: Yes, but you better not tell her that; she would not like that. But, she is someone helping the movement along. She is quite a singular, original voice. She is an iconoclast, I guess like myself. She likes to break the rules, upset people. I am very interested in her work.

c: Iconoclasm is definitely a theme in your plays. What is the ends of the antagonism or confusion in your plays?

EB: Ultimately what I am trying to do is tell a story. Part of the story is chaos, especially in the black dimension—hundreds of years of chaos in a microcosm and even macrocosm. Showing the chaos, but still showing the life routines show the viewer one who is still trying and hoping for survival. Out of the wreckage comes the central figure.

c: Who might that be in *Salaam, Huey Newton, Salaam*?

EB: Marvin! Marvin is still tainted, but he still goes on. He still has hope. Not only for himself, but for the new found Black nation of the West.

c: In our last issue we published a long poem by Antonin Artaud, the founder of the Theater of Cruelty, among many other things. He was trying to expand and reconsider values and trying to define a new moral code. Are you consciously saying that there are different moral codes or universal codes that are not "Judaeo-Christian values?"

EB: Yes. There are parallel worlds, parallel values, parallelism all the time. I saw what Artaud was getting at with his work, but I could not write like that. For one thing, I could never stage something like that. I see the apocalyptic vision, but I think there is something beyond that. There has to be or why write at all? It will never be read. I think I owe it to my children and their children, otherwise they would be very depressed. I have to work towards that, a better world for them. There are varying parallel structures, paradigms. I do not know who has the answer. God is dead, but some people need God. The Black Revolution has come and gone, but some people need that. If that is what it takes, that is fine with me as long as you do not bother me.

c: You said someone had just staged *The American Flag Ritual*, and you were surprised. Suppose someone asked you to do the *Death List* today? Some of the names in the play are dated. If you were to stage it today, whose names would you include in a new script?

EB: I do not know. I do not feel the same way as I did back then. That was when I was espousing Third World Revolutionary politics, and I thought that some people were traitors. But, many things have changed. I guess whoever was going to do it would choose what names they would want to include. I am sure, however, that I would be accused of choosing the contemporaries. Many times people believed that I was "serious" about the political statements that were being made in my plays. I was not serious.

Either that was a character who spoke a la Farakahan, a la Malcolm, a la somebody, or quoted a nihilist perspective, or an anarchist point of view or a terrorist point of view, but that was not necessarily my point of view. I wrote the story. I am not the story all the time. I think that I was blacklisted because I dedicated one of my books to Al-Fatah. That does not mean I do not like Jewish people or even the nation of Israel, for that matter. It is that I went to Algiers to some revolutionary gatherings, and I was treated well by members of Al-Fatah and impressed by them. So, I dedicated my book to them because it was a book of revolutionary plays!

c: Kids today use the term "nigger" all the time. They have claimed the word as their own. You do quite the same thing by using African-American stereotypes as character traits in your plays. Do you do the same thing in this action that the kids do? The kids say that they are empowered by taking the word back, thus the language. Are the characters in your plays limited or empowered by the ownership of the stereotype?

EB: Not only do the kids use the term nigger, but so do I. The term is a reality. It is used in certain code ways and other language ways. It is the culture. One of the first literary movements used it. It was used in *The Adventures of Tom Sawyer* by Mark Twain, and after that it was used in The Atlantic Monthly and Esquire. Writers like Ernest Hemingway and Jack London and other white writers used it as part of their movement to express honesty and to express the American vernacular. ee cummings used it. It was daring to do back then. Then it was Faulkner who used it. It then became ordinary. It was a way to express the real American vernacular. They did not use it lavishly, but respectfully. Now the rappers "nigger nigger nigger" to death. It does not even have the same underpinnings and meanings that it used to have. It has been saturated. That ain't me! That's what you think. I use it not because I want to call somebody a nigger, but because the character uses it. It is interesting that you brought this up because I am getting ready to stage my play *The Electronic Nigger*. But, for the Northeastern University community I am going to have to change the title because people would get so bent out of shape that they would never get beyond the word. This play was put on Off Broadway. It has been published; it's been translated. It has been produced in England. It has been continuously performed for over 30 years. But, the university community does not know that. I can hear it now, the community's screams claiming that they knew I was going to do something like this, and that is what I find ridiculous.

c: In *The Electronic Nigger*, critics say that the two main characters, Mr. Jones and Mr. Carpentier, represent W.E.B. DuBois and Booker T. Washington respectively. Is this true?

EB: Maybe, but it was done unconsciously. In the 1960s, I did not have any such knowledge of the Booker T./DuBois debate. I did recognize the perpetual schism in the black community between the Judge Clarence Thomases and the Judge Thurgood Marshalls, the radical right and the radical left. To me, Carpentier personifies the radical reactionary Black who has destroyed all other Blacks just to keep his imagined position or to acquire his imagined and desired position. In *The Electronic Nigger*, the radical left, the teacher Mr. Jones was ineffectual because he was using the wrong tools against Carpentier. Mr. Jones was trying to beat Carpentier at his own game by using a Western frame of reference and dialectic in just trying to match one Western era against another Western era. In that game Carpentier or the Clarence Thomases will always win, well usually.

c: The character of OD in *The Duplex* reminded us of Bigger Thomas? Was this done deliberately?

EB: No. I did not take the character of OD out of literature, but I was familiar with Bigger Thomas. OD is the house bully, shack bully, the domestic violence man. You can assign a lot of forgiveness to him for what he had to endure, but he cannot be excused. OD had a job. He had a wife, who could have been a loving wife. He just cannot be excused. ODs are causing a lot of stress in the Black Community and not all because of poverty. Some of them are working class and middle class men. They exist with the character, and Black audiences recognize that character. OD bursts through the door and attacks his wife. Sadly to say, he is recognized.

c: All your biographies say that you were the former Minister of the Black Panthers, and that you left the Panthers to go to New York to join Robert Macbeth at the New Lafayette Theater of Harlem. Can you talk about what it was like to be a Minister of Culture for the Black Panthers, and why did you leave?

EB: I did not spend that long of a time in the position; I was purged. But, I did function with them even after after I was purged and lost my title. I was purged because we were existing in the Black House in San Francisco. Marvin X, Eldridge Cleaver, myself and others operated out of there. Bobby

Seale was in one of my original acting companies, and Huey Newton would come in and out of the company. Both he and Bobby landed there in the Black House prior to the Black Panthers. Cleaver's idea was more on the armed and dangerous track, while Marvin and I were into culture and art, though militant too. We saw them as the soldiers/security, and they saw us an obstacle. In any case, we parted company and Marvin and I got purged. After that I was on my way to New York, and Cleaver asked me to help him raise money. I organized a couple of benefits at the Filmore East for them. Then I went to Algiers where Cleaver had fled to visit him. That was about the extent of it. We all went our separate ways and had our own separate histories. I was the fundraiser and courier of truth—revolutionary truth. However, my main preoccupation was the theater.

c: In *Salaam, Huey Newton, Salaam,* you talk about the different paths that Huey Newton and Marvin X went down. What have some of the other members of the Black Panthers been up to?

EB: Bobby Seale was working at Temple University, and I think he had a barbecue restaurant. Eldridge has been having health problems and police problems in Berkeley, California. I have heard that Marvin was in New York or Newark. Those of us who have survived are still around.

c: What about Kingsley Bass, Jr. and his *We Righteous Bombers*? Is there any truth to it being an alias of yours?

EB: What have you heard?

c: On record you will not take credit for writing the play.

EB: I have been accused of many things. I think that somewhere I admit to being the culprit, but I have also been accused of being a liar.

c: Did the New Lafayette Theater represent to you the next step after the Black Panthers ministerial position? Was it that your perspective at that time did not afford you an audience?

EB: The New Lafayette Theater became the quintessential dream. We fulfilled all of our artistic dreams except one—SURVIVAL. But, we learned from the passing of the theater, too. I worked out of the New Lafayette Theater for seven years, and then I began my teaching career. I then had a couple of years of freelance before working for Joe Papp and the New York Shakespeare Festival. After that I was ready to get out of New York, so I went to California for a long, reflective period. But, I wrote some things, and I came back with some scripts. Hopefully, you will see them in the next several years.

c: Where do you see the theater going?

EB: I was wondering if it was going to die like they thought I had died. But, theater is special. It has survived.

Snickers
Ed Bullins

Snickers was first produced at the Playwright's Lab of the Marin Theatre Company, Mill Valley, California, as part of their Shorts Festival, a two-day event of fourteen new short plays. Bernie Weiner, Artistic Director (protem). It was directed by Jonal Woodward, with settings by Alicia Daniels.

Characters:
GUARD, Late 30's
MAN, mid-40's
ANIMAL, late 40's
GHOST, late 20's

Night. City Jail.
Jail bars cast shadows across the deck. Footfalls are heard on the sound system, approaching. A flashlight beam points across the stage.

Enter MAN and GUARD. The GUARD is female.

GUARD: You'll only be in this cell a short while … until we get a call from downstairs.

MAN: That's okay by me.

GUARD: Couldn't put you in the holding tank. Too crowded with drunks.

MAN: Yes, I know. I was squeezed into the courthouse van on the way over here. Felt like one of the herd.

GUARD: Wish we could kick more of you guys out of here faster after you make bail. We got some real hardcases here. No good for you to be around them. Lots of them should be in maximum security or in quarantine, but the state doesn't want to spend too much money on this human garbage. Got to think about the national debt, you know.

MAN: Human garbage. All these prisoners can't be worthless.

GUARD: Look, you don't have to live and eat with these animals day in and day out. Say … I shouldn't even be confiding in you like this.

MAN: Well, don't stop … Miss … Miss …

GUARD: You see my name tag, don't you?

MAN: I was really wondering about your first name. Does it fit your beautiful eyes?

GUARD: It's Diane. Did you use that line on your ex-wives?

MAN: What?

GUARD: I have every bit on you that's relevant. Computers, buddy. What do you think? I'd just talk to any inmate?

MAN: Well, I don't …

GUARD: Your being a single parent of two teenagers was the most impressive thing about you. And so was your career. Since you've got no rap sheet, it makes you almost human, you know.

MAN: Almost? Ah … thanks.

GUARD: I have a girl … in high school … like your kids. But look, we're almost to your cell. Just remember, you'll be out of here very soon. Some of these others … they'll be part of this penal system forever. Just watch yourself and don't accept anything from anybody in here.

MAN: Anything?

GUARD: Anything!

Footfalls soften. Lights up on cell.
ANIMAL and GHOST are in opposite
corners of the cell. ANIMAL stares
defiantly out; GHOST lies hunched in his
corner, his back to the wall.

202

The MAN and GUARD reach cell.

ANIMAL: Hey, what's happenin'? You ain't down here to see me in mucho days, Anderson. You forgettin' that you got a special spot in my heart, baby?

GUARD: Back up, Animal. I'm opening this door and putting this prisoner in. If you start anything funny, you'll spend the rest of the week in the hole.

ANIMAL: You didn't hear me, honey. I loves ya. Hahaha!

GUARD: Like those old ladies you raped? Or the ones you ripped off?

ANIMAL: That was then, mommy. This is now.

GUARD: Get back, you ape! I got your print-out. You're less than what you call yourself, Animal! Rape, grand theft, attempted murder, suspicion of murder. Child molestation! I'm glad I got the keys, so I can lock you up for a long time. (to MAN) You! Get in there.

The MAN enters cell.

ANIMAL: Yeah, come on in, man, we one big happy family in here. Ha ha!

GUARD closes and locks door.

GUARD: You better not bother him, Animal, or you'll get yours, I promise you.

ANIMAL: What's this? You got a teacher's pet, Anderson? And he's bunkin' with me?

GUARD: Remember what I said, Animal. (Points to GHOST) What's the matter with him?

ANIMAL: (shrugs) Who knows? I can't understand his gook lingo. Maybe he's anti-social. Ha ha ha. Maybe he's on his period.

GUARD: (to MAN) Hey, stay away from both of these guys, especially the one in the corner. Okay?

MAN: Okay.

ANIMAL: How cute.

GUARD: Good. I'll be back and get you as soon as I can. Behave yourself, Animal, I mean it.

SHE exits.

ANIMAL: Oh, teacher … you forgot to give me my beddy-bye kiss an' tuck me in. Hey, teach! One of these days I'm gonna shove my joint down your slimy tonsils and rip off ya stinkin' tits. Ya hear me! Ya hear me!

ANIMAL looks at the MAN.

ANIMAL: (half-grins, half-leers) She's gone. Deputy Dawg … better spelled Deputy Bitch … But we're here. Animal. Howdy. That's Ghost over there. He don't say nothin'. Not in English leastwise. Not so you can understand. They picked him up off a raft in the ocean. Don't know why he's in here, but he can't tell me now, can he?

MAN: No, I guess not.

ANIMAL reaches under his bunk
mattress and pulls out something.

ANIMAL: Say, ya like a Snickers?

MAN: Oh, no thanks. I try and stay away from sugar.

ANIMAL: You do?

MAN: Yeah, that's right.

ANIMAL: You stay away from sugar—Ha ha—What you in for?

MAN: Tickets.

204

ANIMAL: Tickets?—Ya mean parking violations?

MAN: Well, I do have a moving violation or two—And the rest are parking.

ANIMAL: Movin'—movin'—ha ha ha ha!—Hee hee—hee hee—ya got ta be kiddin'! Locked up with me 'cause of tickets? Its a joke. I'm starin' forty years in the mug, pal. And you're here—ha ha—you poor sucker.

In the corner, GHOST begins crying. The sound is eerie.

MAN: Is something wrong?

ANIMAL: (disturbed) Shut up! Shut up, ya goddam spooky creep!

GHOST tries to supress his sobs. His body heaves and is wracked by surpressed emotion.

MAN: What's the matter? Shouldn't we call the guard?

ANIMAL: Just hold your pants on, junior. No guards—Say, they didn't put you in here to spy on me, did they?

MAN: No. I'm waiting for my bailbondsman to call. Then I'm leaving.

ANIMAL: You getting' out? How you rate? I been waitin' for my trial date for ten months and you come in and walk right out in the next minute.

MAN: Well, tickets aren't—

ANIMAL: Yeah, I know … What do you do on the outside?

MAN: I'm a teacher.

ANIMAL: A teacher! Ya got to be kiddin'. You sure you ain't undercover?

MAN: No, I'm just waiting …

ANIMAL: (serious) How much money you got?

MAN: Nothing—They have my things down in the property room.

ANIMAL: You ain't got nothin' and you getting' out soon—Say—you want a Snickers?

Suddenly, GHOST begins to cry louder and wail.

ANIMAL: Shut up! Shut up, you geeky gook, or I'll smash your—

ANIMAL moves menacingly toward GHOST. The MAN moves in front of GHOST.

MAN: Don't hurt him. He's frightened to death of you already.

ANIMAL: You in my way, Teach. This ain't none of your business. He belongs to me.

MAN: You helped him?

ANIMAL: Yeah, I gave him my last Snickers.

MAN: So what.

ANIMAL: You're a smart one, ain't you? Well, listen to this ... he ate my Snickers.

GHOST cries more, in apparent fear.

ANIMAL (cont'd): He ate my Snickers and I later asked for it back. With his stupid sign language and monkey talk, he let me know that he didn't have any money either, like you, but when he did get some he'd pay me back—ha ha ha ha!

GHOST cries unabatedly.

MAN: What was wrong with that?

ANIMAL: Ha! Ha! Everything sucker. I told him I wanted the same Snickers that I gave him, not a new one.

MAN: But I don't know what you're getting at.

ANIMAL: What I mean is that if I couldn't have my own Snickers back, then I'd have the hole where my Snickers came out. And I did. I took it! And took it! And took it!

GHOST screams. ANIMAL pushes the MAN aside and attacks GHOST, kicking him brutally.

The MAN regains his legs and pulls ANIMAL off of GHOST. ANIMAL turns and charges the MAN. The MAN holds his ground and strikes ANIMAL in the solar plexus with a reverse punch and kicks him in the groin, doubling up ANIMAL. ANIMAL groans as he grovels on the ground. The MAN helps GHOST up, exchanging words and gestures.

ANIMAL: (groans) Ohh—ohh—how did you do that? How did you do that to me? A punk like you—How did ya?

MAN: One of the things I teach is karate. (to GHOST) Take it easy. You'll be all right.

Footfalls. Light. GUARD ANDERSON returns.

GUARD: Is everything all right in here?

ANIMAL: Ohh—ohh—Guard, I got a complaint. I been attacked.

GUARD: Shut up, Animal. I wish I were zippering you in a body bag right now—Okay, you two others—you're getting out.

The MAN leads GHOST out. GHOST talks to him in a pidgin French, which he can understand a bit.

MAN: Okay—okay—we'll get you some help.

ANIMAL: Guard—I'm busted up. Help me!

HE reaches for the bars. SHE raps his fingers with her nightstick.

ANIMAL: Ooowwww—

GUARD: Get back, scum!

ANIMAL: Oww! Why you all treatin' me like this? I'm stayin' in here an' you two are gettin' out. Hey, what you two jabberin' about like monkeys?

MAN: The Ghost says he's got AIDS. Picked it up in American jails.

ANIMAL: AIDS! That stinkin' fuck brought it here when he go outta his canoe.

GUARD: Let's go, guys—It's near the end of my shift.

MAN: Oh, maybe you'd like to have breakfast with me, at a nice place. I've got an American Express card.

GUARD: I know. And we could drive there in your BMW. Remember your print-out has everything on it. Yes, maybe we can. Our kids are in school—and we have the whole day ahead of us. You think you could show me some self-defense techniques?

MAN: Striking or holding?

THEY exit.

ANIMAL: But what about me? You're not going to leave me here, are ya? I gotta see a doc. I need help. (begins to cry) Oh God Jesus, help me!—sob—sob I—didn't mean it. I'm sorry. I ain't been understood since Viet Nam. I just want to be friends. Does anybody want a Snickers? Huh? Ya want a Snickers? Anybody! Just one little fucken Snickers!—Hey, take it or I'll kill ya!!!

Lights down. Curtain.

Marija Says
Jean Pedrick

Grandmother said, they come from the ears,
on horse. Watch the plain there
for the long cloud, thicker than smoke.
Hide what you can, potatoes, turnips,
anything that will keep, nothing to call
the bees. Then filthen and uglify yourself.
Roll with the swine till you retch, I beg you.

Mother said, they come from the north, tanks
like giant insects, beetlebacks on the feet
of millipedes. Whatever obstructs, they mount
and topple. When the ground shakes, when the crows
scatter, do everything she said. The food. The pigs.

They came from the sky. The pig exploded.
I was pasted with it. Even so, grew up, grew old.

Organ Donor
CHS   [3 poems]

When I die I want to be fed to the sharks
No burial where worms eat through your skin
No cremation where you reek like gasoline for eternity
Just the sea
And the sharks
Ripping
My dead
Muscle
From bone
Nurturing
Feeding
Living

.

FOR THE BLAKE BABIES

I. CHANT TO ME SIR GINSBERG
YOUR WORDS OF WISDOM COCK
YOUR FOUL MOUTH IN THE FACE OF A JUDGE
HOWL AND SCREAM MY LUNGS TO LIFE

CONNECT THE SILVER TONGUE
TO DOOM THE LINES TO COME
WAIT BETWEEN THEIR PAUSES
AND SMILE AT THE PAIN IT CAUSES

I FALL ASLEEP IN THAT CHAIR WHILE
YOU'RE FUCKING ME WITH POETRY
I'M DREAMING A SPIRITUAL REALITY
A CHANTING DANCE WITH A SKINWALKER

A SLAVE'S GHOST WILL WALK ALL OVER YOUR SKIN
QUIVERING DOWN THE CROTCH
TINGLING AND TITILATING THE NIPPLES
OH! HOW WE FLIRT WITH THE DEAD

SWIMMING SPIRITS SMITE I IN SLEEP
AROUSE MY DESIRED DREAMING OF DREAMS

SWIMMING SPIRITS SMITE I IN SLEEP
AROUSE MY DESIRED DREAMING OF DREAMS

SWIMMING SPIRITS SMITE I IN SLEEP
AROUSE MY DESIRED DREAMING OF DREAMS

II. WALT WHITMAN I ASK YOU IF TWO BLADES OF GRASS
            BECOME ONE
DO THEY MAKE THREE? OR DO THEY SPREAD DISEASE
            TOWARD
ARMEGEDON?
THAT'S JUST WHAT HAPPENED I GUESS THE BOOK DIDN'T GET
ACROSS TO ENOUGH PEOPLE AND NOW LEAVES OF GRASS

ARE MOWED OVER BY GAS GUZZLING LAWN MOWERS
SPITTING MONOXIDES ALL OVER THE PRINTED PATTERNS
        OF NATURE
AND THE PEACE TO REST UNDER THE SUN, IS BLOCKED OUT
        BY FEAR
OF OZONE OPENING UP AND SUCKING ME UP TO THE SUN
        TO BURN
AND BROIL ME INTO A ZODIAC SIGN, TO BE ANALYZED
BY ANCIENT SCRIBES
THROUGHOUT TIME AND SPACE
THEY KNEW MY SHAPE AND FORM
LIKE YOU SIR GINSBERG,
WHILE YOU WERE
FUCKING ME WITH POETRY.

The Jesus Freaks

WELL NOW THE JESUS FREAKS HAVE GONE AND DONE
            IT AGAIN
WE REMEMBER JONESTOWN AND NOW WACO, TEXAS.
THE GUN IS IN ONE HAND
THE BIBLE HOLDS THE OTHER.
BE CAREFUL AND LISTEN
OR I'LL SHOOT YOU, "MY BROTHER."
SO BRING ON THE CROWDS
AND LET THE GAMES BEGIN!

WHEN THE BUREAU KILLS HIM, AND HE'S ON T.V.
THEN HE'S REALLY GONNA SHOCK US
AND BE THE RESURRECTED JESUS WITH A GUN

SO BANG, BANG, BANG

 AND THINK OF THE SEX.
"I"LL SHOOT THEM ALL, AND SLEEP WITH THE REST."

IS IT JIM JONES, OR IS IT THE BOOK?
IT'S SO DAMN OBVIOUS, SOME OVERLOOK
THE SIMPLE TRUTH THAT IS NOT ANY WORD.
SOME PEOPLE THINK THEY SPEAK TO GOD
SOME PEOPLE THINK THEY BECOME GOD
SOME PEOPLE SEE NOTHING BUT WHAT'S IN THEIR EYES
SOME PEOPLE SPEAK NOTHING BUT LIES
SOME PEOPLE WILL LISTEN TO LIES AND BELIEVE THEM
SO IF THE HOOK SNARES
SNIP
THE
LINE

Whiskey Worms
Charles Hancock

I like state fair cotton candy
(I always have)

Saw Jesus in the rainbow
once when I was small
(haven't seen him since)

Just then flaming black poison
exploded from every pore
and orifice

My head was a flowing mane
of shiny snake hair with
snapping turtles on the ends
Evil & Ugly I was

The whiskey worms done had me
Nothing I could do about it
Their barbed probing tails burrowed
into my brain past the latches,
padlocks, & boards that guard
the deepest recesses and
secret voids of my
mind

Torrents of Evil Black Ideas & Crazy
Notions gushed out
sludgey green donkey dick shit
genocidal race hate
goose steppin kill em all talk
raged forth

(Repeat slowly shaken not stirred)
Whiskey & Vodka
volatile by themselves
a mushroom cloud rising when

combined
fueled this impersonation of a
blind drunk loser fuckhead
that I had become

Now my girlfriend is pissed
                    at my hideous behavior
friends look at me with new
found revulsion

If only I could remember what
I had done—the alleged
outrages

Instead I must rely on the snakey
testimony of lesser drunks
with their booze garbled
hearsay recollections
from what I can piece together
it seems that I have
behaved badly

If I offended anybody I am
truly sorry

I'd be more ashamed but
I just
can't remember

Puer
Theresa Iverson

You do not mature, immortal boy.

Not the horizontal, not the plod
of a mundane plot, you sidewind,
squirm, crab scuttle from vertical
to vertical. You do not mature.

Visionary, futurist, epicure. Icarus
with a parachute: an accelerating
breath launches you, diving
from a plane's ledge backward

into the sky. You do not
mature, but flit lubriciously from
flower to flower, distilling a lush
illusion of freedom, while the cut

roses you wired hang drying above
the radiator vent, a bloodless trophy,
like the over-sized catfish heads once
nailed to a tree beside the Rio Grande.

Meditator, dervish whirler, worshipper
of a god you devised: the god of Choice—
and you choose it all! Sampler
at a sacred and profane smorgasbord;

Mr. Desultory Desuetude
—such a dry mouth!—aging
Peter Pan, you do not,
do not mature.

Red River Crossing
Fred Marchant

for Nguyen Quang Thieu

i.

The current burly,
hired cars trying to sneek up at
        the crossing. An angry
guard in red silk armband waving
        the too-eager ones back
with a baton. Rice shoot bundles,
        a farmer bent over,
planting in the flooded paddy
        one green blade at a time.

ii.

Warm sun on a teashop's rusty,
        thin, corrugated roof.

iii.

A wobbly wooden stool,
        Worn smooth. A pretty girl
refilling your cup says she's not
        sure she'll every marry,
and you say if it was up to
        you alone, if a poet
could do long without cities,
        if he didn't need other
poets for more than tea or tobacco,
        then he would live here
in the flower of beauty forever.

After Wartime
Ben Mazer

She has not been to war, but she can see
That he has been to war. They touch, they meet,
In darkness where he dreams his private nightmare.
He does not know that she has seen him in sleep.

She, touched by the years of war, is lovely.
Sympathetic, she meets him mid-way on the stair,
Tailoring humour to his lack of tact,
Tailored by a lack of shoes on the shoe rack.

Her father, sore as a mirror after drinking,
Plumbs the depth of the years, one language, and one culture.
This is the way things end, and things begin.
A let-down shade lets sunlight in, and darkness.

A Murder, After Goya
Christopher Millis

Tell me what you mean by going south,
the art of barren kitchens, the lover
you don't sleep with. Tell me

what you mean by the fencing match
framed above the sofa in which
a smooth-cheeked boy gets stapped

by a man whose face no one else
can see. You make him up, the angry
lover whose love is sharp and deadly

while the other's eyes roll back
and blood emerges dark beneath his shirt.
Tell me what you mean by your sunny

fingernails, the money you spend, the island
where your shirt's open and the darkness bakes in.

Jack Powers

Whatever the Flesh Suffers, the Soul Suffers First.
(William Everson 1912-1994)

For the poet is dead. The giant wolf
Crawled out to the edge and died snapping.
He said he would. The wolf
Who lost his mate. He said he would carry the wound,
The blood-wound of life to the broken edge
And die grinning.

The Business Ethics of Poets
Richard Moore

Give me my money back,
you fink, you fancy liver,
or I'll wrap you in a gunnysack
and toss you in the river.

My methods when I'm pissed,
brutal, you say? A shame?
Recall: your favorite dramatist,
Will Shakespeare, did the same.

Hear America Singing: A Gallery of the U.S.

How Should One Live?
A Conversation with Martha Nussbaum   [1994]

c: Being a contemporary philosopher in America today, and one that considers herself part of a discourse which Aristotle started thousands of years ago, we would like to start out by asking you about your life. How have you chosen to live your life? How have you incorporated your philosophical ideas into your daily life?

MN: One of the things I've always stressed about Aristotle's view of the good human life, is that it has a number of distinct components that are not commensurable with each other and that all have to be present if you are going to have a reasonable, rich, and complete life. Among those are intellectual self-development and thinking, political participation and planning, love of friends and family, and the attempt to be just and courageous—all the moral virtues—so you can say that I've tried to combine these things with whatever strain that plurality of components often produces. I have never been content to just be a thinker in the academy; I've always wanted to combine that with some sort of involvement in social and political life. It is hard to find ways to do this.

One way that I've found is to try to write in a way that would engage a wider audience. I don't see why philosophers haven't done that more in America, but I think that they haven't. I think that there is a tremendously large audience who would like to hear about the issues philosophers worry about, like the nature of the emotions, the nature of choice. If only the philosopher thinks enough about writing that can be accomplished, so I've tried to do that. I also try and write in publications like *The New York Review of Books* and *The New Republic* that do reach a wider audience. I do that by mainly reviewing peoples' books.

But, I've really wanted to be more concretely involved in political action. There are two ways I've found to do that. One way is to get involved with international development ethics and to get involved with people who are doing grassroots work and public policy work in thinking about the foundational issues of global development; asking questions such as what does it mean to measure the quality of life in a country; or what is it to ask how the quality of life in country A compares with that in country B? Usually that is done in a crude way by just looking at gross national product (GNP) per capita. The group that I was involved with wanted to urge a more Aristotelian way of gauging the quality of life, in terms of a variety of different human functions that are all very important and in each of which needs a distinctive kind of support from the governmental and private sectors.

The other political area that I've gotten myself enmeshed in increasingly is law, because in America the most direct and politically effective way a philosopher can speak to the general public is through a link either with medicine or law. I found myself getting involved in law more and more just because Aristotle's views of practical reasoning were of great interest to law. They seem to provide a principled defense of the common law tradition against the law and economics movement. Aristotle's views are a justification for saying that the human life contains many incommensurable goods, contrary to what utilitarian economics would like to say.

I've gone so far in that direction, that now I am actually moving to Chicago and my principal appointment will be in the University of Chicago Law School. They've had economists who don't have law degrees teaching there, as resources for the lawyers. This will be the first time that a philosopher will have an appointment at the school. Of course, the lawyers there know that I'm one who has repeatedly argued against the law and economics movement, and essentially the staff is in favor of intellectual debate and plurality. However, I will teach the usual variety of courses in other departments in the university. I'm excited by that; I like the idea that I'll be teaching people who will go out and be clerks for judges, and of course the clerks write most of the judicial opinions these days, anyway. So, if you want your work to somehow get into the public realm that's one very natural avenue. I like the people that I'm talking to there. I think it's exciting to talk to people that are involved in public life. But then I also think that it is very important to have personal relationships and family. My daughter just graduated from Brown University, and I'm really proud of her. It's wonderful to see one's own child become a distinct individual. So those are some of the ways that I've tried to live my life; I don't think of it as trying to read Aristotle, and then going out and putting that into practice. Maybe my interest in Aristotle partly came about because I thought these things important.

c: Can you talk a little bit about when and how you came to make this your way of life?

MN: When I was in high school, I went to a wonderful women's school outside Philadelphia called Baldwin, which is still an all women's school. It was a very intense, very feminist, experience although, of course, I didn't see it that way at that time. In retrospect, it is clear that I had strong feminist teachers. Already in high school, because of what my teachers were urging me to write, I was thinking about a lot of the same problems that I later wrote about, for example about how one can gain knowledge and self-knowledge through the emotions I wrote about when I was fifteen. When I was a senior in high school, I wrote about how one relates allegiance to abstract principles with love of particular individuals. I wrote a play about Robespierre and the French Revolution which had that theme, and I'm sure it was very crude and embarrassing if I were to look at it now. But I was already hooked by those issues.

I thought that I might become some sort of writer. But then I went to college and I began to think that I wanted to become an actress. All along I did a lot of acting. I think I wanted a different way of life. I've always loved artistic people. I love actors, dancers, musicians and creative people. I think it was the love of that world and wanting to go into a much broader world than the one I grew up in that lead me that way. So I left Wellesley College half-way through my sophomore year to take up an acting job in a repertory theatre where they did Greek drama. I did that for six months, and then I went to New York University School for the Arts to study acting for a year. Then I began to see this wasn't a life I could stand. I saw how the New York theatre scene operated, how cut-throat it was, how little security, how little support for the creative life there is in the theatre—very unlike the life of an orchestral musician where you could count on a whole life course. An actor doesn't have that security here in this country. I also didn't think that I was that terrific an actor. I thought probably I wanted to think and write about those things rather than to act.

I then went back to the regular school at NYU. At that point I took up intellectual issues from Greek tragedy and continued straight on. I thought that it was classical literature that I wanted to work on, primarily because I was thinking about ideas, about emotions and moral conflict that were in the tragedies. But then I went to graduate school at Harvard in classics, and what I then realized was that these were actually philosophical questions. Literary people in the classics were not all that interested in these questions at the time I was in graduate school, but the philosophers were. So, I got quickly involved in the Greek philosophy program, and I had wonderful teachers—G.E.L. Owen, Bernard Williams—who had a great influence on me in making me just terribly excited about doing philosophy. From that point on I've known sort of what problems I'm working on, but not necessarily what to call it. There is a slight problem about what to call it; at any time in my life I might be talking to economists, political scientists, philosophers or people in religion. In fact, in Chicago I am going to be partly involved with the divinity school, also. The issues of the nature of practical reasoning, the nature of the emotions, the quality of life lie at the intersection of so many professions. I like that interdisciplinary aspect and the links with literature are very important to me. I've always had a slight problem about what department or departments I would place myself in, but not about what problems I would work on. And the law seems to me to add a huge dimension. My father was a lawyer, and when I was very young I was hooked on watching Perry Mason. I always wanted to be Perry Mason. Not that I'm going to be a legal scholar now, but I'll probably go so far as to write occasionally something about a legal issue.

For instance, I have a colleague at Chicago, and we're writing a paper about concepts of the emotions in the criminal law. It is interesting because the law tends to absorb philosophical conceptions without articulating them. Then often when time has gone by you can't quite recognize how some language came about, and in this case we find two quite different conceptions of the emotions in the history of criminal law. One conception is a rather Aristotelian one in which emotions are part of a character that you cultivate for yourself. You're responsible for being the sort of person who gets provoked by some things and not by others. The way reasonable provocation is defined in the law of homicide is around the idea that a reasonable person will be provoked by some things but not by other things. But, then more recently there was this more mechanistic conception that crept in where emotions are just impulses. Emotions have no intelligence about them; they vary in strength. This has had actually rather pernicious results because people who commit hate crimes can now say that it is not a question about the unreasonableness of his or her emotions. The emotion was very strong, and I was really and truly very angry when I saw these gay people. The point under the mechanistic conception is that one can't distinguish different sources of the emotions; one's behavior is just a matter of an emotion's strength. Of course, then quite vicious people can have just as strong emotions as those with righteous indignation. So we want to bring back the Aristotelian line. It's never completely dropped out, and we just want to bolster it up.

c: You were speaking of your strong background from your high-school years and your home. Can you speak about the source of your strength growing up, being a woman and going into philosophy—the thinker's academy—which predominantly happens to be a man's field?

MN: My father gave me tremendous encouragement, and from the time

I was young I was given the message that I was his junior partner. I was encouraged to play lawyer with my dolls—although I think that I imagined that the dolls were listening to romantic stories that came from opera. So it was a funny way of playing lawyer with my dolls. My father would often complain about the fact that when they hired women in his firm they left to have children. He thought it was possible for women to both have their family and keep their careers going, and he sent me very strongly the message that I could do that. My mother had given up her career to get married, so I think that there was a little bit of a discrepancy between what I was seeing and what I was hearing. I think that that's not too surprising at that time. My mother was an interior decorator. Later in life, she went back and did a bit of volunteer work, but I don't think that she was happy when she was not working. I think I saw that in her, too.

I always felt that I would keep my career going, but I haven't thought very much how to do it. When I got married I was twenty and we hadn't really thought about these things. I think maybe people your age do much more thinking and talking about how responsibilities will be distributed. People your age are much more conscious of sharing child care and such. We were in the generation that improvised on all the traditional marriage arrangements, and it was not easy to do. There were a lot of conflicts. I don't think my ex-husband, to whom I was married for eighteen years (although it was a very good marriage in many ways) was altogether prepared for the fact that I was going to have a career. Although he knew intellectually that I was going to have a career, I think that we really did have to struggle with that. I think that the professions were struggling with these issues at the same time. Again, my thesis advisor really gave me a lot of encouragement. He did certainly send very strongly the message again that women should combine work and family. He would tell me all these stories, when I was pregnant, about women who dropped out of the profession after they had children. This encouraged me, but also made me very anxious. I brought my Aristotle text to the hospital when I had my daughter, Rachel, because I had to prove to myself and everyone else that I was still a scholar. It created a lot of anxiety, but it was still good rather than bad to keep hearing that I wasn't going to be one of the ones who was going to give up her career. However, the professions weren't entirely prepared for the fact that women had child-care duties and that, of course, men did too.

There was one great moment, when I was an assistant professor at Harvard with a three-year-old child to care for. I was constantly making all the child-care arrangements because my husband taught at Yale in

Connecticut. He was away then five days of the week. I felt that my colleagues did not recognize this, the difficulties of child care. In the middle of a visiting speaker's discussion period, a well-respected colleague of mine, Robert Nozick, stood up and told everyone he had to leave because he had to pick up his son from hockey practice. I thought that his announcement was wonderful, and I breathed a big sigh of relief. I thought it was all right to mention family responsibilities, and I now had encouragement from the top. I think people like Robert Nozick and also Hilary Putnam, who had young children at the time, were very important to me in making me feel encouragement. Of course, at the time there were no tenured women in philosophy at Harvard.

I faced a lot of adversity in my career that came from being a woman. I think men don't quite know how to deal with a woman who is their equal. Some men don't and some men do quite wonderfully. Some men feel more threatened by a woman who has a new way of doing things than they would by either a woman who did things in the old way or a man who had a new idea. It's the combination of being a woman and having a new idea that is very threatening. When I came up for tenure at Harvard, the philosophy department voted positively. The classics department voted negatively by a small margin, but there were many issues involved in that, some certainly involving sex discrimination. I was urged to bring a grievance or a law suit against the classics department. I decided not to because I thought my own psychology wasn't one that could have stood the tremendous hostility that would have been generated at that point. And I didn't love Harvard very much anyway. I didn't care whether I stayed there or not. I sometimes think for the sake of other women I should have brought a complaint, but I didn't. My colleagues at Brown have always treated me remarkably well. One of the things I've been so happy about at Brown from the beginning was its extremely fair work atmosphere. I think there is a sense of generosity about peoples' family lives. Now I have three younger male colleagues who have little kids, and they all bring their kids to the office, even to department meetings. It's a very good atmosphere for that. At Chicago, I hope that that will also be the case. I expect it will. I am one of only two women in the law school. So they have had a shortage of women because it is quite a large faculty. It will be a good challenge to see how issues of affirmative action and hiring of people to teach feminism will work in that setting.

c: You've talked about how you incorporate your philosophy into your life. Can you talk about how your philosophy and your love interrelate?

MN: I try to do that in my writing; I do it through adopting a lot of different masks. I try and find a literary work that fascinates me through which I can speak about this. There are so many angles to that question. One is what have philosophers had to say about love, and this is one of the things I'm actually thinking about now. The book I'm writing now is a book on the emotions, which is my attempt to give my own account of what emotions are. About half of it is on philosophical proposals for the reform of love—the old metaphor of the ascent of love, the ladder of love on which one climbs upward from the daily or messy kind of love to something that is somehow more refined or purified. I think philosophers have generally been very suspicious of love, even more than of the other emotions. Part of the suspicion seems to be caused by the fact that erotic love is in tension with general social concerns in a way in which other emotions like compassion or indignation wouldn't necessarily be. This is something that fascinates me greatly. Erotic or romantic love is a very valuable part of the richness of life, but it does require a kind of exclusivity of attention and a singling out of one person on the basis usually of morally indifferent characteristics—not just because of beauty and goodness as Plato would have it but for other reasons. The question then is, what is the justification for that in moral terms when the world contains so much need and suffering?

The philosophers I think about a lot, the Greek Stoics, have a way of addressing some of those concerns when they ask the question, why should I love my own children more than somebody else's? They reply by saying the whole world is better designed if each parent focuses on his and her household rather than trying to take care of all the children in the world, thus no one would get cared for that way. But that doesn't take you all the way to a justification for romantic love, because that love is by its nature more exclusive than parental love. Furthermore, it is a form of love you might just not have at all. You could do away with romantic love completely, and certainly many philosophers have wanted to do so, in order to make more room for general social and political concerns. The best I can say right now is that I think that romantic love is an important part of life's richness and a source of an energy for everything else. If it is intrinsically valuable then it ought to be in your life, even if it's in tension with other things that are good and valuable. But, I keep worrying about this problem.

The last chapter of my new book is about James Joyce's *Ulysses*. I think of Joyce as a great writer to read after one has puzzled about philosophical reform proposals because he in effect tells you that it's all right to go to the toilet. And it's all right to just love people in the messy way that you do. It doesn't have to be pure in order to be a source of generosity, even of social concern. After all the reform attempts, I thought it was the time to turn the ladder upside down and look at Joyce's attempt to get back to the ordinary world and to embrace the ordinary with love and delight. I think it's important that neither Leopold nor Molly Bloom ever wishes harm to another person. I think that it is important that Bloom is a figure who combines in some peculiar way erotic love and fantasy with social commitment.

c: You will probably go down in the *Guinness Book of World Records* as the one who held the most academic appointments in different departments. You say that you are just pursuing your questions; how does that make you feel about how the academy is set up today? Do you think the disciplines the way they stand in the university might not be so well equipped to answer the types of questions which you believe need to be asked?

MN: I think it ought to be easier than it is to cross the boundaries. I'm very lucky that Brown and Chicago are both interdisciplinary places where it is fairly easy to get a group together to do something interdisciplinary, to create a little program or a little committee. In Chicago they have these things they call workshops. When I get there, I'll run a law/philosophy workshop. There's a rhetoric workshop. These workshops make it easy for people to group and ungroup again when they are no longer so interested in a particular topic. They don't have to go to the extent of creating a department; I think that's a very good thing. I think that when you create these new departments sometimes the work loses its impetus, and then you're stuck there. The traditional disciplines perform a good function in keeping people substantive and disciplined. When I work on the emotions, that is on interdisciplinary topic par excellence. There is hardly any discipline that hasn't written on emotions. These days even economists write books on the emotions. But, there is something good about the fact that the work isn't all in one place and stirred altogether. I learn more by reading and talking to a real professional anthropologist, an anthropologist who has really gone and done that kind of fieldwork and has thought about the methodology of doing fieldwork. I can profit by the outcome of that research, although I could never go and just do it myself. Again, psychoanalysts who actually treat patients have an understanding of emotion in a clinical setting that someone who's not a professional analyst or a psychologist would not be able to have. Then there are the experimental psychologists who look at animals or who have done years of experiments with dogs or with rats. They know something that I don't know. So for me it's better that it is interdisciplinary rather than with no disciplinary boundaries at all.

c: We believe the way you look at literature dovetails with compost's mission. Your attempts to broaden literature's significance by reconciling the literary imagination with the public life is more the position we believe in, rather than how the literary world has limited the scope of literature and marginalized itself in society. However, some of our friends look at us and ask why we even bother with literature? In today's world of Cyberspace, Pulp Fiction and MTV, why should one spend time reading literature and books and asking philosophical questions?

MN: I think literature has a tremendously important contribution to make to public life. I have a short book that's coming out in January 1996 from Beacon Press that will be titled *Poetic Justice: The Literary Imagination and Public Life.* In the book there is a chapter where I apply all this to the reading of some judicial opinions. I ask how judges use their ability to narrate, their ability to imagine the situation of another person or, as the case may be, how do they fail to use their abilities in what they write. I think it does make a tremendous difference. In all parts of public life, but especially in the judiciary where individual people have so much broad discretion, I think the ability to imagine with sympathy what it's like to be another person of a concrete sort is an ability that you don't get—I think Charles Dickens is absolutely right—from a technical education in economics. But you get it, or let's hope you get it, from early childhood, through the interactions with your parents and the stories they tell you. To have it in a mature form, as a public actor, you need to read complex literary works such as novels and dramas, because those works are going to put you in contact with the way in which people try to live in a variety of different social settings.

There is a moment in Richard Wright's *Native Son* when Mary Dalton and Bigger Thomas are riding around—close to the University of Chicago Law School, in fact. They look up at the tenements. Mary Dalton says to Bigger Thomas that she's always wanted to go up into one of those houses, and she wants to know how his people live. The reader has been in the tenements since the first page of the book. Then she chatters on in her well meaning way, and she says that he, Bigger, is human after all just like everyone else. What the reader knows is that this is true, the inhabitants of the tenements are human like everyone else. But, in a very crucial way, it isn't because of the way in which their humanity has been deformed by hierarchy and oppression. Not just their circumstances but their thoughts on emotions themselves are formed and deformed by racism. The reader of that novel has an experience that Mary—in her University of Chicago education, which she didn't take very seriously—just doesn't get.

When I read that novel in my law school class last year, it was a high point because the students couldn't fail to notice that there was a chain link fence behind the law school parking lot. Everything is pretty well unchanged from the mid-1940s. Here are people who are going to have to understand problems of race, as judges, clerks and lawyers. There was a class of seventy-five with just one African-American student in it, and he was a middle-class kid and had relatively conservative views about a lot of these issues. I don't think he had more experience than the others with that kind of life. We had great discussions about these issues. I think it's that kind of expansion of one's imaginative possibilities that literature can contribute.

Some judges are able to think this way and some not. Let me give an example. There was a very fascinating opinion in a recent prisoners' rights case. Both the majority and the minority agreed that malicious searches and seizures of prisoners' cells are unacceptable, but they could not agree about whether this particular search was or wasn't a malicious search. (The guard had entered the cell and found a picture of a family member and a letter from home. These items are perfectly legal under prison rules, but the guard tore them up.) The majority opinion stated that it was not a big deal. But Justice Stevens, dissenting, asked: what does an act like this mean to somebody? What does it mean to have the last vestiges of connection with civilization destroyed for no particular reason? He went on to write a very eloquent opinion stating that it was, in fact, a malicious search and seizure, and prisoners have rights against an act like this. This was one of my examples, where the ability to imagine the life of someone who is an outcast was crucial to the outcome. I think that kind of understanding is very much what one wants.

In his confirmation hearings, Supreme Court Justice Breyer was questioned about what he had read recently. I thought that that was an interesting question. He started talking about *Jane Eyre*, saying that when you read Charlotte Brontë you understand that in each house there is a distinct person, and each story is different from every other story. One might think from the outside that all stories are alike, but when one reads them in the manner of a reader of a novel one understands that each person's story is different. I would add that novels also offer particular kinds of understanding of social problems, social asymmetries, the experience of disadvantaged groups. I think those kinds of understanding are particularly important when you are going to be a public actor in a society that has to come to grips with the problems of diversity.

c: How do you choose the texts which you investigate, and what questions do you ask of them?

MN: Sometimes I choose from what I've been teaching, but other times I teach from what I've been working on anyway. It's a two-way relationship. I choose texts that I happen to be gripped by. I never want to write about a literary work that I don't feel some real love for, love for the work or maybe love for the characters or character. I believe that there are many novels that I think very highly of that would be hard for me to write about because I just don't have a particular kind of intense feeling about them. Then there are other texts that I do have a lot of enthusiasm for, but I feel that there is no mystery to them, that I couldn't find my way into them. George Eliot always strikes me that way. I think George Eliot is absolutely marvelous; but I never find myself wanting to write about her work because she already said everything that needs to be said. There is a sort of closed door in that sense. Whereas with Henry James and James Joyce, there seem to be more avenues through which I can find my way into the work. For the law school I knew I wanted to teach some more contemporary novels for the reasons just stated. We read Sophocles' *Philoctetes* and Charles Dickens' *Hard Times*, when we talked about more general issues about imagining and the role of compassion. But, then I wanted to hook the discussion more directly to the students' experience. So we read *Native Son*. We also read Andrea Dworkin's *Mercy*, Joyce Carol Oates's *Black Water* and E.M. Forster's *Maurice*. We read *Maurice* when we talked about gay rights issues. I found that having chosen those works for reasons of the class, I now am interested in writing certainly about *Native Son*. I wrote a review of *Mercy*, but I think I understand it much better now as a result of having taught it.

c: And, the questions that you ask of the text?

MN: I find things coming to me. Certainly with Henry James, all through the things I wrote on James, I was on the track of a group of questions that I would take from one James novel to another. Then sometimes I do things that are a little bit strange like looking at all the places where water is mentioned. I used to do this a lot with Greek tragedy, where they have these wonderful word indexes. If you wanted to find how many times words for deliberation are used in the *Antigone* you could do it in five minutes. I discovered that with James or Marcel Proust it was very difficult to do the same kind of work that I was used to doing on the Greek tragedies. I would make these complicated marginal notes and symbols and make endless lists, noting, for example, every time in *The Ambassadors* where images of light occur. This would often be very helpful groundwork in just getting me closer to the text and getting the sense of its texture. I think that especially with James that was very important because things are so concealed and sometimes they would come out more forcefully so that I could start pursuing them. To give another example, I asked where does "we" occur in *The Golden Bowl* and where does "I" occur? You discover very interesting things if you do that.

My methodology varies. Sometimes it's from the top down, other times from the bottom up. I'll usually bring in some questions that I've been thinking about, but then I also feel that it is very important to not just clamp down those questions but see if I can get very close to the texture of the work and let it throw back its emphases toward me.

Teaching is a good way of doing that because very often the students notice something I didn't. This then makes me see that I ignored something. In many respects I've always found literary dialogue with students more rewarding than with colleagues because most of my philosophical colleagues do not like to read novels. Most of the teaching assistants I get in courses on "Philosophy and the Novel" have not read the novels, so it is really a struggle teaching that kind of course.

c: Do you ever take a look at science fiction?

MN: No, it's funny, I don't. One of my best friends is a big science fiction fan, so I've been lured in that direction. Why don't I like reading science fiction? I do not know because I love reading detective novels of all kinds. I think it is something about the human drama having to do with crime and discovering that is fascinating to me. But science fiction, I think there is great intellectual interest in it, but it isn't a psychological interest. Maybe it is because I do not know the right writers. I think it's human psychology that fascinates me.

c: Would you consider yourself a neo-Aristotelian? Could you tell our readers what a neo-Aristotelian is, and could you speak to the value of a neo-Aristotelian in today's society?

MN: I think I am a neo-Aristotelian, but I think there are so many different understandings of Aristotle and so many different ways of being a neo-Aristotelian that that probably isn't being very informative at this point. There are natural law Catholics who consider themselves, with good reason, to be in an Aristotelian tradition, the one descending from St. Thomas Aquinas. Then there's Alasdair MacIntyre who's closely related to that tradition but is doing something rather different with community and functions within a community. What I think is important to say about my Aristotelianism is that it is a liberal Aristotelianism. If one wanted to give it an historical pedigree it would be in the tradition of the British perfectionist socialists like T.H. Green and Ernest Barker. This view gives a large place to political liberty. Mine is also a universalist Aristotelianism. I think Aristotle's own writings do show or try to show that one can justify a single conception of human flourishing as good for all people regardless of their concrete setting, at least at a high level of generality. But certainly the work I've done myself and the work I've done jointly with Amartya Sen has very much emphasized the defense of a universal notion of quality of life. Of course, one has to be sensitive to local conditions, local understandings and local traditions, but one can still say at a very general level there are certain human functions that we think are important for all human beings. In that way, our Aristotelianism is very close to many peoples' Kantianism, to the kind of Kantianism especially that you see today in people like Barbara Herman, Onora O'Neill and Nancy Sherman, who are presenting Kant in a more human light, stressing Kant's virtue ethic side. I've also been thinking a lot about Kant because it is the two hundreth anniversary of Kant's *Perpetual Peace*, a little work he wrote to sketch a plan for world peace—not exactly for a world government, but for a kind of world understanding deriving from republican traditions in each of the countries. It is a powerful and incredibly moving work, and one of the things that is most moving about it is the sad fact that people are turning away from those ideals and back toward ethnocentric particularism and nationalism. I find this very pernicious. I feel in these circumstances the need to accentuate up the Kantian side of my Aristotle and the Stoic side, if you will, for I think that Kant read the Stoics far more than he read Aristotle.

For me being a neo-Aristotelian primarily means thinking about the human good as composed of a number of different human activities that are not commensurable with one another and thinking of friendship as being a terribly important part of the human good. Aristotle considered the human being by nature as a social and political being. He held that practical reasoning needs to grapple not only with universal rules but with the concrete particulars of social circumstances, and that humans have to find a way of bringing those together fruitfully. Those are the things that I think being an Aristotelian means: I also think being an Aristotelian means giving the emotions and emotional development a substantial place in your conception of what a good person is. Aristotle thought a good person was one who thought of emotions as intelligent rather than unintelligent, having the notion of character as part of one's goal. But I would make all this part of a liberal cosmopolitanism. I was at a conference recently, and I said in the question period that I'm a Kantian cosmopolitan. People seemed very surprised at that. They thought that they had gotten me wrong and I felt that maybe they had. I think that in some of my earlier writings I didn't talk a lot about political issues, so my universalism did not come out so plainly. I think that it was always there, and in the preface of *Love's Knowledge* I did talk about the search for an account of how to live as a completely general project. But now I believe that one should accentuate these things more and also accentuate more the role of political liberty. In my development work the issue arises whether one shouldn't just put economic and social well-being first and forget about political liberty or let that come in second. Both Sen and I increasingly stress that we think political liberty is not only intrinsically of enormous importance, but a *sine qua non* of any lasting economic and social well-being. There is so much bashing of the Enlightenment that is going on right now that I want to accentuate that side of what it is for me to be neo-Aristotelian.

c: In your essay, "The Literary Imagination and the Public Life," you look at Dickens' *Hard Times* and analyze his critique of neo-classical economics. You and Dickens both speak to how economic methodologies are conventionally used. You show how crude aggregations of individual utility maximizers, or GNP, are inadequate as quality of life indicators. In the beginning of the paper you state that economists, lawyers and judges should use novels in integral ways in their disciplines and in our own public life. Could you elaborate how economists or how development economics could actually use novels, not just to critique, but to evolve their disciplines of thought?

MN: It's easy to see this in the law, because it is actually happening in the law. What's very interesting is that courses in law and literature weren't just dreamed up by us philosophers or literary interlopers. They have been in the curricula for some time. There has been an ongoing dialogue between legal economists and people who teach narrative. There has even been an ongoing dialogue within certain individuals. I am thinking of Richard A. Posner, who is obviously the prototype for Mr. Gradgrind, in my essay, but who is also a great lover of literature. He was the one who taught the course in law and literature before I came to Chicago. In fact, he wrote an incredibly literary and imaginative opinion in a sexual harassment case which I discuss in *Poetic Justice*. It was the case of the first woman who worked in the tinsmith shop in General Motors. The only way that he was able to consider her situation to determine whether the harassment that she endured was sufficiently intimidating and damaging to her work performance was to allow his imagination to empathize with the woman. The argument ran as follows: one side said, everyone used foul language in the workplace. The woman pointed out that she was the only woman and the men were doing things like defacing her toolbox, cutting out the seat of her overalls and so on for five years. Posner had to listen to these stories and imagine the situation for himself, asking what was plausible and what was not. There one really saw Posner's literary imagination coming out, and the fact that he had been teaching a course on law and the novel. One saw the fruits of that in his opinion, and I would like to foster that sort of dialogue in the law school. I certainly aim to do that.

As far as economics goes, what both Sen and I tried to do when we co-authored the introduction to *The Quality of Life* was to say if you just think about *Hard Times*, for example, you'll notice components of life quality that are left out of account in the usual economic calculations. Just the habits of reading, thinking and caring about a novel like *Hard Times* will make one notice what is wrong with some of these ways of economic modeling. How does one promote that kind of noticing? If you're in the undergraduate curriculum, people take two different courses and maybe even connect them. It is harder to make inroads on the professional disciplines, like economics. The reason is not because these people can't see the point, but because very often the technical models that are in use are built over the foundation of a certain way of conceiving things. These technical models are themselves extremely sophisticated, and that is what people really want to work on. It is very hard to convince people to go back to foundations and to reconceive the foundations. I don't think that there were very many economists in our project who were willing to do that. What would happen and what does happen is that people say X has stopped doing economics and X is doing philosophy now; isn't that interesting? This is their prejudicial way of describing the fact that X is no longer doing technical modeling and recognizing what they recognize. There is a tremendous resistance and foundational critique in economics. The other social sciences are more open because they are technically less successful. In a sense, it is the technical sophistication and success of economics that is the obstacle.

What can one do, but try and engage the people who appear interested in being engaged? Interestingly enough, you would think that the Chicago school would be the most dogmatic in some respects. But, someone like Gary Becker, the Nobel Prize winning economist, on the other hand, has been a pioneer in taking economics into other areas of human life, like the family, which is not a usual scene for technical economics.

For this reason he's very open to other people's new ideas. He's always been more engaged with ordinary life than many economists, and I look forward to speaking with him. I've been to Becker's Rational Choice Workshop, and I think that in that kind of setting, which is an interdisciplinary workshop, you would hope to have those ideas filter into the profession.

c: Why is the novel your focus?

MN: Of course, I'm interested in drama, too. I think the novel certainly in its rise, as Ian P. Watt showed in *The Rise of the Novel*, was strongly associated with the rise of democracy. It was the genre that drew your attention to ordinary people and their life stories with a new kind of focused attention and delight. Ordinary people, of course, appeared in Greek tragedy, but as figures of fun. It wasn't so often that you had the mundane facts of daily life of an ordinary person presented to you as if that's the person you should really care about; that's the person whose story is worth your sustained attention. This interest in the ordinary attracts me greatly when I think about the role of reading in a democratic citizenship. And, the novel has the ability to move you around from rich to poor and make you aware of differences and fortune, and how the differences in fortune make a difference to human flourishing. Because of its concreteness the form is well suited to investigate the shaping of human projects by concrete circumstances of class and gender. Due to these it surpasses other forms.

c: What about the value and virtue of lyric poetry?

MN: I love lyric poetry and I've written almost nothing about it. The only lyric poetry that I've written about is Walt Whitman, who might actually be an exception, because he is such a narrative poet and, in a way, a novelistic poet. I think lyric poetry, like music, is very difficult to write about. I think it's of greatest interest in thinking about human emotion and human desire, but immensely difficult to write about for many of the same reasons I think it's difficult to write on a symphony of Gustav Mahler. Maybe that is why I haven't done much of it. I actually do try and write about music in the emotions book, because I believe it is such an important part of my life. If I didn't try and say something about music, it would be a cop-out. So I do try and talk about Mahler and emotional trajectories in a Mahler symphony. However, I think there is what Mahler himself called a halting translation when you try to put something that is crafted and shaped in another symbolic medium into your own prose. There is something like that problem when you try to express a lyric poem in your halting prose.

c: You tend to use the prototypes of the classic novel in your writings. In our last interview, we interviewed Jean-Claude Martineau, the former spokesperson for Haitian President Jean-Bertrand Aristide, and in that interview Martineau states that today sons and daughters of slaves are starting to master writing. They are now the ones being recognized as writing the important contemporary novels and are being awarded Nobel Prizes in Literature. Do you think that today the classics have something more ethically relevant than current literature worldwide, or is it that you have more of an affinity to the classics?

MN: No, I don't think that at all. In fact, I just bought and started to read James Kelman's *How Late It Was, How Late*, because I am fascinated by what he said about the Booker Prize scandal. He recently talked about the effort to win recognition and acknowledgment for the lives of ordinary people. He said that it is easy enough to use the high literary language and to write as if the working-class peoples' imaginations use the same language. But once the language of the working-class is on the page everyone is scandalized and upset because four letter words are being used, and so on. When thinking about *Native Son*, which does stay within the category of high language, one must look at more recent novels to see how their language has evolved.

I find that when I travel to other countries I very often run into problems when presenting examples from contemporary fiction. It's very interesting to ask which works I can talk about, that people have read? Take for example Proust. While I was recently in Sweden I could talk about Proust without any problem. Most people know Dickens, so Dickens can also be used as an example in one of my presentations. Henry James is not very well known, because his style is hard to render in Swedish. While in Sweden, I wanted to talk about *Native Son*, because I'm so enthusiastic about it right now. Not one person in Sweden that I encountered in three cities had ever read or even heard of *Native Son*. If I were to go from *Native Son* to James Kelman then I'd really run aground. I think this is a real problem. If one sticks with Sophocles then the result is an international audience.

Take people from India, for instance. If I'm at an international development meeting and I want to give an example from literature, I can use the *Antigone* without a problem. But, the minute I move away from an *Antigone* and toward the novel at all, I enter a localized medium. I don't know what to say about that except that I think that it is a problem.

While in Sweden I participated in a Dialogue Seminar in Stockholm where we publicly discussed emotions and reasoning. I gave a talk on emotion and reason, and a poet named Agneta Pleyel talked about emotions in her poetry. Two actors from Ingmar Bergman's troupe read speeches by Sophocles and Euripides. The actors never would have read a text by Richard Wright, because it would not have had any resonance for that particular audience. Choosing particular examples is a real challenge. Each country is different. I find in continental Europe, Proust is fine and Dickens is pretty well known. Shakespeare, of course, you can always talk about, and I might move more toward Shakespeare probably for that reason. Another contemporary piece that I'm interested in talking about is the Indian writer Vikram Seth's *A Suitable Boy*, but that would be unknown outside England, North America and India. Because I visit India I'm fascinated by the country, and Seth's *A Suitable Boy* is quite a Dickensian novel and slightly anachronistic. But, I love it, and I like to talk about it.

c: Do you think the world's scope of literature will be opening up?

MN: I certainly hope so but I think a lot depends on what gets translated. I do think the Swedes are tremendously energetic about translation, even though most Swedes read English. In countries like Germany, people can really make a living as a translator. But then I also think a lot about the imperialism of the English language, and how that is going to play itself out. But, maybe literary reviews like compost could foster an international climate.

c: How do you find Whitman accepted outside America?

MN: I'm not sure. I did talk about Whitman in Sweden. I didn't get much of a response. I don't think that Swedes read Whitman very much. I spoke a bit about Whitman when I was responding to René Girard at a conference. That was quite fun. I think René Girard and Whitman's sensibilities were quite different, and that's why I wanted to talk about Whitman. I think at the conference, both Girard and the audience, the people working on his work, all knew Whitman. They were mostly Americans, and I think that Whitman probably isn't read outside America. Is that your impression?

c: Whitman has been translated heavily into Chinese Mandarin. He is also fervently read in Latin America, because Frederico García Lorca loved him. Lorca wrote "An Ode to Walt Whitman," and Pablo Neruda, Ernesto Cardenal, and Octavio Paz all loved Lorca so they too were interested in Whitman. Paz's essay on Whitman may be the best written on him in the Americas. I recently worked with a poet from Turkey, and beside Nazim Hikmet, Whitman was his favorite poet. He had a Turkish-translated volume of *Leaves of Grass*. I'm sure poetries of the bardic tradition have translated Whitman due to him being the American bard.

MN: Whereas probably in Germany Whitman might be viewed as a bit rough.

c: Approximately one-quarter of the world population that resides in the northern industrialized countries consume three-quarters of the world's resources leaving the other three-quarters of the world population the remaining one-quarter resources. How could we as a population live a good life and flourish democratically with these limitations upon us? Do these limitations carry a different responsibility?

MN: People don't know the answers to a lot of important, practical questions, such as how agricultural development could serve the needs of increasing numbers of people. All that is stuff that has to be worked on, and we have to keep working on development while trying to reduce consumption. These issues of international justice really ought to be at the forefront of every major discussion of political justice. In fact, in our quality of life project, we knew we had to begin with the idea of the nation-state, because that is how international agencies measure welfare. We thought if we make the information available to the public in comparative form, as the United Nations Development Program does in its human development reports, we would at least have an informal incentive to begin a discussion of global justice. The discouraging thing to me is how little interested politicians really are in this.

A deep form of isolationism is emerging. In Sheldon Hackney's Planning Meeting for the Conversation of American Identity, the issue of how America is related to the rest of the world wasn't even on the agenda, at least not initially. But, several of us fought to get that included, and it was added. The idea that we are not just a nation but a group of human beings who have obligations of many sorts to other human beings and the rest of the world is the central idea of Kant's *Perpetual Peace*. Not even the ancient Greek Stoics have been taken on board by political discussion and political institutions. It's scary because I think that if those discussions are not held, and not held in an intelligent way, things will happen in a random and destructive manner. I think that's quite terrible. What I try to do is focus on education and the curriculum. I think by focusing on things such as education and the curriculum individuals will be more aware of the rest of the world. I think that is happening, and I think it needs to happen much more. When I teach feminism I always spend a third of the course focusing on the status of women in developing countries while most feminist courses focus on the problems of European and North American women. Many feminist courses do not focus on this. As a result, students don't learn about what the lives of other women are like. I think the more knowledge one can pack into the curriculum the more that will provide at least an incentive for people to continue learning. Usually people have good intentions, but they are lazy. They're ignorant. If one could get them going then hopefully something will happen.

c: The focus of the June 7, 1995, episode of Nightline was on the fact that religion can no longer be a means of teaching morals and ethics. Rather what we are seeing now is a manifestation of how to deal with that through the teaching of literature and ethics. *The Book of Virtues* is a good example. Can you talk about how the displacement of religion with literary ethics affects the high school as an institution of learning?

MN: I reviewed William Bennett's *The Book of Virtues* in The New Republic. Of course, Bennett is talking much more about young children than high school students. I think you can certainly discuss novels that have a religious dimension, and I think that it is probably an important thing to do in high school. But I do think that at all ages—and this is Bennett's idea, too—having narrative examples of virtues is an important way of teaching. One can't understand what the virtuous action comes to in the abstract for very much the reasons Aristotle gave. Virtue consists so much with grappling well with concrete particulars of a circumstance that one constantly asks the question: how would the person of practical wisdom behave here? Or as the law usually says; what would the reasonable person do? Stories help individuals discover how people of many different cultures can face different situations with courage, compassion and so on. Often we interpret our own lives through the lens of stories. If we don't have narrative structures from literature in our minds we lack a crucial tool for decoding what's happening to us in our own lives and projecting into the future what we might be and what we might do. So, I do think that high school education should definitely continue to do that, but I think it is also important for precisely the reason—and here maybe I'm differing from Bennett—that a high school literary education should include works of literature that bring students in contact with the experience of groups in their society that they might urgently need to understand. Bennett does make a point of this concerning race and the history of slavery. He devotes a lot of space to that. He also comments on the history of the struggle for women's independence, notably the suffrage movement. Unfortunately, he didn't get closer to the present day than that. But internationalism he is equivocal about. He does include some stories from other cultures, but not much about the struggles of other cultures.

Psalm for My Pilón
Jack Agueros

Lord,
you placed a wooden
chalice in my kitchen,
my mortar, my pilón.

I mashed millions
of garlic cloves,
poured oceans of olive oil
sprinkled little leaves
of oregano like endless autumns
and now they all live in the wood
like sap in a tree
blood in my veins.

Sometimes, when I am hungry
I stick my nose in that pilón
and inhale and raise it over my head.

Lord, then angels rush to my side
ring bells and set tables
open the dam on my salivary glands,
and together our spirits dine
on fumes alone.

Interview with Victor Hernandez Cruz   [1996]

Cindy Schuster: How long have you been back in Puerto Rico? How has returning to the island affected your writing?

VHC: I've been back here in Puerto Rico eight years now and I'm beginning to publish in Spanish. The body of my work is in English; it's an English sprinkled with Spanish words, especially my early writings, where I was still cultivating a form of English that you could say was Spanglish, at points, though not all the time. I more or less moved in books like *Mainland* and afterwards into an English that's more English. English with an occasional visitation of a Spanish word, which doesn't change the fact that I'm thinking in Spanish on occasion, and that the syntax of the English writing still has a Spanish interior. Coming here was nothing easy. I was discouraged much at the beginning, and I thought perhaps of going back. It's not like flipping over an omelet; it's something more complex. It's living a language, it's dreaming in a language, and it's feeling insect bites in a language; feeling this humidity, swatting at mosquitoes is part of writing for me. So, I'm beginning to feel the Spanish more, as a language actually closer to my body. It's closer to my mestizo body, it's full of all the invasions, it's full of imperialism, it's full of colonialism, it's full of the age of the Conquest. Spanish has Arabian words, Jewish words, Gypsy words, African words, Taíno words; it has the story of my body. So it's a much more interesting thing for my soul and my mind to come out writing in Spanish, which has all these ingredients, whereas in English I have to do somewhat more explaining. No matter what the poems are about in Spanish, they're always about this mestizaje, they're always about this body. They're always about history.

CS: How does that play out in terms of what happens to the language?

VHC: They have told me I do things awkward in Spanish too. Just like I have an accent in English, I also have an accent when I speak Spanish. It's like I grew up totally in stereophonics; so I grew up with the initial layer of one language being erased by English, but never so much erased that it changes from one into the other totally. There's always the lingering shape, rolls of the tongue to keep the accent. Now I'm learning on both sides of the fence; it's always a study of myself in that particular intersection where history touches me as a person and where my person enters into history. In my case it's a Caribbean stance, a Puerto Rican stance, an island stance, it's the content of the migrations of going into the States, what happened to us there, and the kind of cultural discussion that goes on there, of growing up with the subtropical memory. So that is possibly happening in both languages at the same time. The thing is to filter them finally to one side or the other. More and more, I write either in Spanish or in English, and less and less I write in Spanglish. I figure languages are already mixed, as it is, and all languages partake of each other in their processes of evolution.

CS: So your writing is coming from a different place now.

VHC: Yes, because here the difference has been not just in terms of language, but also the personal life that I'm leading. I'm filling in certain gaps that were put there by the migration, when I was five. I grew up in New York hearing stories of a place that was not in my presence. So I was hungry for that presence, for that place. By coming here I'm filling in the content of things that were in me as memory or nostalgia, so that things actually become more concrete—everything from the name of a fruit to the name of an insect that I run into, that I finally see, a word that I used to recognize and hear and know, without knowing what it was connected to. Now I'm learning.

CS: So you imagined them differently...

VHC: I would imagine them differently; I would transport them to places that they didn't belong. My poetry was always kind of out of context, definitely out of physical, geographic space. I mean, pineapple under snow in New York City, or seeing someone with a stick of cane through a snow blizzard. Some people might call it surrealism, but it was just my memory working at a cultural level/layer that was constantly wondering about and juxtaposing these things. My poetry has always been about a memory of some other place, no matter what place that was. So even now the same thing occurs with the United States and the stuff I do here in Spanish.

CS: Are you writing about New York?

VHC: I can write about New York splendidly from here. And about California, where I was for 20 years. So my poetry, like my life, is pretty much that discussion between geographic spaces and cultural tinges.

CS: It's interesting to me that you locate your writing at an intersection. I used to conceptualize the process of bilingual writing as one of always looking with two sets of eyes, from two different places at the same time, which is quite different from being at the center of where the two linguistic and cultural experiences intersect, or, as you say, where the individual intersects with history. It has different implications for your writing.

VHC: Of course, languages are sound. So for the first years of my life English was sound, some form of yakety-yak. I didn't really start learning English until I started going to school. But in terms of what I was actually hearing, and I think this is true for other bilingual people in the United States, it's a form of sound cubism. It's like distorted geometric space. You keep hearing the two languages, so if you get creative with it there's all kinds of potential possibilities for writing, for describing things, and all kinds of awkwardnesses that come out.

Foreigners have always done guerrilla warfare against the English language. Because of my bilingual situation, I tend to read a lot of people who have migrated from one language to the next. Like Joseph Conrad, who comes from Polish way in his mid-20's when he starts writing in English. If you read some of those sentence structures that he has, they're quite beautiful, but also quite awkward, some of them. And if you read other people like this Russian guy Nabokov, if you take a novel like *Ada*, you'll see that there are a lot of foreign words—Russian words, French words—in it, and there are also a lot of words that drive you to a dictionary, where you have the sense that he's always writing with a dictionary in his hands, always searching for a word that's very far from common usage. Why? Because his sense of the language is not one of common usage, but of a writer who is not used to English sounds. So you constantly see that in his work, these beautiful words. Whereas an American writer would use the most immediate word to describe something: Nabokov would go out of his way to make you go to the dictionary. He would use some dormant, elaborate word that you are not quite familiar with. Then there are all these Indian writers; there are 176 languages in India and I think English has become like a common denominator for many of them. So much of their great writing is done in English, whether or not they're dreaming it in Tamil, or some other language.

The phenomenon of bilingualism is the center of literature in any given time, for any given people, in any given geographic space. That happened to me against my will, in a sense, because I'm part of a migration that moves from here, for whatever the reasons were—they've been blaming it on Muñoz Marín, the economic situation, international capitalism and their games of moving international campesino populations away from one space and into another. Whatever the reason, I'm part of that crowd that was manipulated and that moved around with an agricultural campesino culture into early 1950s Manhattan, and that's how I grew up, slowly coming to an understanding, blending into an English, perhaps against my will. It wasn't a choice as it was for Nabokov, or perhaps for him there was also no choice; he was part of that Russian aristocracy that had to leave after the Revolution. I don't know what Joseph Conrad's reasons were for changing from one language into the other, or Jerzy Kosinzky's, or Fernando Pessoa's, or a whole lot of other writers who have switched; there have been different reasons for those switches.

Actually, I don't know of a poet I can think of who's not steeped in another language. I mean if you take the *Cantos* by Ezra Pound, there's like 22 languages in there. And there's the case of William Carlos Williams, how he dealt with growing up in two languages. He was half Puerto Rican; his mother was from Mayagüez. So he has all these refrains and all these Spanish flurries throughout his work. I would even say he's one of the fathers of Spanglish as a literary form, in his book *Kora in Hell*, in 1921. And then he had a book called *Al que quiere*, which was titled in Spanish, but the poems were written in English. That was in 1917. So he is one of the fathers of the bilingual poetry movement, and William Carlos Williams was one of the great American poets. Williams, Pound, and Eliot are the three modernist American poets. He grew up listening to the broken English of his mother, and you can almost see that in some of his work. There's a sense of foreignness in the way he approaches his English. And in my language the same thing is constantly happening. I'm doing poems in a language that the thought process is not in, and that's what I think would be interesting in my poetry and that of other bilingual poets in the States. We're doing guerrilla warfare against English, the same guerrilla warfare that Nabokov, Conrad, and the Indian writers did. And we just bring it home in a much more dramatic way since we're immediately within the source of our differentness, which is always resupplying us.

CS: Do you find there's an interplay between freedom and limitation when a writer goes from one language to another?

VHC: Cabrera Infante, the Cuban writer, has been writing very well in English now. His writing in English takes him away from certain customs. There's a lot of custom in the Spanish language and in the Spanish and Latin American culture. There's much more ritual, festival, and ceremony. You get away from that when you write in a different language. And you get away from refrains. For example, he won't say *se lo comió*; that's a popular

Cuban saying to make the point that someone excelled, did something well. A Cuban would say *se lo comió*, "he ate it up." But you might say that differently in English, and you might not be enticed into finding that connection or that vocabulary, or that flurry might not show up as quickly. So you tend to explore a different area of originality. You open up; sometimes you might be even freer if you get away from the strictures and the grammar of the Spanish language, which is much more elaborate than English. Spanish is less free than English. English is more anarchistic because it is more possible to create your own style as you go along.

CS: It really changes our perception of literature and writing if we take bilingualism as a norm as opposed to something out there on the margins.

VHC: It's the center and not an aberration. Multiculturalism and multiracialism are the center of human progress and human culture. There's a certain mid-American point, a certain mid-population point in the United States of frightened WASPS that could be involved in a massive schizophrenic dementia with regard to what true history is. If they had read their own Greek history they would know that Alexander charged into Egypt, that during another invasion 10,000 Greek soldiers married 10,000 Persian wives, that these things constantly went on and people changed not only cuisines but looks. This was the beginning of their own greco-romano-western-occidental history. So if that's one of the roots that a certain middle point in the U.S. wants to get to, then they're certainly out of it by being paranoid about multiculturalism, multiracialism, and bilingualism. They're the aberration, they're backwards, paleolithic. I notice that when I'm in the States. I don't notice it as much here. The whole word minority, all these kinds of words…

CS: They don't make much sense anymore.

VHC: Not here.… Thus the debate between us and English, and also North American culture is, how much is that culture willing to change? We're not going to change, because we're at this other source, drinking from this well that we think is richer. I don't know how other immigrant groups have negotiated their process of Northamericanization, whether it's one generation or a generation and a half, and then they're doing pretty much a North American thing, perhaps with some memorial glances at certain aspects of their ethnicity.

CS: But it's been with that idea of blending in and the whole melting pot…

VHC: And it's the end of the melting pot with the Latino element, because the Latino element will not melt within the pot, but will change the ingredients, will change the dish so much that it creates a discussion of "we all have to change." Look what happened here in the Americas. The Spanish were here, but who here can say they're Spanish now, who can say they're not partially African, or who can say they're anything in this sense? And that's a debate that the Latino-American poets who grew up with English in the States are bringing to the North American scene. This is going to change radically; it's not going to melt, it's going to change right now. The idea of multiculturalism, of different cultures sitting next to each other changes, because then it becomes not so much multicultural, but cultures that blend and mix into one. Each becomes something different in the process, something that wasn't there before, which is what's happening in Latin America, and in Caribbean America. And it's funny how even though that happens, still each particular ingredient stays stronger than it does in the places where there's a conscious effort to separate cultures and races. The place where it begins to be like the Caribbean, there, is New Orleans. That's a place where there is a richness in cultures. You have gumbo, you have the origins of jazz, you have the influence of the Latino, the Caribbean, the Spanish, and the French there.

CS: One of the things that has always intrigued me about your poetry is how you create what I think of as "bilingual metaphors." To me this reflects a more complex articulation of bilingualism than simply sprinkling a basically English poem with a few Spanish words. For example, in "Snaps of Immigration" you write:

> I dream with suitcases
> full of illegal fruits
> Interned between white
> guayaberas that dissolved
> Into snowflaked polyester.

This non-idiomatic rendering of *soñar con*, really makes the reader do a double take; it multiplies the levels of interpretation and in a sense reveals the two languages to each other. Whereas in English we normally say "to dream about"; the simple change of preposition alters our perception of the experience. If you dream with something you accompany it, you are closer to it, together, rather than watching it as an observer. To dream with suitcases brings the history one carries into the present and then on to the imagined future. It also blurs the line between dreaming and sleeping.

VHC: Because it means the same thing in Spanish. The noun *sueño* is both dream and sleep at the same time, whereas in English you have "dream," and you have "sleep." They're different. There's a lot of things like that in Spanish. Also the order of things is what I find interesting. Sometimes what in Spanish you would put first, in English you would put last, so that it's not a direct or literal flipping over of things. It's a way of ordering, of rearranging.

CS: Your metaphors are very explosive. Those suitcases might as well be full of bombs.

VHC: Linguistic bombs. That's what I bring; it's a tool to change the language to meet my own needs, to the mix of a person who's thinking, who's living a life with these pendulums between North and South, the Caribbean and urbanity, English and Spanish, and a debate with history from a personal point of view. My poetry is research in that direction. It's an unreading of the tapestry that history has made, with the confluence of everything in the Caribbean: music, cuisine, architecture, the combinations of things that have come together, which to me is the center of real human history. Its purpose is to continue to inform from that point of view, to make humanity more aware of that.

It's not a poetry written at random, or, "Oh, I've got a fanciful idea," or "I've been inspired." I mean I might have those inspirations but they have been filtered through a system, through a thought pattern, through a process, to filter with what my concerns are. So if they don't meet those necessities then they're just words that come rambling through that I don't need. And they're useless to me; they don't serve my purpose, my poetic mission. I truly believe in poetic centers and missions; there's an ecological sense in Gary Snyder's poetry, a political sense in Carolyn Forché's poetry, a gender concern in Robert Bly's poetry. Other poets have different concerns. You can feel them churning and searching and centering their language to this mission, no matter what their poetry is about. It could be about something haphazard down the street, but it has to connect back to what their center is. There's something higher than the discussion of the narrative or the metaphors. You have to bring it to the plane of sensual ideas, and into a discussion with history rather than an individual. So I try to do those things in my poetry. Of course, the first thing is whatever the poem is about; it's about that plus the way I make it meet this concern that I have with immigration, bilingualism, Caribbean history, multiracialism, the way we are down here.

What does it mean, to be playing this note in the world? To be in a sense, what Benítez Rojo says in *The Repeating Island*, from chaos. The Caribbean is organized chaos. And it's interesting to be at least at a single point of it, as if you were in a spider web, and from your particular string you can step back and see the whole thing, the connections, and to be able to describe and decipher them constantly, whether it's through dance, music, the cuisine, a drink, a juice, the fruits… To know we have native fruits still growing, to know that that's being Taíno, that you're feeling that right now in the post-industrial age. All these things are simultaneously going on. There's simultaneity and chaos and different time zones also going on, at the same time. If you were to drive out now to my hometown, you would find a different time sense there. It's still agricultural, more campesino. You have jokes about fruits and vegetables. And if you go deeper you're not just going into the island, you're going back in time. All these ages living one next to the other, different time spaces in people's heads, and how they connect being together, is interesting to see and to feel, as a writer. People are next to each other but not necessarily in full communication. Only aspects of them communicate with each other. There's somebody in the 1940s, somebody in the 1950s, and somebody in the year 2010 around here. And that is interesting because you can see that curve from agriculture going into industry a little bit more down here, especially when you leave this metroplex area. That's another reason I wanted to come down here, to feel that kind of curve that goes from the vegetable to the saran wrap. And to talk with people who still converse as an art form, who hit the balconies and converse rather than watching CNN or MTV, because they're still not obsessed with news as information. People who still have a sense of local color. So I wanted to be able to come back and see that, as opposed to feeling it from memory or nostalgia back in the States. All of those things influence the tempo and the structures of my poetry.

CS: What do you think of the *chupacabras*?

VHC: It's an interesting phenomenon. During the 40s and 50s they had all kinds of sightings of the Virgin Mary here, under the mango trees and on coconut palms. Back when the economy was real bad. So I don't know if it was like campesino hallucinations were going on collectively because of the bad conditions; *o sea, no había comida,* there was no food, and people

251

might have been literally hallucinating. But also, there might be another aspect. There might be some experimentation going on, at some very high government levels, using third world countries, perhaps even the island of Puerto Rico, given our situation as a territory, to bring together spermatoza of humans with animals, and incubating them either in women or in some contraption, and creating creatures. That either is going on or has been experimented with, sort of like some form of *Rosemary's Baby*.

CS: Or the X-Files.

VHC: Or the X-Files. People have spotted this creature which is like half-dog or goat or bull, half-human with something like fish scales on the side, that hops away or flies away real fast, or that comes around like Dracula and drinks animals' blood. Nobody has brought this thing in, or perhaps some people have found it and the government has come in right away and taken back their inventions. On this island there have been all kinds of experiments in the past, chemicals that have been used illegally without workers' knowledge. Men have grown breasts here, and women have grown moustaches. This was all in the past, but I don't know exactly what the *chupacabras* sensation is. I guess if you know about it, then it's pretty widespread.

CS: There was a story on the front page of the *Boston Globe* recently saying that it had been sighted in Cambridge. And it's all over Mexico, where it's become a political metaphor for former president Carlos Salinas, who is portrayed as sucking the economy dry.

VHC: What I heard in Puerto Rico was the first sighting, and then Mexico, and Panama, maybe Venezuela, so they all happened in countries on the Caribbean rim. I didn't know good old middle-class Cambridge with all those scientific intellectuals. You know, if they're seeing it up there, then it's beyond Latin American campesino hallucinations, and there could be something there; I don't know what to think of that precisely.

CS: What are you working on now?

VHC: *Panoramas* will be out in 1997 from Coffee House Press.

CS: Which is poetry and essays?

VHC: Yes. There's a long introductory essay called "Hometown," which describes my hometown, and the life there when I was a kid. I reproduce a lot of things there, and I imagine some too. I also do that in my poetry. I imagine from facts, so I'm not always precise as to history, but then I'm not a historian, so I can take those liberties. There's essays in there, and short stories, and a very long poem based on Puerto Rican landscapes, "Panorama." There's been a rich tradition of Puerto Rican poetry describing the landscape. Some important Spanish poets made this their home for a while, like Pedro Salinas, and Juan Ramón Jiménez, who won the Nobel Prize while he was teaching at the University here in 1956. And if you read the poetry of the last period of their lives, it's full of Puerto Rican terrains, and light, and ocean waves, and fruits, and all of that; it's rich in our landscape. So I've done a very long poem, which to me is like a landscape poem/painting.

I'm also working on my first collection in Spanish, which will be all the stuff that I've written here in Spanish directly, and I'm also thinking of translating some stuff. I'm going to translate knowing that they're going to become new poems anyway, versions, or what I call reocurrencias. *Ocurren otra vez el poema y el espíritu*, the spirit of the poem occurs again, as I write it from a Caribbean point of view. I want to do that a lot with the English poems that I've done. And of course I'm doing this novel, which is now in its third version.

CS: Tell me about the novel.

VHC: The novel is called *Time Zones*, and it has to do with the sense I was talking to you about that I have of people being in different epochs, with the industrialization of our island, how we took a rocket into the new age of machines and factories, from basically an agrarian, campesino structure, and what effect that had on the psyche of the people. I think it debilitated people, it kind of took their pacing out of them, and it changed their stories. It did something to the home remedies, the old poetry of the *declamadores*, the singers. Not that they're not there anymore; they're still there, but it changes them. They're less there. They'd be more there had it not been for the industrialization of the island.

I believe that writing needs a certain sense of non-writing, of oralness, of communication. And its form as writing is secondary to its form as human communication. So to me, human communication, people conversing, refrains, that which is alive in a language group is very important to my writing. For that's the state of the language that you have. The other thing is not language, the other thing is literature. If you want to look at the stuff that's in books, then you're dealing with the state of literature that's based on the stage of people who are working on the language as sound, especially poets. And narrators to a certain extent too, because they have to listen to gossip, and hear people's language and the way they communicate with each other. Poets should always be able to have access to the sounds of things, the sounds of nature, trees, and rivers, and the sounds of people conversing in different types of human communities, whether it be gypsies, or southern sharecroppers, or southwest cowboys in Colorado, or dock workers in San Francisco, or street people in Chelsea, New York. Each one of those is a special kind of vernacular; they each have a certain kind of verbal territory. And it would be important for an artist, or for a writer that's coming out from their midst to be connected to that, and not just to learn the language, from books about them. In Spain, for example, all the great writers came from Andalucia, which is the most illiterate part of Spain. And they have the best, the most interesting singing traditions, and oral traditions, and they have the gypsies, the flamencos, and rich oral folk customs.

The campesino group is a vital thing to nourish, to keep alive, so there can be a balance between them and what urban life has developed into, or what a university student is, or a technological worker, or a computer programmer. Those things are being nourished now as professions of the future, but we have to nourish the handicrafts, the folk remedies, the artisans, so that we can keep good wood, good leather, good things done with gourds, good crafts, good language, and good conversation alive all the time.

We have to think about the future and not bring one group up to destroy the other group, the way we're doing to certain species, to nature, and the wild preserves of the world. All of what I see is connected, the language of a campesino telling a story is just as important as a tree in El Yunque. We have to water them both, so he can keep telling his story and his children can find a place to hear that story and to use that story, even if his children grow up to be yuppies, and become computer programmers. They have to find usefulness in their lives. Everything cannot be futuristic. We have to use what is in the past, which is always here. So that's what the novel is about, and that's why it's been real complicated writing it.

CS: Is that why you moved back to Puerto Rico?

VHC: That's one of the reasons. I wanted to be able to talk to the tobacco makers who used to roll tobacco with my grandfather, who was a tobacconist. They're notorious storytellers and they used to pay a reader to come in and read the paper, or a magazine, or Cervantes, or Victor Hugo in Spanish. They'd be working and there would be this guy reading the chapter, and these guys would be listening. So, I wanted to feel some of those people, pre-television people, pre-ELA or pre-Muñoz Marín society people, and be able to talk to them.

CS: Does it all take place here, or does it go to New York?

VHC: It has flights into New York. On one occasion there's a flight into East Harlem, and from East Harlem I have a description of the Palladium nightclub in New York City, the famous Latin spot, around 53rd and Broadway. There are also letters that come in from New York, of people describing life on the eastern seaboard back to people here who have to hear about things that they have never seen. Trains, subways, snow, fire escapes, wrought iron, rooftops of tar, the imagery.

CS: It seems in a way to parallel what you said about being a kid in New York and hearing about Caribbean fruits and imagining what they were like. It's kind of the flip side of that, people hearing about a place they've never been to; they don't have nostalgia about it, but they hear about these things and have to imagine what they're like.

VHC: There's also the fact that in the early 50s, television was not as diffused as it is now. So when Latin American people started moving into the North American scene at the time, from 45 to 54 or so, they had no visual pictures of where they were going. There was nothing to prepare one. Whereas today you could be in the Himalayas and have a T.V. and you could see the Manhattan skyline, you could have an idea of what that's about so if you move to New York you more or less have a visual sense of what you might be getting into. Media and television have made the world smaller and brought people together so that the shock of moving around is different now.

CS: Even so, those T.V. images are obviously very different from the reality that people actually encounter when they migrate. Visually they might be able to recognize it, but their lives aren't going to be like that.

VHC: There is a saying, "*no es lo mismo llamar al diablo que verlo venir.*" So it's never the same. You can call the devil all night long, and things are going to be all right, but when you see him coming, that's when you're going to have a real experience.

255

from The Lower East Side
Victor Hernandez Cruz

Where did the mountains go
The immigrants ask
The place where houses
and objects went back
Into history which guided
Them into nature
Entering the roots of plants
The molasses of fruit
To become eternal again,
Now the plaster of Paris
Are the ears of the walls
The first utterances in Spanish
Recall what was left behind.

People kept arriving
as the cane fields dried
Flying bushes from another
planet
Which had a pineapple for
a moon
Vegetables and tree bark
popping out of luggage
The singers of lament
into the soul of Jacob Riis
Where the prayers Santa Maria
Through remaining fibers
of the Torah
Eldridge St. lelolai
A Spanish never before seen
Inside gypsies
Once Cordova the Kabala
Haberdasheries of Orchid St.
Hecklers riddling bargains
Like in gone bazaars of
Some Warsaw ghetto.

Upward into the economy
Migration continues—
Out of the workers' quarters
Pieces of accents
On the ascending escalator.
The red Avenue B bus
disappearing down the
Needles of the garment
factories—
The drain of Man hat on
For the icy winds
Of the river's edge
Stinging lower Broadway
As hot dogs
Sauerkraut and all
Gush down the pipes
of Canal.

After Forsyth Park
is the beginning of Italy
Florence inside Mott
Street windows—
Pelermo eyes of Angie
Flipping the big
hole of a 45 record
The Duprees dusting
Like white sugar onto
Fluffed dough—
Criss crossing
The fire-escapes
To arrive at Lourdes'
rail road flat
With knishes
she threw next to
Red beans.

Roberto Tinoco Durán   [2 poems]

Mexicans are not mustaches

he and she
say
they
really do
appreciate our culture
but
don't like the way
we act
doing it

.

Edward Hopper's Excursion into Philosophy
Diane Bonds   [2 poems]

> *The open book is Plato, reread too late.*
> —Josephine Hopper

Outside the window, glare
rims a hill. On the bed lies a woman.
To say her back is turned would be a politeness.

Bare from hips downward, she is shadowed footsoles,
illuminated calves, and haunches,
like the analogous dunes outside, touched by sun.

Or is it moon? No matter.
She is neither parts—and a hank of hair
(auburn, fanned across the pillow).

By her, lies an open book. By it,
fully clothed, her companion sits, staring
at the floor. He studies a patch of light,

not like a man struck by an idea,
but like an animal
stunned by a mallet. The light is a doorway

leading nowhere if not to the shifting sand
beneath the house, so he broods as if
he has always suspected

what now is confirmed: that he's failed to see
the world aright. That the woman—
always a closed book

and never more so than now—is a mystery
not because she is unknowable,
but because she is not there:

her elusive shadows, which drew him ever deeper
into the wilderness,
are merely shadows of shadows.

Yet she is there, unquestionably—
formidable and fleshy, dead
to the world, while the man sits on the edge

of the bed, no creature bludgeoned
out of his pain, but the lover of a woman
whose back is turned. Mesmerized

by a scrap of light
on which obtrudes the tip of his brown
and material shoe, he can discern nothing,

no shadows by which he once knew himself
and others, no reflections
he still loves.

René Magritte's Attempting the Impossible

—a portrait of the artist painting a woman on air

1.

She rises in the only speech
he knows, an accretion
of brushstrokes. The room
is bare, their work
unthinkable. They stand
as if being erect, one knee flexed,
were the only suitable pose.

How did the woman begin?
You cannot imagine the artist crouched
at her feet in his three-piece suit.
But it's pointless to speak
of ideas. What idea
ever had such dark hair or nipples
so hard and protuberant?

He most adores the stillness
of his creation, the repose
that enters the world
as he fixes her body in the air.
He steadies his brush on the unfinished arm.
When the limb is complete,
her hand will lie over his heart.

2.

She scarcely believes her own
presence, how substance complies
with the strokes of his brush.

She knows she began as intention.
Her serious gaze meets his
because he willed it so. Isn't that why
he's clothed and she is not?

Her breasts are heavy
with his desire: not to create
a woman but to possess a soul.
Her flesh is poetic commonplace,
alabaster touched with rose.
Her outstretched arm, when complete,
will hold the artist at bay.

"O Wert Thou in the Cauld Blast"
Sam Magavern   [2 poems]

My landlord, Royal Jello, came stomping up here this morning.

—Did you use the laundry machine?

—No, I didn't.

—What?

—No, I didn't use it.

—When I find out who did I'm going to kick his ass the hell out of here.

Royal was a lot nicer, they say, before his wife died. She stole part of his self, and he was too tired to replace it.

The Burial Problem

After the last battle of Ishnu,
The corpses lay so thick
We had to hire
Giant birds to drop them into

The sea. Now the
Waves curse us when they break,
They lash our empty cliffs.

Fishers of the Morning
FW Rabey

Across the fitted sky they pin up boats to start the morning,
And then lowering the first long nets, then pulling up the sun;
And when they're through:
A man walks straight and silent out into the early blue.
He moves: this particle of time to pass, a finger touching to the glass
Beneath the hint of half-cut moon that haunts the pink horizon.

    And here the right is all at fault
    And then the left is all at fault,
    And somewhere back behind
    The center has long fallen out
    To launch a space for the extremes:
    And on outside edges, things exist
    With complicated names; but
    Izquierda o derecha, que no es importante—
    People die in both directions
    And the death is much the same:

    They come in through the night
    And then they shut it back behind them,
    And in the mornings lives are emptied out
    Of parts they can't reclaim,
    Left in woods and found as buried bones
    Of 26 such bodies
    Brimming over with the dirt from years
    Of hopeful lies withholding tears—
    Because the military, it appears,
    Patently prefers no little displays of emotion.

    They say: the money trickles down from trees
    Of telephones and coffee,
    Copper mines and used canals:
    But in the foreign student stores
    It seems Marx never holds the gun,
    And la gente would have won
    If the gringo's trees were fallen
    And the leaves had never come.

A man walks off into the glass, his lungs fill up with salt.
His eyes bulge like the great, weird fish:
Yes, I suspect that he will drown—
And across this fitted sky they'll drop their nets to start the morning,
Haul him up in early-blue out of the half-cut red horizon:
His fingers clutching after straws that he could never find.
And then he looks at nothing for a while and the fishers close his eyes.

Sometimes there are questions
About meaning in our lives,
At the ends of afternoons
After the miles of nets and fish:
You pull them in, you throw them out,
You pull them in and then—
All you really have is rope
And not much else to do with it.

The Poetry of Things: Interview with Alan Dugan [1999]

c: You've said that "Any artist is in competition with God in trying to make an objective physical creation which is meant for the experience of other people." Who's winning?—The artist or God at this point on July 17, 1999?

AD: Well, since there is no God, the artist is always winning; except the artist dies and his work is often forgotten.

c: What is a poem to you? And what do you mean when you say that a poem is a physical object?

AD: A poem is a physical object in the sense that it is made out of words that are written down or recorded, so therefore, a poem in that sense is a physical object in the external universe. It exists independent of the mind that created it. So a thought or a feeling from a person takes us beyond that person. So, in that sense, it takes us beyond that person. As for a poem, it's a collection of words, that's all. A poem is less particular at the end of the nineteenth century, when poems lost their line breaks and their rhyme schemes and became, in a way, pieces of prose. You can't define a poem by any structural means as being different from prose. If you call a thing a poem, then it's a poem; if you don't then it's not a poem. There's no way of defining an assemblage of words as a poem unless the person that makes it calls it that. That's the only way of defining a poem. There's no way of defining it otherwise, except for as a collection of words that gets called a poem by the poem-maker or by the people that look at it. There are no standards and haven't been since Whitman. Period. Name a standard. You can't.

c: On that note, what makes a poet?

AD: One way, perhaps, is that a poet is a person who makes an assemblage of words that don't necessarily tell a story, but try to transmit a powerful emotion verbally. If that succeeds then the pleasure of words transmit an emotion, and if a person keeps on doing that, time after time, then that person can be called a poet. Except that the fact that some of these people write stories that are broken up into lines all the time, so they're story-writing poets, so how do you include them in it?

c: What made you a poet? When was it when you began seeing yourself as one?

AD: What made me a poet, probably, is what made other people poets, and that is the family scene. I had a competition with my father. He used to recite terrible poems at family gatherings and things like that. We'd suffer again and again and again. I resolved to better him. When I got to be an adolescent, with the first agonies of sexual awakenings, I used to walk around incensed, saying things that I thought were prose. I thought that what I was writing was prose. I wouldn't dare to be a poet because all poets were faggots and I was going to grow up to be a man. I got convinced that it was more dangerous to be a poet. When I got to college, my freshman faculty advisor convinced me that I was really a poet and it was more dangerous to be a poet and be called a "fairy" and to fight anybody that called me a "fairy" and to be brave. So I took a poetry workshop my sophomore year at Queens College and started writing poetry. I learned to make poems, to type them, to submit them for publication, it was a treat. I was drafted into the Air Force and published in New York University's magazine, *Lens Horizons*, during basic training. I've been teaching poetry workshops myself for 30 or 40 years now.

c: How does the act of writing a poem come to you? Has it changed over time?

AD: It varies with time. Right now, I've got kind of a split personality. Half of me hates the idea of writing and half of me wants to, so I write out of the corners of my mind. My unconscious wants to write, so part of me dictates lines of verse and part of me wants to not be bothered. I write things on scraps of paper, I have these collections of things that I'm pretending not to notice what I write. There are piles of stuff and with luck the piles will result in becoming poems, where the words dictated by the unconscious count for more than any conscious intention that I have. One part of my mind is political, rational, that works when I want to make a point in an argument, or vote for so-and-so. If I do that in a poem it's nonsense. That unconscious part of my mind just wads up a flow of words that don't mean a goddamn thing and that's nonsense too. The things have to meet somehow. That meeting place between the unconscious, emotional flow of words and the conscious demand for an intelligent search for order in the universe. The two things being at war with each other. The war between the unconscious flow and the conscious desire, this is what makes the language of poetry. Sometimes it goes off in the dopiest directions, like the moments that I find myself writing haikus. An absolutely stupid thing. Haikus are absolute nonsense in English because we don't have that inflective language like Japanese. Anybody could write seventeen-syllable poems and they're all crap. Richard Wright wrote thousands of them before he died and they're all lousy. They had a competition in California for flight tickets to Japan and 30,000 people sent in poems. They were all bad. I have a half-a-dozen Haikus that come out of my pen—They're all bad. Age … age!

c: When you're asked to give a reading and begin considering what you will read, how do you go about that process and which of your poems stand the test of time for you?

AD: Well, I try to not read the ones that get anthologized all the time because that bores me. And I find that I cannot read political ones because the political crisis that dictated the poems have passed, so those poems are dead. So, I'm left with the remains. That's the problem. I'm going to give a reading a couple of weeks from now at one of the local libraries, so … "What am I going to read?" I'm trying to finish a poem about libraries and maybe I'll read all the poems I've written about Cape Cod. I'm going to read all of the poems that I've written about animals … about butterflies and not about politics. Should I read all the poems I've written about war? For example, I spent most of my youth in the army and as a consequence I'm what they call a premature anti-fascist, a mature anti-fascist, and a post-mature anti-fascist, so I wrote an awful lot of poems dealing with that struggle, which are pretty useless nowadays. Should I read those for historical purposes?—Or not, I wonder … Those are the things that I think about. I haven't published that many poems. I've only published six volumes. I'm trying to get together a seventh volume now.

c: You've said the American novelist Thomas Wolfe was a major influence. How does a writer of 1,000-page manuscripts influence the writing of a twenty-line poet like yourself?

AD: When I was a kid—an adolescent—Wolfe was the one that I imitated when I was walking around talking to myself. The same word, after word, after word. When I was afflicted with logorrhea, all this stuff came pouring out of me. I didn't have any sense that the words should result in any form. I had a formal crisis during World War II. I walked around the streets talking like Thomas Wolfe, then on the same day, I discovered the poems of T. S. Eliot and William Carlos Williams. I saw that T. S. Eliot could play around with forms, break forms any time he wanted to, and William Carlos Williams was a gorgeous poet and he could cut everything down to the minimum and use short, perfect lines. I figured that those two poets were the masters at the time. But I thought that it was possible to write long lines of poems like Whitman. At the same time, it was World War II and one felt the necessity to be writing political poems that would appeal to as broad an audience as possible. Afterward, Auden and Spender were writing rhymed poems that sounded like popular songs that were anti-Nazi, so that everyone should become anti-Nazi, anti-fascist. I was pulled in that direction too. I was far to the left, not quite a communist, but a radical socialist. I thought I should write popular songs for soldiers like myself, so that would have to be rhyming poems that would be like the popular songs that they sang. So I should write rhyming songs, but I was lousy at that, of course, because I didn't write radio songs, right? So there were those things—write rhyming songs, write tight stuff like William Carlos Williams, write long lines like Whitman—those were the contrary poets working on one's style. Any artist has those pulls.

c: Do you think there is an emerging American language?

AD: Of course. Language is always a process of invention. Just like the name of your magazine, compost, it's part of the process of the invention of language. That's what happens all the time.

c: What do you think some of the major influences are on language and where is it heading?

AD: It's hard to say. We had lunch the other day with a young musician who's playing some stuff with a black singer. We couldn't understand a word that the black rap singer was singing and after a while the horn player said to us, "This is the way language is going, this is it." So, the language is coming up from the streets, it's coming in from television, and down from government nonsense—in from all directions as usual.

c: Are there living poets that you read often?

AD: At the moment my favorite poets are Charles Simic and Bogdanovich. He's great.

c: Who is Bogdanovich?

AD: Zbigniew Herbert!

c: You spoke about how the unconscious plays a role in your poetry. How does humor play a role?

AD: For me, I tend to use humor as a defensive mechanism. I'm afraid that if I show myself as too serious a poet that people will laugh at me. So, I use wit to make people laugh with me instead. It's a trick that I use to get myself off the hook. I've been criticized by people saying, "Why do you bother joking all the time?" I try to avoid it now, try to not be too jokey now, but I joke to get myself off the hook.

c: Critics have said that there aren't enough politics in poems these days and that all of these people are just writing about their own personal experiences. You've said that "All poets are political even if they only talk about personal life in a regimented mass culture."

AD: The thing is that most American poetry today is autobiographical. I see between 250 to 300 poetry manuscripts a year. The autobiographical nature of poetry is political in the sense that the individual is saying, "I am me!" What a state organization does, they'll go on existing. It's a way of saying that there is no organized politics anymore. There is no political movement worth my attention, so I will talk about myself. That's what I write poems about, that's what people do. It might also have something to do with the age business. Conventional wisdom is that the most interesting poetry is written by people between the ages of 17 and 20. But right now we're living in a time when a lot of people grow to be very old. You get an awful lot of people who are old, who are writing poetry, and that's an entirely different situation. It's the first time in history in which we have millions of very old people, like me, people older than 70, and an awful lot of them are writing poetry. Most of it stinks.

c: Where is "Asshole State University in Nowheresville America?"

AD: That could be very many number of places, now couldn't it?

c: You've discussed the academy as a necessary place for a contemporary poet to make a living, but how are students in such environments to come out alive?

AD: Oh boy. How many universities are there in America? Two thousand? Do you see any educated people around? There must be something wrong.

c: How do you simultaneously teach your students and help them hear their own voices?

AD: I do a classic class, where the poet reads his or her own poem aloud to an audience, and by hearing the poem rebound from other people the poet should be able to find out what it's like in a social setting. That's the only purpose a poetry workshop can possibly have. It's a release from privacy. Most people in poetry workshops are unable to take advantage of it, so you never hear from them again. The truth is that poetry workshops do very little in terms of improving people's performance and way of writing poetry. I've had four or five very good poets come through my poetry workshops—Carl Phillips, Ai, Cynthia McDonald, and a couple of others. When they came to my class they were excellent poets and when they left they were excellent poets. There was not that much difference. The only thing that they could have learned from me was how to present their poems to a magazine and how to present themselves to university bureaucracies. So those two things are what a workshop can do. That is what a workshop did for me when I was a sophomore. It taught me how to get myself, my poems, presentable enough to send to magazines. I have students that come back to my workshop year after year after year and they get no better, they get no worse, but they go on producing poetry that is satisfactory to them as a way of displaying their own personalities to themselves. That's a method of retaining our own sanity and celebrating our existence to ourselves and the people that read our poems. Whadda you gonna do, that's about the size of the situation. Several of the good poets that have been through my workshops go on to do workshops themselves. Carl at George Washington University of Saint Louis, Cynthia McDonald at Houston are in charge of those programs and they're doing the same thing.

c: You mentioned that you translate poems, particularly Borges and Neruda. Have any been published? Are you still doing them?

AD: Yeah, I'm in the middle of doing that right now. I'm preparing for The Favorite Poem Project right now, it's going to take place August 7th in Provincetown, MA. Pinsky's organizing it. I'm translating poems right now by Borges. I'm able to translate Borges from Spanish because Borges wrote Spanish with a very English accent because he spent many years in England. He was very Anglicized, so his Spanish has a very English flavor to it. It's easier to translate than people like Lorca, who is very difficult to translate. It's very nice. The poem I'm translating is a translation of a translation from the twelfth-century Arabic, it's called, "The Poet Declares His Notoriety."

The Poet Declares His Notoriety

The circle of the sky is the measure of my
    glory.
The libraries of the East debate about my
    verses.
The sultans send for me, to fill my mouth with   gold.
The angels in heaven already know my last poem   by heart.
The tools of my trade are humiliation and   anguish.
I wish to God I had been born dead.

c: Who is a hero in the world today?

AD: The dead Kennedy. What we have in America is a very good system where we can have a worship of royalty without the legality of it. It is very fortunate that we can have a constitutional system of government while at the same time we can have an unofficial royal family. We're very, very lucky to have a religion without content. It's the same thing with organized sports that are religious in nature. The Olympics come from Olympos, which has to do with the gods. Big time sports or religious functions are religious by nature—a lot of people don't know that, so they worship when they spend all their emotional energies on sports but without all the violence and murder that attended Christianity in the middle ages. So we have royalty without official power, like the Kennedys and sports as religion.

c: Just to shift to the politics of the poetry world, I just read David Lehman's book, *The Last Avant-Garde,* and was struck to find out that Auden, when he was choosing the winner for the Yale Younger Poets, hated all the manuscripts that year, and the rich owner of a gallery in Manhattan handed him Ashbery's manuscript and he chose it.

AD: Literary politics vary from year to year. I dunno. Yeah, I won the Yale Younger Poets Prize because the age limit was raised to thirty-five or something like that and I won it because my brother-in-law, Jonathan Shahn, was a good friend of George Starbuck who won it the year before. He showed some of my poems to Starbuck and Starbuck liked them. He then showed them to Dudley Fitts, who was running the Yale Younger, and he said, "Give it to this guy, Dugan." The guy said, "Dugan's too old." Then they raised

272

the age limit, so they gave it to me. So, I won it that way. Somebody told somebody, my brother-in-law told somebody who told somebody. I've never worked an honest day in my life since.

c: Are you working on another book and will it be continuing with *Poems 7*? And why that title?

AD: Yes. It's my seventh volume, so that's the name. People get mad at me for doing that because they say, "Now nobody else can do that." But I tell them, "Well somebody started naming symphonies 1, 2, 3..." Other people did, so they can if they want to.

c: What do you see as the role or place of the poet in the twenty-first century?

AD: I don't know. Minor. I don't see much of a role at all, as a matter of fact, what I see is the fact that there are 3,000 (at least) of these classes where people write poems and are criticized. I have a sense that we'll see a mass movement of people writing fairly lousy poems and at the moment I don't see anyone that's particularly great. So, I see a huge number of people that are writing mediocre poetry for themselves as an autobiographical medium. That's just the same as the thousands and thousands of people that write these terrible haikus. Writing poetry is a popular medium, but people don't realize that. But it is. Every college has a poetry writing program. Just like this class that I conduct every week. Three thousand of them. And each class has at least a half a dozen students in it, so, you do the multiplication.

c: What do you think, in an ideal sense, that the poets' role could be for society? Looking at your work, it seems that society's not what you think it should be, if it could be there, what kind of a role do you think the poet could play?

AD: Oh it doesn't make sense to engage in wishful thinking like that. I have no reason to think well of poets as human beings. A lot of poets have been absolute bastards—Robert Frost, Ezra Pound. Poetry does not make for virtuous practitioners. Some are good people, some are lousy people, some are just neutral, like everybody else. Art is a very difficult thing. It doesn't neccesarily improve people or ruin people, it just is. It just is. The IS! And that's my last word.

Oaf
Connie Deanovich

he eats hillbilly tiger
and washes his red hair
with gasoline
he has promised to make a movie
to drive an Electra 225 onto a stage
and spit on it
to make a movie of this
to call it Combat

he has a taste for bone
and washes his grandmother
with rubbing alcohol
he has promised to take her to a movie
in her old Electra
promised her she could spit out the window

he drinks red oil
and fantasizes washing a mountaineer
with snowmelt
he was promised a movie of this
by a liar friend
he'd now like to spit on

he chews an orange blueprint of Tony Curtis
just exactly like a spy without a hat
or Nazi Beer to wash it down with
he has promised to keep the secret
so he only spits out the nonessentials
       the shoes
       the tip of the nose

he drinks from the pink water's edge and
as he promised himself
he laps it up like a tiger crouched at a watering hole
during an electric storm
when lightning spits blue strikes across the sky
       really

Unfurl the Snare
Ryan G. Van Cleave

All I can be really sure of
Is that I was better off
Before I read Nietzsche

God is dead
And we have killed him

I sure didn't help
You sonovabitch
So don't try to drag
Me down with you
On this one!

But even as I curse him
For the cynic he was
I recall a young woman
Outside a supermarket
Or a drug store, maybe
As a single brown shape
Spiraled to the pavement
Like a sick. withered leaf

Some sort of bird, I realized
And not being an animal lover
I didn't recognize what type
Despite its strange white stripes
And sapphire-colored head
But even to my untrained eyes
It was clear the bird was hurt
Broken wing or something like it
I figured

The girl coddled it
Against her prepubescent chest
Like a Barbie toy to hold
Maternal instinct taking over

I headed toward the store doors
When I heard the crack
She had whipped the bird
Against the brick wall
A dark red blotch
Marked where it had smacked

I was stunned,
Numb even as she put
The heel of her shiny
Leather boot against its
Head and crunched down
Until the squirming stopped

I was as guilty as she
Nietzsche would've said

Though I don't go to church
I can't help but belong
To the religion of humanity
Therefore I am to blame
As much as anyone
For hefting God like a robin egg
Or a tiny crystal ball
And crushing him into oblivion

I was so much better off
Before I read Nietzsche

Abecedarian
Steve Ratiner

Amazing. A
maze, A to Zed.
The ear races
ahead of the mind's formulation,
the tongue outreaches the arm.
The first utterance
disarms this volatile paradise, offers
the barest hint of what may come.
The syllabic croon as easy
plucks a pin from her hair
or the moon from the sky,
and owns each for an instant.
One word mothers all otherness.
The world dresses and undresses
before your unashamed eye,
named and namer commingling
then thrust passionately apart.
You make your way along, struggling
to spell this eruption of being.
A teacher? Sound it out.

B

B is the body—
backbone straight and sturdy,
breast, belly, the muscles undulating.
As a boy, I made my letters
too ripe, too fleshy,
the voluptuous bottom curve billowing out
like a woman in the last month of pregnancy.
The teacher exed out my B's in red,
demanded a full battery of proper characters,
parading down her blue-lined streets
before she'd grant me recess, release.
Too young to recognize this
bitch for the curse she embodied,
I'd simply mark time until three p.m.,

fly home to my own room, my own book,
where my brash and fecund alphabet
could holler and give birth
to all manner of words, wishes, worlds.

C

The C is the one we
don't broach
in mixed company.
But alone, admit it, it's
all we boys think about.
Little c, large C, tender openings.
Some pure as a cresent moon and as elusive.
Others are steely, a sickle, stropped and gleaming—
sooner cut you off at the knees
than smile at you.
"Country matters," the Bard called it.
Mrs. Chevat offered an imperceptible wink
to the English class. Could the C's concupiscence
be plainer than that! Still,
scrawling this recumbent letter,
I remember the summer night,
the couch in the basement,
her sweaty skin sticking to the vinyl.
How she opened her legs, lifted her knees—
and there, I could see it, the smooth crest,
the cranium barging through distending lips,
a blood-streaked moon emerging
into my waiting hands.
Later, in the hospital, as the child
slept easy in the crook of her arm,
I felt myself lost in the C's declivity
and thought: could I ever lay my head
in her lap again without hearing
that first curt breathless cry?—

Leavers
Virgil Suarez

Though I remember leaving, the act,
        I do recall a big suitcase and my mother
cutting the curtains down and sewing

them into liners for the suitcase, my father,
        who smoked in those days, stepped out
on to the porch of his house, our house,

bought on his policeman's salary, smoke
        clouds in front of him, clouds by the fronds
of the plantains he touched

the porch columns. He kept pacing
        and out, and the last time he threw
the cigarette down and stepped on it to rub

it out, and he told us it was time to go,
        and I saw the resolution in his moist eyes,
the anxiety had turned his hands into birds,

"Listo," he told us. Ready, it was time to leave,
        and I heard my father say "adios vieja," toward
the room where my grandmother had died,

as though she was still there and we were simply
        leaving on a short vacation trip, and I knew better.
I must have fallen asleep in the taxi which was no

taxi but Talo, our next door neighbor who gave
        us a ride to the airport, and next thing I opened
my eyes to was the entrance to the Jose Martí

Rancho Boyeros Airport, a few relatives waiting
        to say goodbye-how they got there from so far
away, I'll never know, other than family calls

to family, and everyone knew what I didn't
        which was that it was the last time, the last
time for my father who died in exile, never again

saw his homeland, the last time for me who
          keeps his son promise not to go back until…
In a damaged country, people learn to sacrifice,

learn how to say goodbye. We were on our way
          to Madrid, Spain, the nuns in the family provided
visas for us, them and my paternal uncle who sent

the dollars. Next I remembered the hallway,
          all the glass they call la pecera, the fish tank,
because once you are in, you cannot touch

your relatives, but you can see them and they you,
          my maternal grandmother Donatila stood behind
the glass, already a specter. My uncles and aunts,

cousins, all learned to wave goodbye, as if in a trance
          we waved back, boarded the plane—I think an Iberia
jet, the first time I was to fly, its doors the gateway

to freedom, as my father said, we climbed on board.
          Sat in silence, my mother leaned into my father's
shoulders and cried. I gripped the armrest, a boy

of eight, my oldest daughter's age at this moment,
          and saw my fingers dig into the thin padding,
and when the plane took off, the silence, I'm sure,

made the ascension possible, a steel bird weighed
          down with so much melancholia, so much sadness,
my father looked out the window and smiled,

I looked out at the lights of the distant homeland,
          A flicker and wink of lights saying goodbye,
for the last time, and we were soaring through

the air toward the unknown, so much left behind,
          and I, I too, have learned this intricate art of leaving,
of saying goodbye to everything home, memories

like fire, a leaver's goodbye to all things irretrievable.

On James Laughlin
Rosmarie Waldrop

We all know James Laughlin's achievement as a publisher is extraordinary. But I was astonished by how much he personally entered into relation even with a latecomer like me. For instance, he did not simply accept what became my second book with New Directions, *A Key Into the Language of America*. This book of poems is based on Roger Williams's book of the same title (of 1643), which is a treatise on the Narragansett Indians and their language.

Not only did he see that the book needed an introduction, he badgered me into writing one—which I am very grateful for. He also suggested pictures and began to send me letters with pictures of Indians xeroxed onto them, especially one of a man gnawing on what was clearly a human arm. I began to wonder if that was a message.

But there's more: he got interested enough to look up Roger Williams's book, and my next letter consisted of three sentences in Narragansett! I spent a lot of time trying to track them down in the book. One I never found. The second translated as: God is angry with me. And the third: Give me tobacco.

James Laughlin was a poet, with a poet's reactions. I had always sent both manuscripts and books to him because it was my dream and ambition to be part of that company of writers he assembled.

But I was surprised when I got a letter from him, in 1986, that he liked my book, *Streets Enough to Welcome Snow*, and that he had used—he said "stolen"—a line from it. Did I mind?

Far from minding, I felt honored. For me, this was the best response to a poem. I was also amused because my poem had stolen lines from Barbara Guest. So this made a nice little chain of reactions, with which I'd like to end:

> Barbara Guest, from "Byron's Signatories":
>
> … They would talk together as long as they could. There were various passages he liked to indulge in and she would follow him there rubbing against the wall, avoiding as best she could the damp …

> Rosmarie Waldrop from "Kind Regards":
>
> we talk as long as we can
> there are amazements
> you like to stray into and
> my body's only
> one of them

"The Maze"
James Laughlin   [6 poems]

I like to stray into the
amazement of your body

where I find treasures
I never found before the

child dreamed of astonish-
ments but never saw them

never touched them never
heard or felt them until

now what god contrived
the maze of your amaze-

ments where I am lost so
happily I never want to

leave this labyrinth.

The Self-Tormentors

It's spring again and that
crazy robin is back from

the south for the third
year bashing her beak on

my window every morning
for an hour or more she

perches on the limbs of
the linden tree on the

terrace then bullets her-
self against the glass

what does she want why
does she do it what is

her Obsession (it hasn't
anything to do with food

or nesting) it's just
self torment each day

until she is exhausted

. . . .

It's spring again and the
famous German film direc-

tor is back in New York
hunting for a distribut-

or for his latest cruel
bitter cynical picture

the cruelty of man to man
the way that men and wo-

men cut each other up and
then come back for more

the mercilessness of fate
(yes those whom the gods

love they hurt the most)
why do I keep on going

to see that wretched gen-
ius's films am I a charac-

ter from old Menander's
play The Self-Tormentor?

*After this poem was written a local ornithologist told me
that a male bird would see his reflection in the window glass,
think it was another bird, and attack it to drive it away from
his territory. I dunno.*

The Love-Candy Teaser

A tall man knows a pretty little cross-stitched punching
        bag, a tease packet, with whom he shares life's comical
        gymnasium

The sweetmeat willows on a string of fast waltz music,
        turning and twisting

The trick is to tag her as she revolves, but always gently,
        not bruising her milkmaid complexion

The tall man wears puff-stuffed gloves like a boy-time
        boxer hustling his birthday party sweetheart

Confetti floats down through strobe-light beams that flash
        and blink in multicolor

It's tickle time in the gym; the more she laughs the more
        he teases, the more absurd and intricate the feinted
        blows become

Spectators in the gym are wondering what the game's about;
        is this a kind of Polynesian courting?

Or does it come from the bust-up of Western Civilization,
        when he plays kiss-kiss teasing like a hyperactive
        midget child?

Roller skates, roller skates, it's a bad, bad world; whisk
        us all up to Heaven, if it's still there.

Have You No Respect for Love

I call you after midnight when
you must certainly be home but

you don't pick up the phone
what have I done to deserve

such treatment have I been
selfish or demanding I don't

care if you've taken another
love (I'd never be jealous

that's not my nature) do as
you wish it's your life not

mine but pick up the phone
so I can hear the voice that

I so much love and remember
our happy times together re-

member our lovemaking please
have some respect for love.

Her Career

Having money and no need
for a job and having a

charming cavaliere ser-
vente for companionship

she made a career of cul-
tivating her feelings each

day became an arena in her
mind where every word of a

friend or acquaintance
was anatomized and a rec-

ord was put down in a pret-
ty hand in a small leather-

bound book anyone meeting
her now would not imagine

that once she had had many
lovers each one replaced

when the feelings he ad-
duced in her were not up

to the hoped for mark
the feelings she stored

up were like a collection
of rare lepidoptera or

perhaps more like a cata-
log of chess moves which

she played and replayed
on her board with a mas-

ter's skill studying for
the perfect combination.

Time Has Many Holes in It

for Edouard Roditi

Holes so big you can put
Your whole arm into them
Not just your fingers,
As when Dawn killed herself in Burgos,
And after I'd buried her in the
      Campo Sagrado,
And found those extraordinary poems
Hidden in her suitcase, I realized
That much as I'd loved her
I really didn't know her at all.
And when word came from Madrid
That, at the age of eighty,
Edouard had fallen downstairs
And been killed, that astonishing mind,
That whole vast world of arcane erudition
He had in his head, six languages
Tripping off his tongue, and with it all
Such kindness, such sweet consideration.

Stay away from me, time,
Keep your holes to yourself! that once she had had many
lovers each one replaced

when the feelings he ad-
duced in her were not up

to the hoped for mark
the feelings she stored

up were like a collection
of rare lepidoptera or

perhaps more like a cata-
log of chess moves which

she played and replayed
on her board with a mas-

ter's skill studying for
the perfect combination.

The Ballad of Mickey and Joey

Robert Daley   [2 poems]

Mickey was a junkie
Draped in mission rags
He wandered lower Broadway
Turning tricks for nickel bags
Mickey screwed his eyes shut
And plugged his ears
He howled for New York City
And the bygone Yankee years

Mickey swore at street signs
Railed at passers-by
But Mickey had a fastball
Back in junior high
Mickey had a pick-off move
Mickey boy could throw
'Til Mickey threw his shoulder out
And filled his brain with snow

Mickey was a white man
Mickey knew a lot
He knew his life annoyed him
Though sometimes he forgot
Mickey went through detox
Mickey went to hell
The state had him committed
To a home in New Rochelle

Joey planted sugar beets
Brussel sprouts and hay
Among infested livestock
On rich Kentucky clay
Joey slaughtered veal calves
Twisted chicken heads
His mind on Cincinnati
And the legendary Reds

Joey was a Christian
Joey couldn't read
But Joey swung a thunderstick
Back in little league
Joey had his timing down
Boy could Joey hit
Then Joey's papa lost a lung
And momma made him quit

Joey was a black man
Joey didn't care
He just got old and tired
In the bright Kentucky air
Joey's farm was repossessed
Joey's mom was ill
He robbed a bank in Frankfort
And was caught near Louisville

The yearly Hall of Fame Game is played at Cooperstown
The fans are men and women
The field is green and brown
The match is a remembrance
Patriots construe it
The Yankees and the Reds were on

Mickey and Joey knew it

Mickey charmed the psych nurse
And picked his day
He hocked a quart of methadone
And made a getaway
Mickey headed northwest
Mickey felt a high
His faculties as brilliant
As a diamond in July

Joey wooed the watchdogs
Joey slipped them steak
He closed their snouts with duct tape
And made a sudden break
Joey traveled northeast
Joey didn't roam
He sprinted into New York State
Like rounding third for home

Mickey sat behind the plate
And ordered up a Coke
The anthem made his heart leak
The windup made him choke
Mickey saw the stitches spin
Mickey traced the flight
A forkball struck the catcher's mitt
Wrong was put to right
Mickey's Yanks were warriors
Mickey's boys could hurt you
Their battle was a catalyst
For Mickey's innate virtue
Mickey thought his life could work
He vowed to try

Joey took a seat at first
And sipped a golden brew
The Reds were dread avengers
Their mission, just and true
Joey watched the wood blur
Joey heard the crack
A double dropped against the fence
Youth came rushing back
Joey loved the pastime
Joey cheered his team
The contest was an antidote
For Joey's poisoned dreams
Joey was reborn again
His savior was nigh

Rain in the eleventh stopped
A nothing-nothing tie

Mickey's clothes stuck to him
He gripped his ribs and coughed
Fans tore up their tickets
Scoreboard lights went off
Mickey saw the warden
Smelled the sniffing hounds
He clambered up the backstop
And staggered to the mound

Joey's nose was running
His skin was drenched
Vendors closed the hot dog stand
Batboys left the bench
Joey heard the megaphone
And knew his fate was sealed
The law approached with badges drawn
He leapt onto the field

Mickey grabbed a baseball
Joey chose a bat
Mickey threw a slider

And knocked a warden flat
Joey laid a sergeant down
And sent him into shock
They tore around the basepaths
Like Henderson and Brock

Joey
Choking up a bit
Mickey
Orb in hand
Stood back to back astride the plate
To make their final stand
Yankees wept to see them there
Reds knelt down to pray

Troopers drew their hammers back
And blew the pair away

The rain's all wet in Cooperstown
The wind is full of air
Nostalgia goes down sweetest with a chaser of despair
Despair's a sin
And so we spin from memory to pain
Erecting halls to men with balls
To corpses in the rain

We love Satchel, Babe and Ty,
Reggie, Nolan, Ted,
Because we know they'll someday die
Or are already dead
So here's to Dizzy, Jackie, Roy,
To Catfish, Pete, et al.
To Sandy, Yogi,
Willie, Hank,
Robert,
Cy

Play Ball

The Satisfaction of Texas: A Tall Tale

We strum out tunes to make a bear dance,
when we would move the stars to pity.
—Flaubert

His doctor suspects the protagonist, Tex,
Was a zygote when chemistry cursed him.
Tex was ugly
And dumb as a newborn can come.
His mother refused to nurse him.
His dad—not a bad one as martinets go—was apt to grow hostile and
                                                                                slug him.
At the baptism, Dad placed his hand on the Gospel
And swore that he'd never hug him.

A stutterer, Tex had severe dyslexia
And was bad at addition.
Grade school marms fractured his arms but failed to reverse the
condition.
They expelled him, declaring,
The kid has no mind.
He's a lout.
A prehuman impostor.
4H, the Scouts and the Baptists in kind struck his unholy name from
their rosters.

Filial Tex, in genetic reflex, crawled in tears to his father
And kneeled in the dust.
The man sneered in disgust, I won't hug you. You needn't have bothered.
His mother drew close to him,
Smacked him and said,
Mommy's not cross; she's just run-down.
You don't brush or wash. You smell like the dead.
Pack and be gone before sundown.

Unemployed Tex lived on whatever flecks he could lick from the trash
he picked through.
He slept in the rear of a burnt Cavalier with a family of twelve from Peru.

Adulthood found Tex doing time in the joint,
Watching Hee Haw, Get Smart, Gomer Pyle.
That's when his life started.
For up to that point he had never seen anyone smile.

Poverty-ridden he
Pawned both his kidneys and purchased a textbook on punning.
Like blind amputees who take up the trapeze
He placed all his faith in his cunning.
Sanguine as guinea pigs bred for dissection, as Custer assaulting the Sioux,
Tex, led by longing for manly affection, believed he was born to amuse.

He erected a cardboard and paperclip booth in a swamp at the Arkansas

  border.
He practiced his lines and hung out a sign:
A laff and a hug fur a corder.
But his timing was random,
His riddles, obscure,
His calcified tongue wouldn't loosen.
Pelted with dung and tipped into a sewer,
He drifted southwest
Back to Houston.

Disabused Tex reviewed his defects from a stool in a redneck saloon.
The bartender, Fritz, served him Ripple and Schlitz.
Tex poured out a time-honored tune:
Why've I always been so all alone?
No man'll hug me in the world.
But dumpkopf, Fritz shrugged, in an obvious tone,
Mens don't hug mens. Dey hug goils.

Ingenuous Tex altered his sex and sashayed to a country store
Where good old boys made a liquid noise spitting 'baccy on the floor.
They regarded his figure,
All lumpy and hard,
For several silent minutes,
Then loaded a Chevy with fish heads and lard
And dumped Miss Texas in it.

Heartbroken Tex tore the pearls from his neck,
He quit his implants and estrogen sessions.
He waved a good-bye to the wide Texas sky.
He howled a streetcorner confession.
He scrawled for his parents a final salute.
(Which was lost by the postal department),
Got naked, got sauced and ascended a butte
To hurl himself off the escarpment.

They flew to caress him,
His brothers, the clouds.
The earth below braced to enfold him.
Tex blew a kiss to the faraway crowds of a race that could no longer hold him.

Thus the quest to confirm his humanity ceased.
His bellows
Resounded
For miles.

An encampment of gypsy musicians below looked up at the creature,

And smiled.

Now triumphant Tex earns sizable checks for his work as a wrasslin' bear.
Nobody pleads that he reason or read or extricate tics from his hair.
He watches TV in a comfortable den.
He feeds upon steak, beer and honey.
His conscience is clear.
He hugs grown men.

And everyone thinks he's funny.

There's Nothing Worse
Leo Romero

There's nothing worse
than not being able
to fall off to sleep
That's what Skeleton Indian
thinks
He's been dead long enough
to know
that sleep doesn't come
easily to the dead
In fact
it's a mystery to them
how the living
can drop off to sleep
so easily
When you think of the dead
Skeleton Indian says
you probably think
they have it easy
Death's like being asleep
forever except
without dreams
that's what
you probably think
Don't believe it
You've spent one night
being unable to sleep
Try an eternity of it
Skeleton Indian moans

Making Bola
Denise Duhamel

Bola is a Filipino sweet talk, best translated as "bull"

Your instep is a black cat arching its back,
your ankle a hill where I want to live,
your soles wear gorgeous halos.
Your fingerprints are art!
I want to connect the dots
of your taste buds, slide down
the bridge of your nose. Your epiglottis
makes my hands sweat! Your elbow
is a perfect tomorrow. Your tear ducts
taste like maple syrup. Your palms are planets
I want to visit. Please, let me undress your fingers
so we can two-step to your heartbeat.

An Emergent Light
Miriam Ventura

I

My dreams were dazzled by older faces
laments, serpents, windmills
my laughter. The grief is no longer mine.
The image cuts across several bodies
silks, lights, cones, colors
the lake rinses out Jupiter, it does what it wants with the living

Like the letters shown by travelers
their loneliness is my own story. Their clothing is seductive.
I think myself one of them. The journey is always everything
all destinations are one

Is it my journey or my doubt?
I am the most common provider of surprises in this life
the one who travels with her dreams turned grocery bag
Half of one. Half of the other.
How many have tasted my coffee, made love unexpectedly
smearing the tongue with sweet clove
not to thank the heavens for their good fortunes
How many have made love in frail bodies
transforming them into diabolic dispersions

I begin to find myself among the figs
a sort of madness that picks up again all my existences
all my previous parallel existences

Pledges have been made. I comb the smile
of untamed pledgers. Their pilgrimage of dreams
is the lie that feeds the world. I among them.
This does not come close to the truth. There is a voice I don't know, a voice that
the poem and I fail to recognize,
a voice that exudes melodies that wrestle with insomnia
and in some place in the world
millions of beings are losing their way. It is meant for us never to be the same.

I throw myself into the light.

Arabesques
Dionisio D. Martínez
translated by Alan West

I

Just like a blind man who develops

his other senses until he sees with them, the Arab
gives life to his alphabet when his religion
prohibits representing the human figure.
The characters become
mouths, veins and muscles of beings
who spend their lives wandering about like the blind.

2

Next to the door of the interior courtyard
of the last house he lived in,
my maternal grandfather prays
in Arabic, lamenting, always
singing some note unknown to suffering.
The courtyard is filled with birdless cages.
My uncle makes cages of cane shoot, traps birds, lets them
escape when they sing: every prison
is cyclical: a waiting room between one freedom
and the next. When my grandfather sings to his god,
something escapes and, in the air, drawn
and undrawn, the unutterable word.

For Gloria, Mario, Mayra, and Juanín
Alan West

From his eyes, doves flew
out from hell.
—Francisco de Oraá

I

You could speak to me of that scent of birds
or fruit on the table, of what you can
see in the morning without opening your eyes

II

Whoever occupies reality does it with the voracity
of those who forget the burning constellation in the mirror

III

To enter the picture like rain
(there's no point in forewarning)

IV

The faces of time
One chosen
                    one yet to choose
But you choose as you choose light,
with your eyes closed.

V

So many things clinging to me
the hidden seed throbbing with four glances
every object has four memories,
or is it four chords, four mirrors?

VI

Two measures of time   two revelations
the metal table, glass top, painted white
The smile of a Chinese sculpture: Mayra
They belong to the same dream, the same roving,
                the same feeling,
        two stars vibrating in a tree

VII

Smoldering the voice of my Aunt Gloria
Smoldering the wind in the living room
         while the shadows of dusk arrived
Smoldering the piano pulsing like a vast
        tooth in the night
To drink glowing embers, betel leaf of my dreams.

VIII

Islands lose their clocks
Sweet, purple, basil aromas reinscribe the years
         against the furious wall.
From the eyes of my childhood,
butterflies scatter longings bathed in obsidian.

Richard Kostelanetz

From 1001
Concise Contemporary Ballets—IV
Any number of which may be selected for
publication, distributed in any order

A good libretto, even an impressionist, double-exposed or
portmanteaued one, follows most of the rules of simple
dramaturgy. Balanchine once said the perfect type plot for a dramatic narrative ballet
was the story of the Prodigal Son. Once there was a man who had everything, then he
had nothing; finally he had everything again.
　　　　—Lincoln Kirstein, Ballet Alphabet (1939)

Two impresarios try to steal each other's dancers, in full view
of each other.

Among the guests at a party honoring a prima
ballerina is a young man who falls in love with her and she with him;
but as she recalls former lovers, who dress to resemble one another, she
realizes that not only is this new suitor beneath her standards but that, of
loving men, she has simply had enough.

Inspired by birdlike movements, this ballet is
essentially plotless.

The girls of a port town find the ship captain so
irresistible that they disguise themselves as beardless young sailors to
board his ship, where they discover, as he makes advances on them, that
the captain must be essentially homosexual.

Two prisoners escape to the home of one whose wife falls in love
with the other, who is persuaded to kill the husband but then, under the
persistent threat of arrest, he remains his den in her house, eventually
realizing that he has simply exchanged one prison for another, the new
one only slightly less disagreable than its
predecessor.

Several performers, as naked as acceptable, smear one another
with chocolate syrup whose smell becomes so overwhelming that

chocolate-hungry members of the audience on their own initiative come on stage to lick spatulas and even the performers' bodies. (Their needs should not be spurned.)

A man with an easily divisible personality is torn severely between body and soul, convention and dissidence, wealth and love; his role can be played by two or more dancers.

In an apartment too large for two people, an attractive young woman tries in vain to get more attention from a husband who is more devoted to cocaine.

A beautiful young girl who loses her virginity prior to marriage is turned into a butterfly, which may or may not in the end represent a punishment.

An American college girl marries a handsome foreign student who could not otherwise stay in the States, incidentally hoping he will eventually love her.

The assassins who appear to be male turn out to be women.

In this updated version of the Orpheus legend, a matinee idol, publicly known as homosexual, descends into hell in search of a favorite lover who recently died from AIDS.

A military nurse saves the life of an enemy officer, who falls in love with her, and she with him; but before they can make their affection public, they must overcome numerous obstacles that are both official and unofficial.

Though from all appearances she looked like a contemporary woman, the prima donna was also a skilled automotive mechanic.

An athletic woman who tries repeatedly to do four jetés in mid-air finally succeeds, disappearing above the proscenium.

In an all-night performance, several dancers represent the planets slowly rotating around the sun, whose role is played by the choreographer.

Thanks to effects possible with videotape, we see on the small screen a man, obviously exhausted,
continually climbing upwards to heaven and repeatedly passing a sign marked only with an infinity symbol.

On the white classic leotards of scores of dancers are projected both radical contemporary political slogans and abstract lines resembling the tread marks of radial tires.

The spook of a murdered woman returns to dance with her husband, who, in honor of the occasion, suddenly appears twenty years younger.

All available spotlights are shined directly at the audience, preferably in steadily increasing number, until everyone leaves.

Among small slender women rehearsing gymnastic routines moves a stocky man holding a television camera devoid of extending wires.

A prostitute enslaved by a demonic pimp is required to murder her customers until she encounters a man who, even though he is stabbed many times, does not die.

When a prophecy made by a psychic proves to be false, disappointed and disgusted dancers throw him into the orchestra pit.

In a black mass, with three archangels presiding, a young woman makes a Faustian wager, transforming
herself, thanks to angelic hocus-pocus, into the
contemporary embodiment of excessive knowledge—a hard computer disc that lies under a spotlight at the
center of the stage.

The protagonist is someone, apparently a dance patron, for whom everyone is continually waiting, even though he or she doesn't appear.

In a ballet accompanied by primitive music, a
devilish young woman, dancing with extravagant
movements, strangles prospective suitors with her extended ponytail.

During an hour of continuous movement, a game of musical chairs evolves into a brawl that requires the intervention of the police.

When a pilot who dies in an ocean crash returns to his fiancee as a ghost, she agrees to follow him to his submarine cave, where they are wed. Consummation is impossible, given their inhabiting different realms, until she too becomes a ghost and an infant is born.

An older choreographer defines the current style of his art by performing selected passages from his earlier works, as well as describing in loving detail those he is physically no longer able to do.

The protagonist falls into an epileptic fit when her father tells her to marry someone other than the man she loves, and she has even more extravagant fits when her father offers yet other suitors.

According to the program, "The purpose of this ballet is to represent male-female relationships realistically—as harmonious as they should be."

From over two dozen famous classic ballets this dance called Inventory, really the epitome of compilation choreography, takes phrases familiar to all dance lovers.

Before any human performers appear, water floods onto the stage and out into the audience who are forced to leave. Their commotion becomes the ballet.

An imperious woman employer gives a young man marijuana, which he brazenly shares not with his employer but with another employee, female, prompting his summary dismissal.

A pretty farm girl, abducted by the brother of the county's agribusiness mogul, awakens in a house graced by a life-sized statue of the mogul. After much confusion and explanation, she consents to stay with the brother.

Two women mount bicycles at the backcorner of the stage and, as they ride forward, crash into each other.

On a cruise in the Caribbean, the protagonist's girlfriend is swept overboard, fortunately near the shore. As the ship's crew is unable to find her in circling around the sea, he leaves the cruise, going from fishing village to village until, to everyone's surprise, he finds her.

The protagonist stakes all he has, including his wife, on a sports wager that he loses.

In this urban horse opera, a beautiful girl is enslaved by a homosexual who exploits her to attract men whom he then rapes and, if they threaten to report him to the police, murders unrepentently until one of his intended victims draws a gun in return, killing the rapist and falsely assuring the girl that she is free, all while making plays in an aside to enslave her for his own purposes.

A man new to town finds lodging with a widow, who finds him desirable, and her daughter, whom he desires instead.

In this war between two gangs of young people, a girl belonging to one gang causes a street war when, to escape an oncoming car, she hops on the back of the other gang leader's motorcycle.

Before a projection of a bombed-out city, the dancers construct a tent from urban scrap.

In this version of Alice in Wonderland, all the dancers working in a studio conspire to crash into a mirror that, when it breaks, becomes a doorway to another world.

Christ is reborn in an urban slum, experiencing again, after a period of miraculous good deeds, a crucifixion and resurrection whose significance is apparent not to those around him but to the audience.

If God Was Chicano ...
Javier Lazo

If God was Chicano
  Would he wear chinos
  wife-beater
          muscle shirts
  a hair net?
Sing oldies
  as if they were
  new songs?
Drive a low rider
  1962 Impala
  chromed-out engine
  complete with hydraulics?
Would he have a tattoo
  of the
Virgen de Guadalupe
  on his chest,
or a small one
  of Maria
    on his arm?
Would he go around
  saying, ora le
            cuida le
            watcha le?
Would he have a
  funny nickname like
    La Omni,
short for
    the Omnipotent?
If God was Chicano
would he walk around
  claiming he's something
    he's not;
or not be seen for what
    he truly is?

Rogelia Cruz
Marjorie Agosin

a Mari Jane

I

Rogelia Cruz curvada
como en un vértigo.
tu memoria
tu cuerpo
sitial de la Guatemala florida y
rojiza.

II

Tu cuerpo
atropellado entre las
sombras
y a pedazos
borrando tu hermosura
tus ojos que reconciliaban
la memoria.

III

Miss Guatemala:
Rogelia Cruz
tanta oscuridad cuando te nombran
tantos silencios cuando
te miran en los callejones
de lo que fuiste
Miss. Rogelia Cruz
cuando te miro estás viva
y me hablas más allá de las raíces
y tu mirada se
acerca a todos
los secretos como sortijas
que acechan en la oscuridad.

The Anthropomorphic Cabinet
Juan Felipe Herrera

They killed the Tlaxcalans. They slaughtered their daughters
and wept only once. When they were satiated with the scent
of Mazapán after their sundry affairs in the harem—
this is when they wept.

Pulled out the robe of their ancestors from Extremadura and wept
aloud, as their banquets resumed in the gardens. I was left behind,
in the palace. In the military dance hall. I called to them once.

I wrote out the name of my gods in cuneiform, in the pink
negative language that I own from my mother, I scratched out
my own contract for transformation.

And yet, they issued the order against me. It was simple and tawdry.
It was as usual. My skin was in their shape now. This was enough.
My skull resembled theirs, except my face was bowed and fell into my chest,
in grayness. My arm resembled a loaf of Spanish bread, my last breast
was held up for exhibition in the Friar's hallway. And my right hip
gashed with a capital letter. My legs folded in an odd fashion.
I could not speak.

Unrecognizable with my hands, with my letters
and the slit below my belly. A rag poured out of my bowels.
How they tried to clean me,
Is it my belly that wonders?
Is it my tongue, outstretched in its grayish abandonment?

They have taken Gala to Vladivostock.
She told me to follow the blue veins, to the yellow ones,
these solar aches—to reach her.

And yet, all I can do is cover myself in the strange foliage.
Make marimbas out of the few tubers left in the ship, La Caldea,
en route to the Philippines.

Arpeggios. Pellets
inserted into every pore.

The Code
Margarita Luna Robles

I can no longer let liars into my life
Liars stick together like maggots
eating the life out of others
(like good little parasites)

One must be prepared to pull them off
They do stick to you
Multiplying themselves, they bring
other liars to suck on you

It works this way:
if you are truth then lies must do away
with you

Never look a liar in the eye
before saying a prayer, lies have a way
of webbing

Never let a liar into your house
untruths create chaos in the air
Your house must remain safe

Don't let a liar get too close
The liar is selfish and wants you
Liars attack the center of being

Never eat a meal with a liar
This is like poison

Never tell a liar your truth
Liars lie and make lies
even of the truth

an inward journey for the outward good of humanity:

Abraham Lincoln
Russell Larkin

I.

He would sit slumped in his office chair or lay flat on his back at home and read to the air. Newspapers and journals, sometimes books, chronicles about the founding fathers, Shakespeare and the Scriptures; peering and listening for what the New World Latins call salsa, and the Americans call soul. That is how he got his prose beauty, concision and rhythm. Gettysburg is late prose yes, but because of that, I call it the first modern American poem. Elemental moods, bighearted and mirthless, cushioned inside the carnage of a collapsed minority nationalism, turned fantasist and earthbound.

Almost everything that was put out in slavery came back to the republic in war: invaded lands, split up families, love harvest and regret, labor unredeemed, the whole sickening absence of normality. A tremendous price was paid for U.S. democracy. All was supposedly tractable except the colors red and black. The old world Mexicans were no different, a mixed people, who came into the union at the end of the Mexcian American War in 1847. Citizens in limbo too, justified ideologically by white, hegemonic nationalism, until the Civil War, and the 13th, 14th, and 15th amendments opened up American democracy to all people of color. The American slave was a precursor, modernist, but modernist with the white, manchild soldier, the abolitionist, and the shut out nativeness of the white southerner. And Lincoln presided over these expectations and his 18th century document, the Declaration of Independence.

It is partially his fault that after this ghastly episode in our history that our white citizens confused patriot with racialist for nearly another hundred years. War and the disabled insurgency of liberty were reparations for the African as a native alien. As citizens, they would assemble and struggle for a full participation that never came. Their "new birth of freedom" was a Dosteovskyian novel: intrigue, strategical and irrational conflicts in politics and economics, static speculum and moral intensity.

A receptive flay of it, the Gettysburg Address is the philosophical antecedent of Eliot's Wasteland. Slothness and melancholy hinged onto the new democratic ethos, but that is only half the story. And what about the queer Whitman?, bewitched by Lincoln and democracy. A colder, passionate critique of the original Leaves of Grass because in that explosion tragedy was mediated through sensate beauty. Lincoln spoke to the living dead at Gettsburg. His way of fighting to gain 20th century consensus; he was the greater representative humanity.

...... an inward journey for the outward good of humanity

II.

Strong bony, hairless and cheekbones salient because of
absent roundness in the face; I can't think of a fresh metaphor,
so I can't speak about the nose. But the legs, whatever
position, seem infinite, and yet in the context of his torso,
proportionately akin to it. Black eyes, or maybe stained brown,
distinct: Sally completely oblivious to the world and Thomas
very warm. Some imagined formality suggests that I talk about the mole on
the right side of his face, and the pressed lips. The neck is the
thing I find really fascinating.
        Precarious, future seeming, because of its precariousness,
is it there or not?, impression: Lincoln comfortably erect in his
dressed-up costume.
        1860, photograph by Matthew Brady, robot with a heart,
extreme humanist. Left thumb, self-sufficient, with four fingers,
tapped on a book; straight up by his right side, right hand rested.
Brady slightly hurried up.
Lincoln did a speech that same day that got him the presidency.
Manhattan. The Cooper Union.
        powerful hints of regular and sensual nastiness around the
mouth area; I see it as far as the bridgetip of the nose, drenched
black, taboo hair.

III.

A primal fatalist who suspected the inward sensibility of the majority,
but believed that they should not only have a right to exist, but a right to
sanction authority and rule in civil society. Republican liberty must have
visions of universal imperatives ineluctably linked to divisions of practical
self-interests. And Lincoln's majority subsisted to gain the middle ground.
No matter how powerful, restrictive, and just are the sounds of the minority,
the principal sounds belong to the majority. That is good democracy. Minor-
ity cohesiveness exists and should exist in a democracy, but not only as an
avant garde figure, but a representative one. Lincoln had no other choice
but to make war on Anglo southern nationalism because it proclaimed its
uniqueness, but refused to suggest an inclusive need for slavery in a demo-
cratic society. Here was an example of a minority so narrowly illuminated
that all forms of voyeurism were seen as a conspiracy to destroy its liberty.

A paranoid style that would be imitated by other minority nationalisms, but without the serious demand of formal isolation from the union. In a democracy, liberty soley attached to a minority is a dangerous thing and recessive if your document is the Declaration of Independence, even if your document is the U.S. Constitution. Yes, the Constitution did compromise the liberty of the African people, but posterity would push them closer to mainstream freedoms that had started with the Enlightenment. Yes, it wasn't a dazzling beginning for freedom, but paradoxically, an extraordinary future, because it prepared itself for its own destruction, seventy years later. Liberty and humanity in the most powerful white supremacist society were the conditions that separated the Anglo Africans from the Mediterranean Africans in the New World. In a formally Anglo European ethos, the Anglo Africans were partly responsible for the considerable wealth in the country and the war. Their elemental presence helped Lincoln to discard sections of the Constitution, issue the Emancipation Proclamation, and oversee the 13th amendment through the House of Representatives, and more crucially, give up the hope of black emigration. The last compulsion was the explicit recognition of the African's birthright to participate in the humanity of the majority. African, black nationalism was blunted and the mixed tradition lead the way. Lincoln, as his contemporary critics charged, became a philosophical mulatto. Writing in 1863 to General Nathaniel P. Banks, in Lousiana, he wanted some "practical system" adopted "by which the two races could gradually live themselves out of their old relation to each other, and both come out better prepared for the new."

The only difference between Lincoln and the abolitionists was the presidency and Lincoln's comfortability with all of humanity. The minorities in his cabinet and around him: republicans, democrats, abolitionists, gradualists, Confederate partisans, shared an exclusive humanity and intermittently, all despised Lincoln's alternative behavior. Chase, Seward, Sumner, Blair, McClellan and others: so strong, so individualist, so cultivated, with great singularity, they claimed their sentiments; yet in the end, Lincoln's democracy won out. The assembled, listening style of the man and his meditations; his ambiguity, his collation of distinct minds to overtake their decisions, and then the final upturn, always tainted with compromise, saved his greatest passion, the Union.

The hope was that no minority nationalism would try to destroy this blessed union again, but if they so wish to, they must become the majority. Representative yes, avant garde, necessary, but the bully, self-contained imposition by the one against the many, never. Democracy is the recurring triumph of the average good.

IV.

Seven Stupid Myths About Abraham Lincoln

Lincoln was poor white trash and this produced a racist. You can't find proof of this anywhere in his writings. The man was a national patriot, not a minority nationalist. First, personally, then, civilly. What he said of Henry Clay makes perfect sense for him: "He loved his country partly because it was his own country, but mostly because it was a free country." The ideology of racism was absurd to Lincoln because he knew it constructed a non-humanity for the African slave for the sake of property and profit. "Mr. Calhoun and all the politicians of his school," Lincoln informed his 1858 audience, believed that the "term 'all men' in the Declaration did not include the negro." Lincoln in fact thought that not only was this an astounding sentiment, but a "new principle-this new proposition that no human being ever thought of three years ago (1855),-is brought forward, and I combat it as having an evil tendency to dehumanize the negro-to take away from him the right of ever striving to be a man." Lincoln used the word inferior never in a biological sense, but in a social sense because he knew that poverty and deprivation eliminated opportunity. Liberty required unchained humanity everywhere if it was going to survive for all time. America was the first beacon of hope, but he also cherished a manifest universality of freedom in the world and not spleened with physical force (he rejected the Mexican American War, rebuked the annexation of Texas), but through example. He was a tribal chief to certain white, northern, western tribes at one time, and then he favored his tribes over others, but constitutionally, and this was manifested in the end, he simply wanted freedom for every living human being. In some frustration, he tried to impress his vision of America on a friend in 1855. Writing to him about the nativist, ethnocentric Know-Nothing Movement, he was emphatic: "I am not a Know-Nothing. That is certain. How could I be? How can anyone who abhors the oppression of negroes, be in favor of degrading classes of white people? Our progress in degeneracy appears to me to be pretty rapid. As a nation, we began by declaring that 'all men are created equal' We now practically read it 'all men are created equal' except negroes. When the Know-Nothings get control, it will read, 'all men are created equal', except negroes, and foreigners, and catholics. When it comes to this I should prefer emigrating to some country where they make no pretence of loving liberty-to Russia, for instance, where despotism can be taken pure, and without the base alloy of hypocracy."

The president thought Jesus divine and God deistic.

A fatalist who had to be a pessimist.

Too modest to consider himself almost at the end of the war crisis, the 19th century's greatest, good leader. Lincoln's motor was the same as Marx's, but Lincoln chose democracy for ordinary humanity.

Abraham Lincoln thought capitalism compatible with his form of democracy. His declaration to Cassius M. Clay: "Clay, I always thought that the man who made the corn should eat the corn;" is that figurative for capitalism, but literal for slavery?

The war crisis gutted his sexual, romantic hunger.

Sufficiently democratic enough to resent and envy the monied and intellectual classes.

V.

At 22, Lincoln left home and returned only twice to see his folks. His mother died when he was only a boy of ten. In 1818, a year shy of that tragedy, he had a stepmother and three stepsiblings. Sarah, his original sister, had the same name as his stepmother. Lincoln had a great deal of affection for Thomas Lincoln's second wife, and always thought of her as a "good and kind mother." A "good and kind mother" might have been visited more often, but Lincoln thought differently. When he won the presidency in 1861, he fetched his horsedrawn buggy, and paid her a visit. About that time, his father had already died and presumably Lincoln's family had forgiven him for his cruel response to Thomas Lincoln's death. He had refused to visit his daddy on his sickbed and didn't come to the wake. In 1851, the stepbrother wrote Lincoln to hurry to his father's sickbed. Lincoln wrote back that his wife was slightly sick and he didn't want to leave her and besides, "if we could meet now, it is doubtful whether it would not be more painful than pleasant." In the letter, he told his stepbrother to tell his father that if fate would take him now, he should console himself with his God, and Lincoln left him in his wilderness town to die. The 1861 visit to the stepmother was full of memory and embrace and it was the last time Lincoln saw her. The "good mother" outlasted him and wept with the rest of the nation in 1865.

An aboriginal curiousity for book-learning apparently was born in him when he was born in 1809, since his family and community thought the habit impractical and possibly wasteful. "There was absolutely nothing," he writes in 1859, "to excite ambition for education." He did acquire some basic education in "readin, writin, and cipherin," which was taught at a distant schoolhouse. Unlucky, or maybe not, during his childhood and youth, his schooling amounted to no more than a year. In his eleventh year, he picked up Locke Weems's *The Life and Memorable Services of George Washington*, which gave him a picture of the national euphoria that had created the country and its first leader. And reading the poems of Robert Burns, and Bunyan's *Pilgrim Progress*, made him a civil romanticist. Between the ages of 14 and 22, the folks saw a manchild with a sense of humour, and a peculiar habit (reading), a storyteller, and a rowdy ruffian at times, a straight forward answer to a straight or round about question; and a young man so melancholy afflicted that he cut himself off from people and then the "hypo" spell would lift, and he would be back again immersed in the misfortunes and opulence of ordinary humanity.

A strong, physical specimen, he was the best wrestler in New Salem, Illinois. Lincoln was simultaneously many people and many things, so that blocked any deep discernment of his character by others. Women were seen as intelligent or charming, exacly like men. He was too democratic and too dumb about them for a different kind of behavior. He wanted women to vote and as Mary Owens found out, bear themselves across a creek river. Mary Todd Lincoln was intelligent, captivating, and faintly eccentric. She was a product of southern Kentucky aristocracy. That appealed to his snobbery against his own kind and the unworthy insatiables in the upper classes. The Todds were against the marriage for obvious reasons; he was not one of them. The engagement was broken off, then renewed; the marriage was quick. He showed a great deal of personal passion towards Todd. Outside the private connections of family, he was enchanted by physical civility in men and physical beauty in women.

VI.

Origins exist not to be chained to one's plot of dirt, but to see how far one could go beyond it. No matter how modest one's beginnings, dreams were realizable. And ordinary humanity couldn't survive without dreams and cultivated individuality. The paradox is that Lincoln was impassioned about the common folks and yet he gave his life to them. He hated the mob and stationary sentiment in them; knew that they were proned to civil anarchy because of their inflexible lot. Democracy must create conditons so they could see the open road. "Most governments have been based, practically," he writes in the 1850s, "on the denial of equal rights of men, as I have, in part, stated them; ours began, by affirming those rights. They said, some men are too ignorant, and vicious, to share in government. Possibly so, said we; and, by your system, you would always keep them ignorant, and vicious. We proposed to give all a chance; and we expected the weak to grow stronger, the ignorant, wiser; and all better, and happier together."

Descent had to be brushed aside so ordinary humanity could get on with their lives of self-invention. Even the well-heeled had to invent themselves because of democracy's dynamic character. The slaves were at the bottom of the horizontal ladder and sympathy for them produced sympathy for all of humanity. He hated slavery because he was a dispossessed product too. Denied his own wages till he was a young man, not morally or intellectually encouraged to learn to read or write, neither to dream beyond his boundary, and stuck with obscure ancestors, he had a lot in common with them. And even his rise from his humble origins to self-reliance is a slave tale, similar to the ascendency of Harriet Tubman, Frederick Douglass, Sojourner and other runaway slaves and free Negroes. So it is fair to say that Lincoln rejected his origins like the ex-slave. Both probably understood the white southerners' claim to their local origins, but repudiated it, because the future belonged to the union.

VII.

4 March 1865
The Second Inaugural Address
a translation

abrahamlincoln

Both parties deprecated war; but one of them would make war rather than let the nation survive; and the other would accept war rather than let it perish. And the war came. Neither party expected for the war, the magnitude, or the duration, which it has already attained. Neither anticipated that the cause of the conflict might cease with, or even before, the conflict itself should cease.

Both read the same Bible, and pray to the same God; and each invokes His aid against the other. It may seem strange that any men should dare to ask a just God's assistance in wringing their bread from the sweat of other men's faces; but let us judge not that we be not judge. The prayersof both could not be answered; that of neither has been answered fully. On the occasion corresponding to this four years ago, all thoughts were anxiously directed to an impending civil war. All dreaded it-all sought to avert it. While the inaugural address was being delivered from this place, devoted altogether to saving the Union without war, insurgent agents were in the city seeking to destroy it without war-seeking to dissolve the Union, and divide effects, by negotiation. One eighth of the whole population were colored slaves, not distinguished generally over the Union, but localized in the Southern part of it. These slaves constituted a peculiar and powerful interest. All knew that this interest was, somehow, the cause of the war. To strengten, perpetuate, and extend this interest was the object for which the insurgents would rend the Union, even by war; while the government claimed no right to do more than to restrict the territorial enlargement of it.

tHE aLMIGHT hAS hIS oWN pURPOSES. "wOE uNTO tHE wORLD bECAUSE oF oFFENCES! FOR IT MUST NEEDS BE THAT OFFENCES COME; BUT WOE TO THAT MAN BY WHOME THE OFFENCE COMETH!' If WE SHALL SUPPOSE THAT aMERICAN sLAVERY IS ONE OF THOSE OFFENCES WHICH, IN THE PROVIDENCE OF gOD, MUST NEEDS COME, BUT WHICH, HAVING CONTINUED THROUGH HIS APPOINTED TIME, HE NOW WILLS TO REMOVE, AND THAT HE GIVES TO BOTH nORTH AND sOUTH, THIS TERRIBLE WAR, AS THE WOE DUE TO THOSE BY WHOME THE OFFENCE CAME, SHALL WE DISCERN THEREIN ANY DEPARTURE FROM THOSE DIVINE ATTRIBUTES WHICH THE BELIEVERS IN A LIVING gOD ALWAYS ASCRIBE TO HIM?

With malice toward none; with charity for all; with firmness in the right, as God gives us to see the right, let us strive on to the finish the work we are in; to bind up the nation's wounds; to care for him who shall have borne the battle, and for his widow, and his orphan-to do all which may achieve and cherish a just, and a lasting peace, among ourselves, and with all nations c: In contrast to other Latino anthologies, *Paper Dance* is quickly being heralded as one of the most inclusive anthologies of Latino poetry. Other such collections have been criticized for what is seen as a heavy Cuban-American and Puerto Rican flavor, but *Paper Dance* seems to be more inclusive of the larger Latino diaspora, which includes a substantial representation of female poets. Could you talk about the process of compiling this anthology? And would you describe this as a Latino canon?

LQ: When Virgil Suarez first called me with the idea of having three different Latino editors compile an anthology of contemporary Latino poetry, I was fascinated. You see, Victor Hernández Cruz is Puerto Rican, I'm Chicano-Mexican and Virgil is Cuban. I don't know if in the beginning we were that aware of the advantages of such a diverse group of editors, but it was very interesting to witness the unfolding of such a democratic process. What we primarily looked for was anyone that had a voice, something to say or that we believed would complement the other poets we thought would be included. Let me begin by saying that there are a lot of people who are not in the book. And there are many reasons for that: there are writers whose agents don't want them to be in such an anthology, or some writers themselves want some kind of item or treatment, or there are writers that didn't send their submissions in time or there are writers that prescribe toward a particular slant, such as a gay or lesbian journal. This could have been bigger had that not happened, and we would have been dealing with something like sixty people. We wanted something representational, so I was especially pleased that we received such a big response from women. That was very important for an anthology being put together by three men. When I'd hear of a writer, I would call Virgil and say, "Does Victor Hernández Cruz know who Gloria Vando is?" and he would run with that ball. Virgil basically told us to collect and send everything. The interesting thing about that is that we all had in mind a vision, but we never said, "Let's make sure that we this, this and that." Thankfully, it just turned out to be a nice salad.

Another interesting point that might answer your question is that *Paper Dance* does give room for several people to voice themselves in their own particular way and style. I think what might be learned from this is that there are a lot of different types of Latino writers but each one has an interesting voice, a particular way of stating something in his or her own style. Unless you attach a label or have an obvious connection you wouldn't be able to say, "Well this one is Puerto Rican, or this guy is Mexican." If you didn't have the names of the poets it would even be hard to classify them in terms of gender. In some ways that is good. We don't have a lot of poems in *Paper Dance* that are strident.

c: Prior to *Paper Dance*'s completion, you said that it was hard to tell the differences in some of the pieces that were to appear in the anthology. However, now that *Paper Dance* is a whole, what are some of the similarities that you see?

LQ: I think that these poets are addressing issues that are relevant to the human condition: raising children, divorce, patriarchy. But there are also issues that are of particular interest, such as: problems with language, alienation in terms of skin color, any kind of "not-fitting-in." I think that *Paper Dance* addresses these issues in some interesting ways. There were a lot of poems that dealt with womens' issues that I thought were particularly fitting. I would have liked to have included at least five more female contributors, but there were problems tracking people down. I think the contributors who sent in materials and those who were easily tracked down were the ones that didn't expect to make a lot of money off this venture, but they were accessible and wanted to be a part of *Paper Dance*. In that sense it was democratic and perhaps why it came out the way it did. These poets knew that this compilation was something new that we were trying to do, so they gave to the project almost instantly. This text has a lot of different types of writings, such as Guy Garcia from New York City who writes for *The New York Times Magazine*. Garcia has more of a formalist style of writing, in many senses.

c: Many of the poems in *Paper Dance* were written in English with Spanish lines or words woven into the poem. Why is that? Is it a choice or consequence of the market? Do these poets write predominantly in English or Spanish? And is the difference in language a consequence of different age groups?

LQ: One of the issues we considered was how to sell the text. For instance, my poem has some Spanish in it that was left untranslated. I thought that was interesting, because some who contributed might complain about that, but the other editors of *Paper Dance* let it go. Most of these contributors do write primarily in English. But people like Victor Hernández Cruz is writing more and more in Spanish now that he has returned to live in Puerto Rico.

c: Traditionally, the Latino writers represented in the United States have been Cuban, Puerto Rican and Mexican. What do you think has been the inspiration to shift to a broader representation of Latino literature?

LQ: I think what has happened is that a lot of the poets in *Paper Dance* are second generation, or more. Most of the people that came to the United States as immigrants were probably literate in one language. But as a result of schools and education, people began to use the new language, the written language, as a means of expression. I don't see many Latino or Chicano writers writing in Spanish within the United States, although most of these writers can. So the question has become, how much is the language in which they write swayed by accessibility that the presses represent? I don't know. There is such a thing that linguists call "code-switching," in which words of two languages are incorporated into the text in order for the speaker or writer to cope with both languages. Another term for this is "Anglo-ize," in which a light switch for example becomes a *switche*, or brakes become *brekas* instead of *frenos*. In order to become a linguistic survivor people revert to a blending of languages.

c: Traditionally in the United States people have come to English through an assimilation process and a subsequent loss of a first language. However, what we seem to be witnessing in this country is a bicultural linguistic system that enables us to better understand cultures, thus creating a bridge between the "home culture" and the dominant "external culture."

LQ: Yes, you can use code-switching or the angloized version of words in school and not be punished because it is seen as a viable means of communication. Maria Mazziotti Gillan, co-editor of *Unsettling America*, a new anthology of multicultural poetry, used an interesting metaphor for this when she spoke to my class. She said, "When I went home and I closed that door, I was Italian. Everything at home was Italian. We spoke Italian. But when I opened that door and went out into the world, I was American." I think that is a very real and valid way in which language is preserved. There's got to be some compromise, so that if you don't know a particular word, you can come up with something.

c: The poem, "Dusting" by Julia Alvarez or the prose poem, "Muchacha" by Cecilia Rodríguez-Milanés are insightful because each represents a female role and a rejection of those roles as women in a very male-dominated Latino culture. Are these pieces representational of the women of the second generation who reject traditional female roles? Are these female poets our witnesses to the reinventing of a culture?

LQ: Well, the older generation, both male and female, have always been the enforcers of the patriarchy. Just because there were women does not mean that they weren't involved in enforcing patriarchy. What we are seeing are these Latino men and women undoing that, rejecting the cultural duties or traditional roles for women. I guess by rejecting traditional roles, in a sense, they are rejecting a part of their culture, and that has to be difficult to do, to go against everything that you've been taught. It's like Gina Valdez's poem on becoming—the concept of becoming is interesting. The idea that someone can recreate him or herself is part of the American myth. Can women really remake themselves? Alma Luz Villanueva seems to think she can and has some very interesting ideas about that.

c: In discussing the poetry of women in *Paper Dance*, the quote by Toni Morrison, "When you kill a part of your culture, you kill yourself," comes to mind. Could you elaborate on what aspects of the culture you see these poets embracing or rejecting in their work? And do you believe that part of a culture is lost by the younger generation's rejection of tradition?

LQ: Just because it's culture doesn't mean it's good for you—man or woman. What Toni Morrison's work says is that women have been very much discounted in all cultures. In a sense by writing about these women, she rewrites or revises them and ultimately frees them. I think that's good because it allows people to see that it's okay to live and be a part of a culture, but that one doesn't have to be tied to the worst parts of his or her culture. I don't have to be either. I believe if you're tying women down, you're tying yourself down too.

c: It has been said that *Paper Dance*'s unifying theme is that of the Americanization process, a struggle to define or redefine "The American Dream." What does the Americanization process mean in terms of poetry?

LQ: I don't know if the reviewers and critics went too far in saying that. But what is interesting is that suddenly there is this anthology that wasn't around thirty years ago when I went to school. The only person that I had any sort of relationship to was Hemmingway, because he used some Spanish. By allowing people to express themselves and to express themselves in their own style is a freedom.

Here's a way I might be able to answer your question. A year ago I did a workshop for June Jordan's class at UC-Berkeley. The class was discussing the poem "Baltimore" by Claude McKay, and I decided that even though McKay was black, he wrote white poetry, because he wrote in the very formalist language of sonnets. That morning I had eaten breakfast at a little diner next to Berkeley and Nat King Cole was on the radio. I started thinking, "Did Nat King Cole sing white songs?" When does something become Americanized? Why did McKay write in rhyming verse? Because that was the zeitgeist at the times? Does that entitle him to be American? Or was he too Americanized to the point that he was no longer black? Take for example Chuck Berry, his songs aren't black songs, "I'm so glad I'm livin' in the U.S.A." They're rhymed for a teenage market and he knew it. Now you have rap, and an age when maybe you have too much expression.

But at what point do you draw the line and say; now this is American. I'm going to answer that point by saying that finally minorities have reached the point where they are a part of that Americanization, WE have access to it as much as everybody else. There's black-American, but it's still American. It's good to have an access, in which we all can learn from one another. This access teaches individuals about the issues of roles, gender and how to feel about being human. That's exactly what poetry should do.

c: The Spanish language has an incredible history of rich literature, in this century alone. How much of that tradition is a legacy in Latino literature and how much of it would you say is "new wood?"

LQ: If you were to go to the biography section of *Paper Dance* you'd see that a lot of the poets have gone to school, so they're obviously aware of the history and language of poetry. Victor Martínez, for example, went to Stanford and you can see a lot of that in his writing. I think you see a lot of the history of the language in these poets. Most of the contributors are professors so they have tradition as a background. I don't think they're writing blindly. I don't know if these individuals necessarily follow a tradition, but they have a sense of being the product of something that they're using in their own way. Then again, maybe there is the blending of what they learned from the United States, as well as the other traditions. So yes, there is a sense of melding cultures. But there isn't an imitation of other writers.

Are you familiar with Sor Juana Inez de La Cruz? She was a nun who owned the largest library at the time. She was a scientist and made her own musical instruments. Octavio Paz wrote her biography. The Catholic church found a way to sanction her. She would go in front of the bishops and they would question her in terms of philosophy and she always had answers for them. Eventually the bishops had to destroy her because she was too damn smart. They took away her books, her life really. She lived in a cell and virtually gave up. She was primarily a nun, and they asked her to do that which is a nun's duty. She ended up losing her own life while taking care of her fellow sisters during a cholera epidemic.

c: Let's talk about Leroy Quintana. You've been experimenting and writing poems about many different themes throughout your life. Can you speak of them? What are you working on now?

LQ: That's a really good question, because how many themes do writers really work on throughout their lives? Some maybe one, some, maybe two or three, but it's really the same stuff. I don't have that kind of objectivity though, but it seems that most of my poems are about people. My poems are all little biographical portraits. I can't really write about a place, but I do it through the people. It's an interesting way for me to connect or document. All I can say is that it's a series of portraits in a community. I guess I try to speak for them. I guess my theme portrays people in their circumstances, poverty, whatever conflict they face, manipulate and survive, that's all.

I have a new book of poems coming out by the end of next year titled, *My Hair Turning Grey Among Strangers*. It's taken from a Korean poem about longing for home, but again it's all portraits. I also have a collection of short fiction coming out next year. It's a book of short stories with reoccurring characters. I hope that by the time I'm through, the collections of poetry and prose will total ten. That seems like a good number.

Nicknames
Leroy Quintana   [2 poems]

The talk turned to nicknames the other day
and Filemón said the man who worked next
to him in the mine and burst into song
all day long was called Caruso,
and the guy who admired his sandwich
and smacked all through the lunch hour,
that was El Sabroso, and the one burned
pretty bad in the smelter, why he
came to be known as El Chicharrón.

Stupids

Filemón, famous now for his particular use
of the plural form of nouns.

When he disciplined his children, always,
in order to be inclusive, ended

by angrily dismissing them as "You stupids."

from Hearsay Sonnets

Atlanta
Beth Anderson

With amazing speed the hills dried out until they were
so decimated that they disappeared. We searched for them
down wide industrial streets others could not believe
we'd survived when later we told stories of our hunting.
But I most want to turn somersaults in winter. I know I'll
forget the language that lives in my building, and this
disconcerts more than the act of departure. Severe stretches
will save the long tendons connecting each finger to a
skyline blip, stop a stack of cards from sliding to your lap.
I habitually conquer all my fears but only in my head
so that when faced with danger I can only freeze or flee.
We are not sorry to have this time together, to count lanes
fanning out from our position in a vast pattern of hoods
and roofs and impatience that might never move again.

Cleveland

My feet hurt but not my sentences. I want this bug out
of my eye and banish it by turning it into a hairline fracture
waiting to happen. When the shore isn't yours anymore,
where the bay becomes the ocean and saltwater taffy is named
for associations rather than minerals, there we will embrace
rust and all things iron. *Instead of* sand, we will make of
this variegated dust a habit. There I'll be, with the instead of
pronoun. So much texture is trapped outside the skyline
and inside machines that churn cement. It will be so hot that
nothing will not catch on fire. But the battles we channel
draw on common names and force insomnia to morph into
vertigo before heading for the suburbs. I shall stick to present
tensions, anticipate not a swim but a search for pure water
and liken this vantage point to the best of the b-side songs.

Cold Fried Fish and Brown Rice
Anastasios Kozaitis

Yeah, the night fell:
it fell so far it kept looking
                        Down.

It couldn't believe it had fallen such depths.
Darker than black...
                        Cold

"Byzantine Empire ruins? 1463?
Are these Bogomils I see?
Do they move?"

Reaching Bosnia it wondered,
how it ever could have gotten there?

"Am I Catholic, Orthodox or Muslim Yugoslavia?
Muslims—dead or cleansed
Bosnians? Croats? Serbs?
Yugoslavians? Yugoslavians?
                        Yugoslavia?

Sure it was majestic, but now what is it?

Freckled with pinholes of light,
which escape every night,
it's the coldest cemetery
the night's never forgotten.